The National Lottery
and Its Regulation

THE NATIONAL LOTTERY AND ITS REGULATION

Process, Problems and Personalities

ANDREW DOUGLAS

continuum
LONDON • NEW YORK

Continuum
The Tower Building, 11 York Road, London SE1 7NX
370 Lexington Avenue, New York, NY 10017-6503

First published 2001

Andrew K. W. Douglas 2001

British Library Cataloguing-in-Publication Data
A catalogue record for this book is available from the British Library.

ISBN 0-8264-5554-9 (hardback)
    0-8264-5555-7 (paperback)

Library of Congress Cataloging-in-Publication Data
Douglas, A. K. W. (Andrew K. W.), 1960–
   The National Lottery and its regulation : process, problems and personalities / Andrew Douglas.
      p. cm.
   Includes bibliographical references and index.
   ISBN 0-8264-5554-9 — ISBN 0-8264-5555-7 (pbk.)
   1. Lotteries—Great Britain. 2. Lotteries—Law and legislation—Great Britain. I. Title.

   HG6185.A2 D68 2001
   795.3 8—dc21

                                                                    2001037100

Typeset by Centraserve, Saffron Walden, Essex
Printed and bound in Great Britain by
Creative Print and Design Wales, Ebbw Vale

CONTENTS

ACKNOWLEDGEMENTS

I should like to record my gratitude to all those who have helped and supported me in this work. My thanks go to those individuals with whom I have entered into correspondence, and who have been prepared to be interviewed and whose names are recorded in the bibliography. I would like to thank in particular the Office of the National Lottery and the National Lottery Commission, and Camelot, whose staff have been so willing to provide support and information. Finally I would like to pay tribute to Bernard Foley for his advice and his even-handed supervision of the MPhil thesis from which this work was drawn, and to Suzanne Hale and Pamela Baker for their word-processing skills and assistance in liaising with a number of the contributors.

INTRODUCTION

In November 1994 tickets for a domestic[1] state-sanctioned National Lottery went on sale in the UK for the first time since 1826.[2] This book examines the regulation of the Lottery, and the rôle of regulation in serving the public interest. In so doing, the design and functioning of the enabling legislation are scrutinized. The work is particularly concerned with the nature of personalized regulatory models and as such is focused primarily though not solely on the Lottery's regulation from the appointment of the first Director General on 25 October 1993[3] to the replacement of the position of Director General by a team of five National Lottery Commissioners on 1 April 1999.[4] The following lines highlight not only some of the inherent difficulties associated with designing and implementing regulatory regimes (especially new structures), but also the enduring problem of establishing and agreeing appropriate criteria which can in some helpful and meaningful way evaluate the regulatory process.

Broadly the book is separated into four sections. The first section (Chapter 1) provides a background to the Lottery. It explains the influences that were at work in determining the venture's regulatory design. This chapter also attempts to set out the different criteria by which the Lottery's regulation can be measured. In particular it addresses those issues appertaining to the nature of personalized regulatory models, which proved to be of such critical importance during the time of the Director Generals. The second section comprises Chapters 2 and 3 and assesses the Lottery and its regulation against the objectives as set out in the National Lottery etc. Act 1993. These objectives, which are also the main duties of the Regulator, fall into three areas – ensuring the Lottery's propriety, protecting the interests of participants and maximizing the proceeds to be allocated to the Good Causes. The third section (Chapter 4) provides a critical appraisal of the Lottery's regulatory design as set out in the enabling legislation. The difficulties that beset the Lottery during the time of the individual regulators are addressed. This chapter also outlines the problems and conflicts which influenced the course of the regulatory process and which ultimately led to the disbanding and replacement of the personalized regulatory model by a commission-based system of regulation. The fourth and final section (Chapters 5–7) looks beyond the period of the Lottery's personalized regulation, appraises the bidding process for the next Licence and examines those issues that influenced the policy options for the project's regulation following the expiry of the initial Licence in September 2001.

Notes

1. Foreign national lottery tickets have been sold illegally in the UK for a number of years. See Andrew Douglas, *British Charitable Gambling 1956–1994* (The Athlone Press, London, 1995), p. 402.
2. C. M. Smith and S. P. Monkcom, *The Law of Betting, Gaming and Lotteries* (Butterworth, London, 1987), p. 402.
3. Director General of the National Lottery, *Annual Report 1993/94* (HMSO, London, 01/11/94), p. 6.
4. Department of Culture, Media and Sport, Government announces names of the new Lottery Commissioners (news release) (25/01/99).

To Pamela and Florence

CHAPTER 1

BACKGROUND AND REGULATORY CRITERIA

1.1 *Political Philosophy*

The National Lottery (and its attendant regulatory apparatus) finds its point of reference not in the state and national lotteries from around the world, but in public administration developments in the UK. The stagflationary years of the 1970s were a period of crisis in the management of the UK economy. These difficult years saw a breakdown in the social democratic Keynsian consensus, which had since the end of the Second World War ascribed a strong social and economic rôle to the state.[1] The search for institutional forms to replace the historical concept of public services delivered centrally by large government departments under the direct supervision of elected representatives can be traced back to the mid-1970s.[2] These new institutional forms were designed to separate out functions and to introduce some aspects of competition and markets in public services.[3] They manifested themselves particularly during the 1980s in the creation of Next Steps agencies and the privatization and subsequent regulation of a number of the public utilities.[4]

In the case of the National Lottery, there is no international precedent to draw on having regard to its design or format. 'Uniquely, this is a state-sponsored lottery, set up to serve the public interest and run by a private monopoly.'[5] The initiative was in part a response to the concern that without a National Lottery of its own the UK domestic market would become increasingly attractive to lotteries from other EC countries and elsewhere.[6] The British public might therefore be able to participate in lotteries benefiting the citizens of other countries but not their own.[7] That it was placed in the private as opposed to the state sector is a reflection of the trends in UK public administration referred to above and in particular is consistent with the privatization policies pursued by successive Conservative governments throughout their 18 years in power (1979–97). The arrangements chosen for the Lottery were thus ideologically informed by the notion that almost all entities that involve the delivery of a public good or service are best placed in the private sector. This is predicated on the belief that the presence of the profit motive and the disciplinary powers of competitive markets will help eliminate the slack and wasteful practices that can (and often do) arise in state-owned nationalized industries.[8] Yet the reasons why so many international lotteries are found in the public rather than the private sector are important in the context of this work. Firstly, most national and state lotteries are considerably older than the UK's Lottery, and many of these were established in the 1960s and 1970s or even earlier, when command and control or dirigiste policies *vis-à-vis* economic planning and management were still the preferred policy option. Secondly, the historical association of the gambling industry with crime has meant that controlling the Lottery and preserving its rectitude and probity have been government priorities which have ranked *pari passu* with the venture's commercial success.

State and national lotteries have been placed under the control of governments on a safety first principle.[9] Today government-run lotteries continue to be the most prevalent organizational model.[10] There are, however, a number of exceptions to this rule. In the Australian state of Victoria the privately owned Tattersalls company (which established its first lottery at the end of the nineteenth century) has since 1953 operated lotteries for the government, retaining a percentage of the profits, under licence which is reviewed periodically.[11] There have also been a number of experimentations with privatizations or part privatizations. In Denmark, The Netherlands, Germany, Italy and Portugal, the direct operation of some of the state lotteries (many European, and all North American lotteries are state- or regionally based, rather than national)[12] have been handed over to corporations, although these corporations typically maintain close links with one or more government ministries and remain dependent on government for policy decisions.[13] In France and in Denmark (for one of its lotteries) the state has granted a licence to a private or semi-private company with the government retaining the major equity stake, and the private sector holding a minority interest.[14] This is similar to the arrangements obtaining for the National Lottery, but falls short of the full-blown private entity model, which is to be found in the UK. It is significant that the attempts by governments in certain European lottery jurisdictions to involve the private sector is often tempered by the ongoing close participation of those selfsame governments in the lotteries concerned; either through the retention of an equity interest or through the involvement of dedicated government department(s) ensuring accountability and setting policy.

Finally the sizeable majority of the 37 states plus the District of Columbia that run lotteries in the USA do so through state agencies. The public has approved, via the ballot box, the introduction of state lotteries in 27 of 38 instances where lotteries have been successfully enacted.[15]

Although they are state agencies, the lotteries operate largely outside the realm of state government as quasi-independent enterprises.[16] These agencies almost always contract out to the private sector those aspects of the lottery's promotion that call for technical expertise, while retaining control of policy and promotional matters.[17] Some states have turned towards private entity or quasi-private/quasi-public entity models including Kentucky, which was the first state in the country to structure its lottery as a corporation in 1988.[18] However, the corporation is owned by the state.[19] Similar arrangements pertain in Louisiana, Georgia, Connecticut and New Mexico.[20] Indeed in the case of Connecticut the state legislature changed the status of the Lottery in July 1996 from a state agency to a quasi-public corporation with the purpose of making the operation less bureaucratic and more entrepreneurial.[21] Among the lotteries in the US, only Texas (in 1992) has contracted out its lottery operations to a private operator with a view to providing more services at less cost.[22] It is noteworthy that none of the states that have authorized lotteries have seen fit to allow competitors.[23] This is a function not only of the need to guarantee the exclusion of criminal elements through government assuming ultimate ownership and control, but also of the desire to ensure that the state can capture monopoly profits.[24]

While the foregoing enumerates the incidence of lotteries with (to a greater or lesser extent) private sector characteristics, it should be noted that the majority of these lotteries are regional or state-based, rather than national. The UK Lottery is the first modern lottery which is both privately run and national. As such it is unmistakably informed by and is a logical extension of the former Conservative government's economic philosophy of extending the involvement of the private sector in the management of the economy through privatization and contracting out policies. The consequence and evidence of this can also be witnessed in the framework established for the Lottery, which incorporates key elements of the regulatory apparatus created for the public utilities following their privatization in the 1980s. However, the Lottery is not a utility and it poses a different set of unique regulatory challenges. Since the early 1980s, the withdrawal of the state from the delivery of many public services in the UK and the ramifications for government policy has been a powerful and formative influence on the National Lottery's regulatory design. But so too have the long-standing policies carried forward and observed by different governments throughout the twentieth century in relation to the rôle of gambling in society, gambling's tendency to malfeasance and the need for its containment. The effect of the stresses created by these different and in some ways conflicting objectives is expressed in the Lottery's regulatory architecture which as a result of these tensions may be said to possess something of a chimerical quality.

1.2 *The Regulatory Challenge*

Having determined on what might be labelled the riskier course of placing the Lottery in the private sector, the priority for the government in its first duty of identifying and upholding the public interest was to determine what structures should be put in place that exercised an appropriate degree of control to prevent or minimize undesirable social costs while at the same time not stifling the flower of enterprise. It may be said that in simple terms regulation seeks to remedy various kinds of market failure.[25] Whether placed in the public or private sector, the Lottery is a monopoly (or near monopoly).[26] As a manifestation of imperfect competition this state of affairs poses classic regulatory questions that fall broadly into three areas: the abuse of market power,[27] negative externalities or spillovers that create social costs, and the consequences of asymmetric or imperfect information which can result in a variety of market distortions, including the monopolist making excessive profits. All three of the foregoing issues can lead to the inefficient allocation of resources and to a resultant loss of welfare if the regulation is in some way deficient and/or if the monopoly in question is not adequately policed. This is a perennial regulatory problem and the National Lottery and its attendant regulation does not enjoy an exemption from this general rule.

In choosing the model for a national lottery, the government rejected competition in favour of a regulated private monopoly to deliver a set of prescribed policy objectives. One of the criticisms of regulation is that it is at best a pallid substitute for competition.[28] It cannot prescribe quality, force (allocative) efficiency or insist on innovation as effectively as competition because this would involve invading the sphere of management, and when government leaves these matters to industry it denies consumers the protection that competition would afford.[29] However, it is fair to posit that competition is capable, in certain circumstances, of being excessively strong and that restrictions on it can induce an improved performance.[30] The ultimate restriction is to remove or create circumstances where there is no or only minimal competition. This is often appropriate for industries which deliver services through fixed networks (e.g. wires or pipes) to consumers.[31] Indeed monopoly may be desirable in such industries in so far as it produces output more cheaply than duplicating the network.[32]

The National Lottery may be described as such an industry. However, in the interests of preserving competition within the market one policy option open to the government would have been to allow more than one operator, but to have placed the computerized retail network necessary to sell (Draw) Lottery tickets under the auspices of a different agency. This is analogous to the regulatory model that was designed for the railway industry with the separation of the network under the aegis of Railtrack from the individual companies that operate rail services under franchise. The regulation and the separation of functions between power generation and its distribution and supply in the electricity industry is also relevant in this context. The most likely reason why this option was not pursued can be found in the fact that while the Lottery may not be a natural monopoly it does possess certain properties which are common to natural monopolies. As in the case of natural monopolies there are significant economies of scale enjoyed by the National Lottery.[33] A variation on this theme is the absolute importance of critical mass (for the main Draw game) in allowing the Lottery to meet its main objective – the maximization of the net proceeds[34] allocated to the Good Causes. High turnover creating high jackpots which in turn generate greater interest and further potential for increasing turnover are central planks in the success of any state or national lottery.[35] Nevertheless there remains an argument to suggest that it may be feasible to franchise more than one private firm as a lottery provider and thus create some competition for certain games such as the Instants game where scale economies are not pronounced.[36]

Notwithstanding the foregoing proviso, if the case for the National Lottery to be run to all intents and purposes as a monopoly is accepted, the question still needs to be addressed as to how, in the absence of competition, management can be expected to deliver an efficient lottery that serves the public interest. In part the answer to this question can be found in that element of the Lottery's regulation that established and facilitated the bidding process for the award to the most efficient would-be operator of a seven-year licence to run the Lottery. Competitive tendering can be used as a valued substitute for conventional market competition.[37] To enjoy the monopoly right *ex post* the supplier must engage in competition *ex ante* to secure that right or privilege.[38] Thus competition in the market was replaced by competition for the market. This issue is addressed below. The following section, however, sets out the key areas of regulation with which this book is concerned, and in particular the critical features that were most instrumental in defining the nature and style of the Lottery's regulation during the term of the first Director General.

1.3 *Personalized Regulation – Principles and Problems*

Since the privatization acts it has largely been the so-called director generals (also sometimes styled Directors General) who have had a 'personal duty' to regulate a variety of industries and utilities.[39] Decisions for which elected ministers were once responsible were passed to a new breed of politically appointed mandarins.[40] Under these new arrangements regulation was supposed to be administered with a light touch, with no vast overlay of rules, but rather with modest scope for discretion, determined on a personal basis.[41] The annual reports and deliberations of these regulators are written in the first person and the individual regulators have come to be seen as personifying regulatory constraints and style.[42] Director generals have been invested with enormous powers to make decisions affecting the services provided to every consumer and the commercial viability of some of Britain's largest companies.[43] Less accountable than ministers,[44] and not subject to the judgement of court or ballot box,[45] it has been argued by some that there are dangers in concentrating too much power in the hands of a single individual and that checks and balances are inadequate.[46]

It was this paradigm that acted as the template for the National Lottery's regulatory design. Yet it would be the problems associated with personalized regulation that were to mark the early life of the Lottery, and which would culminate in the promulgation of new law. The National Lottery Act 1998 introduced a number of changes to the Lottery, the most fundamental of which was to replace the Director General and the Office of the National Lottery with five Lottery Commissioners at the head of a National Lottery Commission.[47] This section sets out the principles and problems connected with the regulatory process and personalized regulatory regimes in particular, against which an assessment of the Lottery's regulation during the time of the Director Generals can be made.

Peter Davis was appointed Director General of the National Lottery by the Secretary of State for National Heritage on 25 October 1993, for a period of five years,[48] although he acted as a regulatory advisor to the Department of National Heritage from July 1993.[49] As a law graduate, a chartered accountant, and a seasoned businessman with former directorships in the retail, financial and banking sectors[50] (although with mixed success)[51] Peter Davis would have appeared to be a suitable candidate for the rôle of Director General. Indeed he described himself as 'a careful, cautious chap who has an understanding of the commercial side of life'.[52]

Yet on 3 February 1998 Peter Davis was forced to resign his position.[53] In assessing the performance of the first Director General and the reasons for his resignation the following pages are informed by classic public interest theory, which is predicated on assumptions of normative regulatory behaviour, i.e. what should motivate policy-makers and enforcers?[54] This is of itself a particularly contentious issue. However, classic public interest theory is not only a normative theory, but also a positive theory that stresses what does rather than what should motivate regulatory agencies,[55] and that lays emphasis on how the effectiveness and independence of the regulator can be undermined or brought into question. In addressing the Lottery's regulation this work is then concerned with both normative and positive aspects of the regulatory process.

It is probably fair to claim that there is no single set of regulatory arrangements appropriate in all circumstances for all industries at all times. Regulation of whatever hue inherently lacks precise or absolute standards.[56] What is needed for good regulation is an 'appropriate' balance between broad and vague policies and policies that are too tight and therefore too specific.[57] However, regulatory unreasonableness and controversy is almost inevitable because regulations especially when centrally formulated will always have a tendency to be either overinclusive or underinclusive as applied to the real world,[58] and in particular to the peculiar, technical and esoteric circumstances of the regulated industry in question. This is likely to be especially true when both the industry and the regulatory apparatus are new and untested. *A fortiori* when there is no ready made or at least readily adaptable model which can be borrowed from a similar industry faced with comparable regulatory problems. Such is the plight of the National Lottery. It follows from this that individual regulators and indeed regulatory commissions or agencies can lack clearly defined standards and policies, and one of their key functions is therefore to interpret statutory provisions as they impact on the industry for whose regulation they are responsible.[59] This raises the hoary issue of regulatory discretion which, while a valid and necessary part of the regulatory process, can also become at once invidious and controversial. This is particularly so in the case of personalized regulatory formats. The balance between how tightly drafted the rules that govern and define the regulator's powers are *vis-à-vis* the amount of discretion and latitude the regulator is given or believes he is given in terms of enforcement is an enduring regulatory challenge. This book demonstrates the difficulties that lie behind the task of adjusting between and balancing these two factors to deliver good regulation, and how this process is made more fraught by the regulator's own interpretation of his brief and rules, and his prioritizing of different and often competing interests.

It is important to emphasize that discretion is not an alternative to rules. Any regulatory system or system of administration is a combination of rules and discretion, and there are advantages and disadvantages to the use of rules as opposed to discretion and vice-versa.[60] The individual regulator qua agent for his or her principal or sponsoring government department is established to perform a dedicated task implying a degree of expertise, knowledge and time not possessed by the Executive.[61] It is not unusual therefore for the agent to enjoy a measure of discretion in performing the task that has been set.[62] Legislation is often couched in language which implies a fairly wide scope for discretion and interpretation on the part of the regulatory agent to make and enforce regulation, with phrases such as 'as far as reasonably practicable' designed to provide a degree of latitude to both regulators and regulated.[63] In the case of the National Lottery, the 1993 Act required the Director General *inter alia* to 'do his best' to maximize the proceeds; additionally the Act stated that the Director General 'may include' Licence conditions as he considers appropriate, 'may vary any condition in a licence' subject to certain procedures, and shall revoke a licence 'if he is satisfied that the Licensee is no longer a fit and proper person'.[64]

While primary legislation tends to concentrate on the general principles of regulatory law, the issue then arises as to the extent by which detached rule-making is then delegated to the Executive or an agency which is to a greater or lesser degree independent of government.[65] The National Lottery etc. Act 1993 devolved powers to the office of Director General through the creation of a licensing system. Under this system, which the Regulator helped to design,[66] the Director General was made responsible initially for awarding the Licence to run the Lottery and thereafter to set standards, to monitor the performance of the Licensee and to award licences for individual games.[67] In addition the Director General enjoyed a degree of authority to vary licence conditions,[68] (i.e. alter existing or set new rules) and to enforce the Operator to observe the conditions of the licence(s).[69] The Secretary of State was charged under the Act with issuing when and where necessary Directions to the Director General having regard to the matters that should be taken into account in deciding whether or not to grant licences and the conditions that these licences should contain.[70] The dispersion of regulatory rule-making powers between the executive and agencies tends to distinguish British regimes from their American counterparts where the concentration of rule-making powers in the largely independent agencies facilitates the creation and targeting of control systems.[71] The more fluid British system invites government interference which may also be difficult to identify and can create instability for agencies as well as shifting targets for complainants seeking to pin down responsibility.[72] The extent of the authority extended to the Lottery's Regulator and the extent of executive support/interference is one of the issues with which these pages are concerned.

Rule-making by agencies can create problems of accountability; yet the expertise that can be concentrated and accumulated in an agency in a way which is not always possible in government departments can if the agency is also responsible for enforcement (as is the case with the National Lottery) beneficially feed back into the rule-making process.[73] Nevertheless, at whatever level rule-making authority is located, the rigid application of and adherence to these rules can lead to unreasonable and unjust regulatory outcomes which may produce legal resistance by the regulated, greater inducements to corruption and surreptitious returns to discretion by agency officials.[74] By contrast the exercise of discretion and where appropriate forbearance by the regulator can enhance the relationship with the regulated, and thereby improve the prospects for compliance. Indeed if friendly relations between regulator and regulatee can be cultivated, then the less confrontational milieu can allow the regulations themselves to be more easily developed.[75] Such strategies may involve the regulator overlooking violations that pose no serious risk, not enforcing regulatory requirements that might prove excessively costly or disruptive *vis-à-vis* the added protection they would provide, granting reasonable time for compliance to be met, accepting substantial if not literal compliance, and making allowances for good faith efforts on the part of the regulated enterprise.[76] Without doubt one of the first questions the regulator has to address is whether his office is there to act as an 'agent' of, or an activist for, the consumer groups, or whether it is there more properly as an important arbiter of the public interest, where public interest includes the interests of the firm(s) being regulated.[77] Yet wherever the agency draws the line it is not possible for consumer interests to be well served without some regard for the well-being of the regulated body responsible for providing the goods and services to those same consumer groups. Good, flexible enforcement by an agency and its compliance or inspectorate teams requires technical competence, toughness, good communication skills and good judgement – qualities which are not only the result of right training but also of right personality.[78]

The regulatory difficulties that beset the National Lottery, particularly during the first half of the initial Licence term, underscore some of the inherent problems associated with personalized regulation. These problems embrace regulatory design, the difficulties faced by the Regulator in interpreting his statutory mandate along with the facility of discretion and regulatory style, the politicization of the regulatory process and the rôle and functioning of the polity. Indeed it was following criticism which centred on the style and judgement of the first Director General, culminating in his removal from office, that the regulatory architecture of the National Lottery was overhauled. Criticism in the media and among key members of the polity was highly personalized and focused on a perceived lack of vigour demonstrated by the Director General in his dealings with the Operator, Camelot, especially in comparison with some of the other main regulators, including those for electricity, gas, water and telecommunications.[79] Thus, Peter Davis was accused *inter alia* of 'lacking curiosity',[80] of being 'a bit of a soft touch',[81] and of providing 'inadequate protection of the public interest'.[82] There was a growing feeling voiced in the media and elsewhere that for effective and fair regulation, monopolistic industries required the regulator to do more than 'sit back and let the wheels turn'.[83] Furthermore, from May 1997 the new Labour government in championing the rights of the consumer was prepared to let individual ministers place pressure on the regulators to encourage them to become tougher within their existing guidelines.[84] Indeed some of the regulators including Peter Davis were arguably in as much discomfort through this process as the directors of the companies they were responsible for regulating.[85]

It is undoubtedly the case that one of the ways for a regulator to gauge his or her performance in upholding the public interest is the response of other institutions to the agency's policies and rules and their implementation.[86] The most important of these is arguably the regulatory agency's sponsoring government department. In theory one of the perceived advantages of creating regulatory commissions and agencies is to isolate them from undue political influence.[87] Certainly this was one of the key aims of privatization.[88] Indeed it was a stated precept of the Conservative government's regulatory policy (during the 1980s and early to mid-1990s) that ministers should set targets and objectives as part of the planning and resource allocation process, and thereafter the agency should be left to deliver on them.[89] The onus would then be on a department to justify any interference with the agreed arrangements, rather than on the agency to justify its independence.[90] Yet too much independence on the part of the regulatory agency, isolates it from the political support and leadership that is essential for successful regulation.[91] In this context the relationship between the Lottery's first Director General and his sponsoring government department is particularly relevant. The book also addresses ministerial involvement in the regulatory process, the level of support extended to the Regulator, as well as the degree of authority invested in the office of the Director General. The response to the Lottery's regulation and the rôle of the Director General from leading members of the polity including the House of Commons Select Committee of Public Accounts (hereafter, the PAC) and the National Audit Office (NAO) is also examined below.

1.4 *Identifying the Public Interest*

Regulation then, is subject to political influence (and interference). But this occurs not only in the party political sense; it is also political in the broader sense of the word, having regard to the rôle of different institutions and interest groups that have a bearing on regulatory processes. The environment in which the National Lottery operates incorporates a variety of bodies with a direct or indirect interest in the Lottery, including think-tanks, consumer pressure groups, charities, the various constituent parts that comprise the gambling industry and those institutions with a more formalized interest in the Lottery – *viz.* Parliament, the PAC and the

NAO. These so called 'external theatres of judgement' serve to provide the Regulator with a flow of success indicators, i.e. actions or responses that express approval or disapproval of the agency's decisions – the corollary of which is that it is quite feasible to argue that any regulatory agency will view the public interest as being served if these success indicators show approbation.[92] Furthermore, it is not unreasonable to argue that in a modern western democracy the rôle of these different actors is a valued and important part of the process that helps to define the public interest. Regulatory agencies such as the Office of the National Lottery (Oflot) and the Lottery's more recent incarnation – the National Lottery Commission (NLC) – operate in the storm centres of politics, where the pressures are intense and where it can be argued that attempts to influence the course of administrative actions is not only normal but even essential.[93] These pressures are often expressed most vociferously from protection-minded constituencies and interest groups and legislators, eager to elaborate and enforce protective rules; a tendency much aggravated by the political climate created often inadvertently (and sometimes advertently) by the media.[94] These pressures are potentially most acute when they are focused on an individual regulator. This feature of personalized regulatory models is a recurring theme, which is explored extensively in the following pages.

The public interest model is perhaps the oldest theory of government.[95] The theory assumes that the instrumental goal of an enforcement agency is to minimize the harm resulting from contraventions of regulation at lowest administrative cost.[96] As already alluded to, the theory emphasizes the government's rôle (when putting in place regulatory structures) in correcting market imperfections such as social and environmental externalities, monopoly pricing[97] and the problems of information asymmetry. The agencies are thus viewed as benevolent maximizers of social welfare.[98] However, the term public interest is particularly malleable, and can be and often is employed as the justification for 'whatever the Government does'.[99] Furthermore, the meaning of the public interest at any given time will be coloured by the political leaders holding key government posts,[100] and arguably it will have different meanings for the same government at different times. In this context it should be remembered that the private entity model and associated regulatory structures appertaining to the Lottery were chosen by a Conservative administration and inherited by a Labour government which, while in opposition, had made no secret of its dislike for several aspects of the Lottery's regulatory design, and its capacity to serve the public interest adequately.[101] Thus the new government was arguably less inclined to extend support or to persist with a model that it had not designed and had not advocated. This was undoubtedly to inform the nature of the relationship between the government and the Regulator and regulatory process as the ensuing chapters of this book will demonstrate.

Irrespective of the vulnerability of the regulatory process to politicization, it remains the case that because of the difficulty of defining the public interest and the concomitant problem of its codification in the field of regulation in a set of absolute laws or rules, one is brought to the question of how to ensure that regulatory design serves the public interest – however defined.[102] The elusiveness of the concept means that the regulatory agencies themselves while trying to serve the public interest can and do have a great deal of difficulty identifying it.[103] Furthermore, when, as was persistently the case during the reign of the first Director General, the Regulator's interpretation of the public interest was at variance with that of a number of different groups with a specialized or particular interest in the Lottery, these selfsame groups were voluble in their criticism and were quick to lay the blame for many of the Lottery's perceived failings at the feet of the Director General.

In the UK, regulation has been historically less rule-based and more discretionary (a feature much vaunted by its supporters), and this has arguably resulted in the tendency for the system to become more personalized.[104] Proponents of the single regulator/discretionary model argue that, as with juries, it seems easier to use several minds to reach agreement on fact where the law is clear than where it is not; and to reach agreement on fact rather than on what the law – the rules – should be,[105] and that 'the more a position requires the use of discretion, the more it requires a single mind'.[106] This contention is one of the central issues with which the book is concerned. For in seeking to identify and uphold the public interest, the 1993 Lottery Act charged the Director General with the ongoing and problematical task of locating an appropriate and acceptable balance between his different and often competing regulatory charges. From 1 April 1999 this same task was devolved upon the National Lottery Commission and its Commissioners.

CHAPTER 2

THE MODEL

This second section (comprising Chapters 2 and 3) examines the National Lottery's regulation *vis-à-vis* the objectives as set out in the enabling legislation. This part of the work also addresses the Lottery's regulation against the backcloth of criteria established in the first chapter. In so doing, the nature of the regulatory design, the problems of identifying the public interest and the difficulties associated with personalized regulatory models all feature prominently. This second section also forms the main body to the work and its overriding concern is to measure the success of the Lottery's regulation having regard to the statutory duties devolved upon the Director General of ensuring the projects propriety, protecting the players and maximizing the proceeds to be passed to the Good Causes.

2.1 *Regulatory Brief: Balancing Responsibilities*

Section 4 of Part I of the National Lottery etc Act. 1993 provided that

> 4–(1) The Secretary of State and (subject to any directions he may be given by the Secretary of State under Section 11) the Director General shall each exercise his functions under this Part in the manner he considers most likely to secure –
> (a) that the National Lottery is run, and every lottery that forms part of it is promoted, with all due propriety, and
> (b) that the interests of every participant in a lottery that forms part of the National Lottery are protected.
> (2) Subject to subsection (1) the Secretary of State and the Director General shall each in exercising those functions do his best to secure that the net proceeds of the National Lottery are as great as possible.[1]

While Section 4 refers to the functions of both the Secretary of State and the Director General, the Act made it clear thereafter that it was the Director General via the licensing system who was responsible for the day-to-day regulation of the Lottery.[2] However, as referred to earlier (p. 8) the Secretary of State retained (and continues to retain) the power to give Directions *vis-à-vis* the nature of the licences issued by the Regulator.[3] The Minister also enjoyed (and continues to enjoy) the power to make regulations in relation to the promotion of the lotteries that formed part of the National Lottery.[4]

In his ongoing management of the Lottery's regulation, Section 4 of the 1993 Act required the Director General to carry out two primary duties and a secondary duty. His first charges were to ensure that the Lottery and its constituent games were run and promoted with due propriety, and that the interests of all the players were protected. It was only after he had discharged his rôle in connection with these two primary areas (i.e. subject to) that the Director General should turn his attention to his secondary duty of maximizing the proceeds to the (initially five) Good Causes set out in Part II of the Act.[5] The dispatch of this secondary objective was in large measure by means of economic instruments – *viz.* a comprehensive competitive bidding process for the award of a monopoly, i.e. a seven-year Licence to run the Lottery. Having established the safeguards of quality, delivery and security, the criterion of projected rate-of-return to the National Lottery Distribution Fund (hereafter, the Distribution Fund) was ultimately the standard by which the head or main (Section 5) Licence was awarded to the successful bidder.[6]

All regulation is ultimately in place for social purposes, yet the employment of economic instruments, while not always a matter of precise science, does at least provide the regulator with some sort of framework within which evaluations can be made, as opposed to out-and-out social regulation (which the Director General's primary regulatory duties may be said to be), where there is no such agreed framework.[7] In crude terms it can be said that economic regulation is more rule-based while the social elements of regulation may be said to give rise more often to discretionary and value judgements. In the case of the National Lottery it was certainly the area of the Regulator's primary 'social' duties that proved to be most contentious and which led to the first Director General's resignation. Yet the problems that beset Peter Davis focused not only on his ability to carry out his regulatory function effectively, but also on his understanding and interpretation of the brief given to him by the Act.

Section 14 of Part I of the 1993 Act required the Director General to make an annual report of his functions to the Secretary of State. In his second report (which related to the first full year of the Lottery's operations) Peter Davis included a mission statement for his agency. This illustrates well, not only the difficulties already described of defining the public interest, but also how the initial purpose and clarity of vision that underpins or should underpin regulatory design can and often does become blurred and prone to controversy almost as soon as the regulatory process comes into action. The Director General's mission statement included in the second and subsequent annual reports reads thus: 'To ensure that the U.K. National Lottery is properly run and regulated, and players are protected, whilst maximising the money raised for the Good Causes.'[8] There is a small, subtle yet important difference between the Director General's mission statement for Oflot, on the one hand, and his office's statutory obligation of seeing that net proceeds were as great as possible 'subject to' the Lottery's propriety and the protection of the players' interests, on the other.[9] The mission statement for Oflot seemingly elevated the maximizing of proceeds to the Good Causes to a status ranking alongside that of ensuring the venture's propriety and the protection of participants. The problems for regulatory agencies are accepted as being especially difficult when the statutory brief is conflicting, for example regulatory versus promotional duties.[10] Some (including the Consumers' Association) called for the legislation to be amended to avoid this built-in conflict of interest between Oflot's different duties,[11] with the growing feeling that Oflot had too close an interest in players' losses being indicative of the success of the Lottery in delivering to the Good Causes.[12] By contrast the charity Directory of Social Change, which promotes the cause and needs of the voluntary sector, argued that: 'If Oflot just did the job set it by Parliament, instead of another it has chosen for itself, all should be well.'[13]

This is perhaps an example of an archetypal regulatory conundrum. It is also arguably a 'positive' variation of classic public interest theory which advances the concept of political actors who operate, sometimes perhaps mistakenly, to further a vision of the public good.[14] The criticism by the Consumers' Association echoed by the Directory of Social Change is that the National Lottery's first Director General misunderstood his statutory duties.[15] They maintained that his oft repeated objective of 'balancing' the maximizing of funds with the need to protect the venture's propriety and the interests of players[16] was flawed, as the Director General's job was not to strike a balance but to put the regulation of the Operator and interests of the players first.[17]

In the author's judgement, criticism that the Director General was not required to balance his regulatory duties, but to give the one unqualified priority over the other is flawed and guilty of reductionism. The public interest model of regulation maintains that it is a central function of an enforcement agency to reduce the negative externalities which come about as a consequence of regulatory breaches – but at lowest administrative cost. In the case of the Lottery, potential areas for negative spillovers or externalities, which the Regulator is statutorily obliged to prevent, relate primarily to issues connected with propriety and player protection. However, regulatory overinclusion will result if the marginal avoided social or external losses from enforcing compliance with a given standard are less than the sum of the compliance and enforcement costs.[18] In other words, perfect compliance is neither practicable nor desirable given that the costs of achieving it will invariably outweigh the benefits.[19]

In the case of the National Lottery, heavy-handed rule-based or inflexible enforcement policies will only result in regulatory outcomes which may be administratively costly and uneconomic. In this context it should be reiterated that the ultimate purpose of the Lottery is to improve the quality of life for the people of the UK by way of the monies applied to the Good Causes.[20] Overzealous regulation could also result in a cost to the Distribution Fund (the conduit which feeds the Good Causes) in the form of a loss of income that might have been generated against the background of a more liberal set of regulatory enforcement practices or strategies. By contrast, if regulation is underinclusive, ineffectual and lax this may result in unacceptable social costs as a consequence of negative externalities such as unsatisfactory standards of corporate behaviour by the Operator, or excessive or under-age participation in the Lottery.

Whether or not the combining of regulatory (propriety and player protection) with promotional (maximizing proceeds) duties was an appropriate remit for the Director General of the National Lottery and Oflot (or the National Lottery Commissioners and the Commission) is a point of some contention, and is addressed in Chapters 3 and 4. However, having regard to this brief and irrespective of the inherent tensions and potential for conflicts of interest to arise, it is entirely possible to defend the Director General's interpretation of his duties, to include that of balancing his promotional and regulatory functions. Neither is it unreasonable for a regulator with less than perfect information in all cases and in all circumstances to adopt a 'satisficing' strategy whereby instead of searching for an elusive optimal solution to regulation, he establishes what he believes to be an acceptable standard and prosecutes regulatory policies that have the best chance of meeting that standard.[21] Peter Davis was certainly an adherent of this style of regulatory realism or pragmatism:

> As with any verification or compliance work a balance has to be struck between the resources and costs devoted to the work undertaken and the degree of assurance required from the work . . . The Director General must exercise his judgement on what is the correct balance between the two poles.[22]

This is one of the quintessential features of personalized regulation. For the balance to which the Director General refers was in the final analysis a matter to be decided upon by him alone and not a committee or commission which would be likely to reach determinations consensually. A single regulator if he is able and consistent can in turn develop a consistent policy in decision-making in a way which, at least to himself, plainly locates his position in the middle ground, even if he cannot express to others its superiority over an alternative series of consistent decisions.[23] There is no reason to believe that a panel of regulators will have such an inner if inexpressible consistency.[24] If in trying to find the right 'balance' in his regulatory duties the individual regulator employs criteria which are consistent, fair and transparent then this makes for good regulation. Yet, in the UK, regulators (including the Director General of the Lottery) have been under no general duty to give reasons for their decisions, and they are therefore often accused of operating on the basis of vague criteria and standards of proof when making decisions.[25] Negotiations between regulators and industry chiefs do not have to be made public, nor do they have to involve other affected parties.[26] This contrasts with the American regulatory model which favours a more open procedural format, with public hearings and a greater degree of transparency.[27] In the UK, judgements and conclusions arrived at have been traditionally identified with the individual regulator; and advocates of the single regulator system argue that it is more difficult to fix responsibility for administrative discretion and managerial decisions on a multiple executive.[28] Yet in the final analysis the expertise of the regulator can only really apply to scientific problems and while this should help to ensure a grasp of technical limitations and possibilities, it does not contribute to a positive elucidation of the public interest.[29] Here even the expert must rely on his fallible judgement and integrity.[30]

The rôle of the individual regulator is, then, a function which carries heavy responsibilities; and criticisms of the National Lottery's regulation during the time Peter Davis was in office were invariably addressed to the Director General rather than Oflot. Not only was he criticized for striking balances where such an approach was deemed by some to be inappropriate, but he was also criticized for striking the wrong balance between his competing regulatory duties by those who would have preferred a different judgement to have been made.[31] The Director General of the National Lottery's search for an acceptable public interest standard was in practice an invidious and thankless task; it remains so for the five Lottery Commissioners. The criticism that the Regulator was not required to balance his regulatory responsibilities with his promotional responsibilities, but to give the one absolute priority over the other is flawed and simplistic and at odds with the views of the Lottery Advisory Group's report, which argued that the Regulator should endeavour to strike 'a balance between the generation of revenue and the public good. It is the duty of the Regulator to achieve and sustain such a balance'.[32]

2.2 *The Bidding Process and Its Rationale*

The establishment of a National Lottery created a rule-making and regulatory challenge concerned with both structure and conduct. Structure regulation is usually said to describe the arrangements that allow certain firms or individuals (or types thereof) to engage in prescribed activities, and includes the creation of a statutory monopoly with the concomitant rules on single capacity and restrictions on market entry.[33] In the case of the National Lottery the Operator enjoys a partial or near monopoly, with the potential existing for collaboration with other commercial entities under Section 6 of the Act. The first section to this work described *inter alia* the reasons that lay behind the model of a monopoly or quasi-monopoly being preferred for the promotion of the National Lottery. Replacing competition in the market with competition for the market helps to reduce the monopolists' opportunities for rent-seeking, resulting in allocative inefficiency and dead-weight losses. The bidding process can thus be seen as a valid response to the classic regulatory problem of configuring the economic system in such a way that individual economic actors make decisions in their own best interest that also achieve allocative efficiency for society at large.[34]

Having determined upon a bidding process to award a licence, it followed *a priori* that the Licensee would come from the private sector. The rationale behind the placing of the Lottery in the private sector was a manifestation of the government's stated philosophy that the profit motive would provide a strong incentive for the Operator to maximize sales and, therefore, the returns to the Good Causes.[35] The implicit argument underpinning the Department for the National Heritage's decision was that only a for-profit organization could raise the start-up capital investment, and sustain a marketing budget on a large enough scale to generate the level of ticket sales necessary to achieve the desired return to the Distribution Fund.[36] By granting a seven-year Licence (effective until 30 September 2001), the Operator of the Lottery would have sufficient time to recoup its start-up costs and make a reasonable return, although the winning bidder, Camelot, has argued that (when the Licence is renewed) the Lottery would benefit from a more lengthy licence period to enable the Operator to make investment decisions over the longer term.[37] On 21 December 1993 'Invitations to Apply' to run the National Lottery under Section 5 of the Act were issued by Oflot, and by the closing date by which applications had to be submitted (14 February 1994) eight applications had been received.[38]

In his deliberations, the Director General assessed the suitability of the applicants against the criteria of his own overriding duties of guaranteeing propriety, ensuring player protection and then maximizing the net proceeds to the Distribution Fund.[39] This area of the Regulator's responsibilities, which was also ongoing, may be said to be chiefly concerned with conduct. Conduct regulation refers to measures that are associated with how firms behave in their chosen activity or activities, and will typically include price controls, rules restricting advertising and measures to guard against anti-competitive behaviour by the dominant incumbent firm(s).[40] A priority for the Director General of the Lottery in meeting his two primary duties, was to satisfy himself that the body and persons making up the body that secured the Licence were fit and proper.[41] The phrase 'fit and proper' is something of a rubric which permeates the regulation of other areas of commercial gambling and as such reflects the underlying and enduring concern of regulators and legislators with the industry's tendency to corruption and misconduct. In connection with the applications, the Director General established a vetting division within Oflot to check submissions and information contained therein, with law enforcement and other agencies, government departments, regulatory bodies and other relevant organizations in the UK and overseas.[42] In all, the Director General undertook vetting procedures on some 1300 individuals and 230 companies.[43] Indeed this vetting procedure was ongoing – the details of which are included in each annual report.

In their submissions the eight applicants were required to provide comprehensive responses to questions falling under ten main headings. These headings are reproduced at Appendix I, pages 199–200. The NAO concluded that the systems and procedures employed by the Director General in evaluating the applications were 'comprehensive, consistent, logical and properly controlled; [and] that throughout the process the Director General acted in accordance with the statutory duties placed upon him.'[44] In determining to award the Licence to the Camelot consortium, the Director General had, of necessity, concluded that the organization and its constituent parts were 'fit and proper'. Subsequent events found this assessment to have been flawed, with the propriety of the Lottery being brought into question. This culminated not only in the Director General resigning his post, but also in a fundamental overhaul of the regulatory arrangements appertaining to the Lottery. This subject will be addressed below.

While the first heading under the 'Information required from applicants' exhibited at Appendix I is concerned with the propriety of the Lottery Operator, sections 5–10 inclusive address either in total or in part the matter of player protection.[45] In studying the Report by the Comptroller and Auditor General, *Evaluating the Applications to Run the National Lottery*, it appears that the decisive factor which determined the award of the Licence was less to do with the issues of propriety and player protection, than it was to do with determining the appropriate balance between the projected monies to be retained by the Operator and the net proceeds to be applied to the Distribution Fund. No applications were rejected on the grounds of failing to meet the strict criterion *vis-à-vis* propriety. Three applicants were found by the Director General to have had failings embracing one or more of the following: lack of experience, lack of state of readiness and inadequate systems,[46] any one of which could have undermined the protection of players and also the proceeds to be passed to the Fund.

In reporting the evaluation process, the Comptroller and Auditor General of the NAO focused most strongly on revenue issues in evaluating the Director General's deliberations. This would suggest that the main differences to be found in the quality of the applications to run the Lottery were indeed less to do with 'propriety' and 'player protection' than with revenue generation and its apportionment. This position was also confirmed by the Director General himself: 'The contributions to the good causes were perhaps the most significant part of the competitive process that we used to select the operator.'[47] Furthermore, the Director General confirmed that he had found no evidence of improper conduct by any of the applicants.[48] Sections 2–5 inclusive of the 'Information required from applicants' at Appendix I deal principally with the issue of revenue and its allocation (section 5 deals with both revenue generation and player protection). It was these categories that proved critical in the award of the Licence to Camelot, as the company 'offered the greatest contribution to the Good Causes over a wide range of revenue scenarios, and retained the lowest percentage of turnover to cover its operating costs and profit.'[49]

In concluding this section on the bidding process and the award of the Licence it is worth observing that three applicants including Camelot offered additional payments to the Distribution Fund over and above the contributions included in their applications.[50] Two of the applicants offered contributions related to the profits they earned, while Camelot offered to maintain in an Escrow account a balance equal to 2.5 per cent of the value of the previous years' ticket sales less £40 million which upon termination of the Licence for whatever reason, including the effluxion of time, would revert to the NLDF.[51]

2.3 *Richard Branson and UK Lotteries Ltd*

At the time of the announcement that Camelot had won the bid to become the Lottery's Operator, there was a good deal of speculation in the media as to why one of the bidders, *viz.* UK Lotteries Ltd which had pledged all its profits to charity, had not been the successful candidate.[52] This consortium, led by the businessman Richard Branson, had provided in its application for all profits to be covenanted to a parent charitable foundation which would then apply those funds to charities of its own choosing.[53] The contribution by UK Lotteries Ltd to the Good Causes chosen by Parliament was lower than Camelot's over a wide range of revenue forecasts.[54] Under the framework of the National Lottery Act, the operating profit of UK Lotteries Ltd which the parent company The Lottery Foundation had pledged to charities of its own choosing could not properly have been taken into account in the calculation of the contribution to Good Causes.[55] Nevertheless, the Director General acknowledged the possibility of UK Lotteries' assertion that more players would spend more if they knew that all the profits would go to charity, thereby generating higher sales and so greater contributions to the Distribution Fund.[56] Although the bid included market research in support of this position, the Director General found it inconclusive as it did not incorporate any estimate of the amount by which total revenue would be increased as a result.[57] According to the NAO the bid by UK Lotteries ranked fourth of the eight applications.[58]

2.4 *Regulatory Structure*

The National Lottery etc. Act 1993 established in Part I Section 3 the new position of Director General of the National Lottery. The Director General led the Office of the National Lottery (Oflot) which was a non-ministerial government department.[59] The Director General was appointed for a term of five years, remained eligible for re-appointment and could only be removed from office by the Secretary of State on the grounds of 'incapacity or misbehaviour'.[60] This phrase (which is also found in the Acts that define the rôles of other key regulators such as Ofgas and Oftel) is included deliberately to help guarantee the freedom and independence of the Regulator from the interference of the judiciary, while at the same time protecting the private Operator from arbitrary interventions from politicians,[61] in response to short-term political pressures. That the Director General's term in office was two years shorter than the Operator's Licence of seven years was certainly of some value in helping to preserve the Regulator's independence and also in preventing his 'capture' by the Regulatee. The personalized nature of the regime was underscored by the framing of the legislation. The Director General was not the Director General of Oflot, he was the Director General of the National Lottery.

The Regulator and his office were charged with authorizing a body corporate to run the Lottery under Section 5 of the Act, and then under Section 6 to award licences to run individual games. Thereafter it was the duty of the Regulator in meeting his statutory obligations to ensure the Operator's compliance with the conditions set out in the Licence. The Licence in turn sets out in detail (the document contains 189 A4 pages)[62] the performance standards the Operator is required to meet in order for the Director General to perform his statutory duties. The funds raised that are passed and applied to the Distribution Fund are under the control of the Secretary of State.[63] These net proceeds are in turn passed in equal proportions to five Good Causes, *viz.* the Arts Councils of Great Britain and Northern Ireland, the Sports Councils of the United Kingdom, the National Heritage Memorial Fund, the National Lottery Charities Board (established under Section 37 of the Act) and the Millennium Commission (established under Section 40).[64] The National Lottery Act 1998 created a new category – The New Opportunities Fund[65] – to share in the Lottery's bounty.

CHAPTER 3

MEETING REGULATORY OBJECTIVES

1 ENSURING THE LOTTERY'S PROPRIETY

The integrity of a lottery is a vital ingredient in retaining the confidence of the public. The design of the UK Lottery and its licensing system is different from most other lottery jurisdictions in that the impact of any fraud in general falls on the private sector operator, rather than the Distribution Fund.[1] Nevertheless, doubts about the probity of the Operator could lead to a withdrawal of public support and as a consequence a diminution in the funds raised for the Good Causes. The importance attached to the integrity of the Lottery is borne out by an extended vision statement for Oflot set out by the Director General in his first report which stated *inter alia*, 'crucially, the Lottery must be run (and be seen to be run) in a fair, trustworthy manner that is beyond reproach.'[2]

As has already been described, the Regulator made extensive enquiries during the bidding process as to the 'fit and proper' status of the applicants. However, these enquiries into the suitability of the Section 5 and indeed the Section 6 Licence holder(s) did not end once the Section 5 Licence was awarded. In each annual report the Director General delineated the measures he had taken to help maintain the highest standards of propriety and public confidence in the Lottery. In the year to 31 March 1997 for example, the Director General's office made vetting enquiries on 524 individuals and 10 companies drawn from Camelot employees, shareholders and main suppliers.[3] During this period, six individuals were found to be not 'fit and proper' – three were Camelot employees and three were employees of key contractors.[4] They either left or did not take up their position in relation to the National Lottery, and in one case they were prohibited by Oflot from day-to-day involvement in the Lottery.[5]

In upholding the integrity of the Lottery an important duty of the Director General's office at the launch was to approve Camelot's on-line lottery systems.[6] The main objectives of this were to ensure that the systems and procedures that had been designed would guarantee that the right sums were collected and paid to the NLDF, that prizes were paid correctly and that Lottery retailers gave a good service to the players.[7] The central priorities for Oflot and in particular its Compliance Division were to monitor payments made by Camelot to the NLDF and to the Players' Trust.[8] The Players' Trust is a trust fund independently managed by Law Debenture Trust Corporation PLC which is designed to protect the prize money due to winners from the default or insolvency of the Operator.[9] In addition the Operator deposited funds in a trust account (which had reached £20.3 million by 31 March 1999) as an additional reserve for the protection of players which only reverts to Camelot at the end of the Licence period.[10] To protect the integrity of Lottery data and Camelot's systems and procedures and thus the propriety of the Lottery, Oflot's Compliance Division also operated a stand-alone computer in a secure computer suite at Camelot's offices.[11] Data from the primary Camelot lottery gaming system was copied onto tape at the close of each day's processing, and these tapes were handed to Oflot before each draw.[12] Oflot then processed these tapes on their Independent Control System software and compared and balanced the results with Camelot's primary gaming system reports to ensure a full declaration in number and value of wagers.[13] This separate computer audit function was (and is) continually developed using more sophisticated interrogation software and risk analysis tools to ensure the compliance of the Section 5 and Section 6 Licensee(s).[14]

Oflot and more especially the Compliance Division of Oflot existed to make sure Camelot honoured its Licence commitments. The annual reports of the Director General listed any failures or breaches of its Licence by Camelot. Most breaches that were listed by way of appendices to the annual reports were generally of a minor or technical nature and were soon rectified.[15] In the Director General's assessment the more serious Licence breaches by Camelot included failure to meet retail outlet commitments, the submission of inaccurate data on this subject, failure to pay unclaimed prizes to the Distribution Fund on time and the use of lottery systems for the launch of the Instants game before official approval had been granted by Oflot.[16] Under Section 9 of the Act the Director General was empowered to seek an injunction in the High Court to prevent or remedy a Licence breach. This power was not invoked by the Director General. However, it is for the type of breaches that are listed above that the Director General sought unsuccessfully to have his powers extended by the Secretary of State to incorporate other avenues of intermediate action including the power to impose financial penalties on the Operator. This issue is addressed below. Nevertheless, in maintaining the propriety of the Lottery it must be said that the Director General had been conferred extensive powers by the Act which included powers to require Camelot to provide information at any time and in any form the Director General stipulated and to seek his approval prior to the introduction of new

Lottery products or other market developments; and to inspect at any time any aspect of Camelot's implementation of its Licence, including any bodies subcontracted to it.[17] These powers are now invested in the Commissioners and the Lottery Commission.

Notwithstanding Oflot's extensive powers to ensure the Operator's compliance, the PAC was critical of Oflot's Compliance Division. In its report on payments to the Distribution Fund in 1997, the PAC expressed its concern that a year after the launch of the Lottery, 11 of 21 compliance programmes had still to be executed, including important areas such as draw procedures, protection of players' interests, and security arrangements.[18] The PAC concluded that the Director General had not given sufficient priority to the compliance programme in the first year of the Lottery, and expressed concern with regard to the limited frequency with which the programmes had been applied.[19] The Director General in defending himself maintained that the priority and frequency of such programmes had been based on his assessment of risk, and that he had met his statutory duties.[20]

1.1 *The Retail Network*

The retail network is also a key element of the Lottery's operations where issues of probity and propriety can and do arise. The number of retail outlets selling National Lottery products rose from nearly 10,000 at the time of the launch of the Lottery in November 1994[21] to over 35,000 outlets by the year ending 31 March 1997.[22] These retailers are contractually bound to Camelot who remain responsible for ensuring that the highest standards are maintained with the threat of contract termination for miscreant retailers.[23] Oflot did not have the power to institute proceedings against such retailers, instead it relied on commercial sanctions by the Operator and/or Trading Standards offices.[24] The same applies to the Lottery Commission. The types of activity at the retail level that serve to undermine the propriety of the Lottery include the theft of tickets, whether by retailers, the public or distributors,[25] and selling of tickets to players under the age of 16 which is prohibited.[26] Under-age sales will be tackled more fully in Part 2 of this chapter. Other problems that have detracted from the integrity of the Lottery relate to retailer fraud. This could include the retailer cancelling a Draw ticket after it has been bought without refunding the money;[27] unless customers win a prize they have no way of knowing that their ticket has not been registered.[28] Retailers could also be tempted to pick at the seal of Instants scratch-cards to discover the winning tickets.[29] While security defects have been minimized by Camelot, at least one retail agent, and possibly more than one, managed to tamper with Instants Lottery tickets in 1995 to discover which cards were winning cards before they were sold.[30] The individual retailer concerned had his contract with Camelot terminated, and the matter was reported to the police.[31] In the first year of the Lottery's operations 27 retailers had their contracts terminated for security breaches and a further 25 for failing to pay monies over on time.[32] From the financial year 1997/98 the Operator agreed to bear the cost of payments equivalent to prizes to any players whose tickets are shown to have been fraudulently, negligently or erroneously cancelled by retailers or Camelot itself,[33] thus helping to uphold the propriety of the Lottery while at the same time providing an improvement in the level of player protection.

Sales of Lottery tickets to under-age players, and fraudulent practices carried out by retailers certainly undermine confidence in the Lottery. These are offences that are committed not by Camelot directly, but indirectly by agents acting on Camelot's behalf. Nevertheless, monitoring retailer behaviour remains the responsibility of the Operator. Yet Camelot itself has been accused of direct commercial activities in the retail environment liable to damage the Lottery's image. Allegations were made in 1996 that Camelot's sales representatives were using aggressive selling techniques to pressurize retailers into removing rival charity scratch-cards from their premises, in defiance of government guarantees to encourage the sale of both.[34] Furthermore, in 1998 Vernons wrote to Oflot complaining of predatory pricing and pressure placed on retailers by Camelot to use their products in favour of other competing products.[35] In the absence of written evidence no action was taken by the Director General or his office.[36] These allegations, if true (they did not result in any legal action), would confirm the tendency outlined in Chapter 1 for monopolists to abuse their market power. The extent of the authority of the Regulator in relation to such issues was (and continues to be) less than entirely satisfactory. If the propriety of the Lottery is being undermined in some evidential or demonstrative way then there is a clear statutory mandate for regulatory intervention. Yet the protection of other organizations from the abuse of the Lottery Operator's dominant market position was not in the first instance a matter for the Director General and Oflot, nor is it for the Lottery Commissioners and the Commission. The Director General confirmed: 'I have no statutory duty to promote competition or to promote a level playing field; that is not a duty laid on me in the Act.'[37] In the first instance reported abuses of market power of the type that were alleged to have taken place would be a matter for the Office of Fair Trading (OFT).[38] In June 1999 the OFT decided not to pursue allegations by the Littlewoods organization of anti-competitive behaviour by Camelot.[39]

1.2 *A Tasteful Lottery/Corporate Responsibility*

When the Lottery was conceived, it was an important element of the government's vision that the enterprise should be seen as tasteful.[40] This meant in particular that the vending of Lottery products should not be intrusive, and hence tickets are forbidden from being sold in the street, by door to door or by telephone.[41] But the good taste and propriety of the Lottery are not only dependent on how Lottery products are distributed or how they are advertised. In connection with the National Lottery, good taste and propriety are issues that are closely linked with each other and with standards of corporate governance and corporate responsibility on the part of the Operator.

During the summer of 1997 the image of the Lottery was damaged by the furore that followed the announcement of the level of bonuses that were to be awarded to the directors of Camelot. These bonuses increased the earnings of the directors by between 50 per cent and 90 per cent[42] at a time (year ending 31 March 1997) when the Company's operating profit (which had also been the subject of ongoing adverse media attention) had fallen from £66.7 million to £60.2 million, and when the annual contribution to the Distribution Fund also fell from £1,416.1 million to £1,272.6 million.[43] Camelot defended the level of payments, describing them as a combination of annual and long-term bonuses which had been designed in part to compensate the directors for the fact that they could not be awarded share options as Camelot cannot be floated on the stock market.[44] These payments were made at a time when there had been a good deal of disquiet and media attention having regard to the level of remuneration enjoyed by senior executives of public companies and in particular the senior executives of privatized public utilities. There was a feeling that Camelot had ignored or misread this 'new mood of the times'.[45]

The reputation of the Lottery was certainly not helped by the foregoing. Yet an unfortunate episode was arguably exacerbated by the individual intervention of the Secretary of State for Culture Media and Sport, Chris Smith, who demanded that part or all of the bonuses – totalling £2.3 million be paid to charity.[46] The Secretary of State claimed that hundreds of thousands of people had telephoned the Heritage department to express their disgust, and that many had boycotted the Lottery resulting in the lowest ever Saturday income.[47] Mr Smith's dismay at Camelot's behaviour led him to emphasize not only that the government was committed to seeking a non-profit making Operator when the Licence expired in 2001,[48] but also to declare that he was examining how much would have to be paid by way of compensation to Camelot if the government overturned the contract before its expiry.[49] Matters reached a head when three of the directors of Camelot threatened to resign.[50] This prompted a climb-down by the Secretary of State who agreed to accept an undertaking from the directors to make secret personal voluntary payments into a charitable fund from a forthcoming long-term bonus.[51] Additionally Camelot agreed to pay over interest earned on the so-called Prize Target Shortfall from 31 March 1997 to the expiry of the operating Licence – a figure anticipated to exceed £20 million.[52] However, this concession had been the subject of negotiation for almost a year and many commentators and Lottery experts were of the view that Camelot's directors believed the Company would have to yield to demands to hand back the interest on the prize shortfall sooner or later.[53]

This episode certainly sullied the Lottery's reputation, and also brought into question the propriety of the Lottery. The *Shorter Oxford English Dictionary* defines propriety as 'fitness, suitability, conformity with requirement, rule or principle; rightness, correctness . . . conformity with good manners . . . correctness of behaviour or morals.'[54] Neither the behaviour of Camelot, nor indeed the Secretary of State could be said to satisfy the definition of propriety. Yet the affair is also important in helping to shed light on the stresses and strains of a political, philosophical and cultural nature that the Lottery is prone to. The ill-judged intervention by the Secretary of State without any statutory mandate served to politicize the Lottery. Whether or not the bonuses were excessive they were paid legally as the result of proper contracts.[55] The implication of Mr Smith's actions is that it is entirely appropriate for government to have an overt rôle in setting private sector pay levels.[56] The difficulty was further compounded by the government's oft repeated statement that the venture is 'The People's Lottery' and as such it should reflect the people's priorities.[57] This in turn is predicated on the notion that the Lottery is not really part of the private sector, rather as a government monopoly administered by a private sector company, it is seen as a hybrid which will remain sensitive to political considerations.[58] The very public steps taken by the Secretary of State can be seen at one level as a logical extension of stated government policy *vis-à-vis* the reining in of excessive profits and pay deals in particular with regard to the privatized utilities. At another level it can be seen as the government preparing the way for achieving its stated objective of having the Lottery, if not transferred to the state, then at least run on a non-profit or much reduced profit basis when the first Licence expires.

Chapter 1 highlighted the importance of the balance and the agreed lines of demarcation between the functions of a Regulator and his sponsoring government department. The nature of this principal/agent relationship holds one of the keys to successful regulation. The challenge is for political leadership and support not to become too frequently expressed, or too heavy-handed and intrusive, as this can serve to undermine rather than underpin the authority and credibility of the agency. The precise application of any regulatory instrument should be determined independently by the regulator, subject to ministerial intervention only in the last resort if the regulator's decisions are perverse or contrary to government objectives.[59] The Secretary of State's intervention falls outside of this definition.

While it is not unreasonable to expect the regulatory frame of reference to shift with a change of government, it is arguably the case that Mr Smith's behaviour in giving the impression of making up policy on the hoof, and then attempting to implement it himself, had 'exposed himself as interventionist.'[60] For it is the National Lottery etc. 1993 Act that provides the framework for the Secretary of State, the Regulator and the Operator. Thereafter the Licence sets out the rules for the Operator which in broad terms are designed to help meet the Regulator's duties. In keeping with most private, regulated firms, the Act and in particular the Licence principally impose external controls on the firm. That is to say control is extended to those variables that link the firm (Camelot) with outsiders and most especially consumers (participants).[61] These external controls are designed to protect consumers while interfering as little as possible in the internal management of the firm that is providing the service(s).

The alternative of issuing more specific instructions can involve those responsible for the firm's regulation in areas where they are less well informed and qualified to make decisions than the managers of the industry for whose regulation they are responsible.[62] The danger of issuing more specific directives is that the regulator is liable to cross over from overseeing a framework of essentially external controls to intervening more directly within the business by attempting to impose certain controls which may be styled internal. Internal controls include control of the firm's inputs and costs, managerial inputs and incentive schemes.[63] The problems associated with such a course of action are potentially made more fraught still when efforts to impose internal controls are made by government and not the firm's regulator. For this can serve to damage any good will that might exist between regulator and regulatee; as well as eroding the authority of the regulator's office. Unless the Secretary of State's powers are used sparingly there is a danger that the government will intervene for short-term political gain and in so doing undermine some of the benefits associated with agency rule-making that have already been referred to.[64] Mr Smith's intervention with regard to the Camelot directors' bonuses, which was both highly visible (being covered extensively in the media) and controversial, may be said to be a case in point. The Director General Peter Davis was sensibly inconspicuous in what turned out to be a very public spat.

1.3 *The GTech Fiasco*

The presence of GTech as a member of Camelot, the five-company Consortium that won the Licence to operate the National Lottery, became something of a running sore that served to undermine the credibility and integrity of the Lottery. This eventually culminated in the resignation of the Director General, the withdrawal of GTech from the Consortium and the subsequent overhaul of the Lottery's regulation and a re-evaluation of its format. This section is salutary in demonstrating the weakness and vulnerability that can be associated with personalized regulation. The Director General's judgement in discharging his individual statutory responsibilities was found to be seriously flawed in connection with the rôle of GTech and the part played by one of its directors (who was also a non-executive director of Camelot). The deliberations of the Director General in connection with GTech were found to lack transparency and to be idiosyncratic if not eccentric, and led to a series of events that damaged the Lottery; events which might have been avoided in the more consultative setting of a commission-based system of regulation.

From the outset one of the Director General's early tasks (under Section 5 (4) of the Act) in making sure the Lottery is run with propriety was to determine that the Operator and any person involved in any part of the business of running the Lottery was 'fit and proper' for the task. Section 1 of Appendix I on page 199 outlines the type of information sought by the Director General in order to make his 'fit and proper' enquiries. In evaluating the competing bids the Regulator designed a series of tests or tasks to help him choose the Operator and so award the Licence. One of these tasks, Task G, involved the checking of declarations completed by individuals and companies associated with each applicant.[65] These declarations were then verified with relevant agencies, such as financial regulators, police forces, and stock exchanges both at home and overseas.[66]

At the time of the Director General's 'fit and proper' enquiries and before the Licence to run the Lottery had been awarded a number of findings in connection with GTech and the Company's business practices were unearthed. These findings brought into question the suitability or fitness of GTech to participate in the UK's proposed Lottery. GTech is an American company and one of four or five in the world that specialize in providing equipment, services and software to the Lottery industry.[67] GTech is the biggest of these companies supplying in one form or another around two-thirds of the world lottery industry's needs,[68] and a total of 72 Lotteries on five continents.[69] The Company was also (until April 1998) a 22.5 per cent equity participator in the Camelot Consortium.

The Director General's investigations into GTech uncovered suggestions of undesirable business practices by the Company in obtaining lottery contracts from the US, including alleged corrupt payments in California, Kentucky and New Jersey made to various persons, one of whom was a state Senator.[70] The Director General explained to the PAC that in deciding that GTech was 'fit and proper', he had considered *inter alia* the proposed rôle of GTech in Camelot, the standing and reputation of the members of the Camelot consortium, that neither GTech nor any officer of GTech had been charged with or found guilty of an offence, that the allegations against GTech related to securing lottery contracts, not operating or supplying them, and that the standards of business practice in the US are different when compared with those in the UK.[71] The Director General told the PAC that he had been concerned that if GTech had been required to withdraw from the bid then he would have effectively ruled out the applicant offering the best return to the Distribution Fund.[72] This raises the issue outlined earlier having regard to the Regulator's statutory remit. It is a primary duty of the Regulator to uphold the propriety of the Lottery. Maximizing the net proceeds to be passed to the Distribution Fund is a secondary responsibility.

Between the announcement that Camelot had won the bid to run the Lottery (25 May 1994) and the launch of the undertaking (14 November 1994) the Director General further weakened his position and credibility. In October 1994 he travelled to the US to visit selected lotteries, during which time he made a number of internal flights in GTech aircraft and at GTech's expense.[73] The Regulator's justification for this had been that the journeys by scheduled airlines would have taken much longer and would have cost the taxpayer much more.[74] However, the then Secretary of State Virginia Bottomley took it upon herself formally to write to the Director General and reprimand him suggesting that his decision to accept the flights had been unwise and that he 'should maintain a proper distance from the company [Camelot] and its constituent parts, and be seen to do so.'[75] The implications of the Director General's actions were that by failing to keep his distance from the Regulatee he was in danger of becoming a victim of 'regulatory capture'; a state of affairs that would compromise his independence. The issue of regulatory capture is addressed more fully in Chapter 4. It was suggested at the time of Mrs Bottomley's letter (which was itself not sent until over a year after the flights had been taken) that the Regulator came very close to being dismissed by the Secretary of State, who had refrained from this course of action only because senior colleagues had convinced her that dismissal would overshadow the success of the Lottery.[76] Even though the Director General had taken flights after the award of the main Licence to Camelot, and even though there had been no attempt to conceal the flights or to gain personally from the visits, the PAC agreed with the Secretary of State, commenting that the Regulator had made a serious error of judgement as he had an ongoing duty to regulate the Lottery, and indeed to issue Section 6 licences in the future.[77] The Director General was also upbraided by the PAC for accepting during his visit the private hospitality of a prominent member and executive of a New York investment house with a shareholding in GTech, irrespective of the long-standing friendship between the wives of both the Regulator and the financier.[78]

It is worth remarking that even after Camelot had been awarded the Licence, the Regulator remained concerned having regard to the seriousness of some of the allegations made against GTech. So much so that he summoned the Chairman of Camelot on the day after the announcement of the winning bid had been made to seek reassurances that the position would be monitored to guarantee nothing untoward happened.[79] As events transpired the Director General was proven to have made a serious miscalculation in determining that GTech and its officers were fit and proper.

1.4 *Bribery and Corruption*

The Director General had been correct to point out that business ethics and lobbying practices are very different in the USA compared with the UK and that what are acceptable practices in one are not necessarily acceptable in the other. In addition to this, another factor that should be borne in mind in connection with the propriety of the Lottery is the mixed reputation and indeed track record of the gambling industry itself. Gambling is an activity in which the only product which changes hands is money – all commercial gambling is therefore cash generating and cash circulating and as such is susceptible to criminal involvement, for example through money laundering.[80] Although it is the 'hardest' forms of gambling, such as casino gaming, that tend to be the most prone to abuse by criminals (and which are therefore subject to more rigorous regulatory regimes), it has been alleged that thousands of UK Lottery tickets have been connected with police investigations into an international fraud and money laundering ring.[81] Lotteries too are then vulnerable to malfeasance. With reservations over GTech's more liberal code of business ethics coupled with their high profile in the international gambling industry, it is perhaps not surprising that their presence in the Camelot consortium would be likely to attract controversy, and require close supervision. GTech was also the only member of the Consortium whose principal business lay in the gambling sector.

In 1991 California State Senator Alan E. Robins pleaded guilty to accepting campaign contributions from a GTech lobbyist in return for voting against a Bill that affected the California State Lottery.[82] Neither GTech nor any of the company's officers or employees were charged with any crimes.[83] However, in February 1998 Guy Snowden who was at that time Chairman of GTech and a non-executive director of Camelot, was found in the British High Court to have offered a bribe in September 1993 to Richard Branson a director of UK Lotteries Ltd to withdraw his Company's rival bid to run the Lottery.[84] Mr Branson had initially made the allegations on the *Panorama* television documentary in December 1995, and the ensuing court case represented a two-way libel action with Guy Snowden suing Richard Branson over the bribery allegations, and Richard Branson suing Guy Snowden for accusing him of lying.[85]

The outcome of the libel case was certainly a serious blow to the propriety of the Lottery and a fatal blow having regard to the credibility of both Guy Snowden and the Regulator Peter Davis. The government was eager to act quickly and decisively to restore public confidence. Yet there were concerns held in some quarters as to how discovery of the bribe had only surfaced two years after it was originally alleged to have been made[86] and, furthermore, for the allegation to have taken nearly four and a half years to be upheld. Notwithstanding the notoriously slow progress of the judiciary there were perhaps two reasons for this. Firstly, Richard Branson had been reluctant at the time the bribe was made to publicize this fact or to report it to the Director General for fear of 'muddying the waters' during the selection process; as this might have served to detract from the merits of UK Lotteries' bid.[87] Secondly, following the revelations of the *Panorama* documentary, the Director General appointed a Queen's Counsel to investigate the bribery allegations. Anne Rafferty QC concluded her investigations by stating: 'I am not able to find as a fact that there was any attempt to bribe Mr Richard Branson.'[88]

Ms Rafferty had arrived at her conclusion in large measure due to Mr Branson's disinclination to cooperate with the enquiry.[89] He had refused to cooperate apparently because of his lack of confidence in the Director General, due to the latter's admitted acceptance of GTech hospitality[90] in the form of free flights taken during his visit to the US.

The result of the court action confirmed the doubts that had been raised by the Public Accounts Committee over the fitness of GTech and its officers *vis-à-vis* their rôle in the National Lottery. Following the verdict the Director General delivered an ultimatum to Camelot, insisting the Company sever all links with Guy Snowden within 24 hours.[91] As a consequence Mr Snowden resigned on 2 February 1998 as a director of Camelot Group plc and on 3 February as a director of GTech Holdings Corporation and all subsidiary and affiliated companies.[92] The 3 February also saw the resignation of the Director General.[93]

The whole episode had certainly brought into question not only the propriety of the Lottery but also the effectiveness of the regulatory regime and in particular the rôle of the Director General. Although the Director

General resigned his post it was clear and widely understood at the time that he had come under a great deal of pressure from the Secretary of State.[94] In accepting the Director General's resignation the Secretary of State announced to the media that there was no question mark over Peter Davis's integrity.[95] Had there been any doubts in this area then the Secretary of State would have had the power under Schedule 2 (1) (4) of the 1993 Act to dismiss the Regulator. The Secretary of State Chris Smith welcomed Mr Davis's readiness to put the public reputation of the Lottery before his own personal position.[96] However, there is clearly a fine line here as to whether the Director General jumped or was pushed,[97] with some commentators suggesting he was dismissed on the direct orders of the Prime Minister.[98] Yet had Mr Davis not resigned it is doubtful as to whether he could have been dismissed as the Secretary of State's powers in this area only extended to removing the Director General on the grounds of 'incapacity or misbehaviour'.[99]

The Director General's 'enforced' resignation was the result of serious errors of judgement on his part. As Alan Keen the Labour MP and member of the Commons Select Committee on Culture Media and Sport rather bluntly put it, Peter Davis had, in discharging his remit to help guarantee the Lottery is promoted with all due propriety, 'obviously failed almost from the beginning to the end because he knew GTech were flawed when he first spoke to them.'[100] The Regulator had taken a calculated gamble in permitting GTech to form part of the Consortium that won the Licence to run the Lottery. While he had reservations about whether the Company and its officers and employees satisfied the 'fit and proper' criterion, he took comfort in the knowledge that GTech would be operating as part of a Consortium with four other companies.[101] It was the structure and standards of the Consortium that the Regulator judged would uphold the integrity and propriety of the Lottery.[102] Because of the strength of Camelot's bid in terms of the returns to the Distribution Fund, Peter Davis had been prepared to take a risk with the presence and rôle of GTech in the Consortium. In so doing he had arguably elevated the maximizing of the funds to the 'Good Causes' to a status above that of protecting the propriety of the undertaking.

Peter Davis's deputy John Stoker was as a consequence of the former's resignation promoted to Acting Director General with immediate effect (the position was subsequently confirmed) and straight away put in train an extensive investigation into GTech's 'fit and proper' status (notwithstanding Guy Snowden's resignation).[103] Sensing the difficulty the Company was in, and with growing public and media outrage, Camelot moved to buy GTech's 22.5 per cent ordinary shareholding in the Consortium (for £51 million).[104] This step, completed on 15 April 1998, was welcomed by the new Regulator (and the Secretary of State)[105] who considered it the right response to the public mood and also a measure which would simplify his deliberations regarding GTech's fitness and propriety.[106] Had this measure not been taken by Camelot it was entirely possible that the new Director General would have seriously considered revoking the Operator's Licence, and suspending the Lottery while the imbroglio was sorted out.[107] This would have been an extreme measure. Intelligent regulation will subscribe to the philosophy that: 'If the golden goose is befouling the nest, the regulator should try to clean it up without stopping egg production.'[108]

While GTech had voluntarily withdrawn as a shareholder, the new Director General still had to satisfy himself that GTech was 'fit and proper' to continue in its rôle as a major supplier of services to Camelot. Historical evidence suggests that changing the running of lottery games or their operators can result in sizeable losses. In the early 1990s GTech lost the contract to run the Arizona State Lottery to a rival company; however, the new company suffered software problems which in turn affected sales and as a result GTech was asked to take up the Licence again.[109] In many ways GTech was the most important member of the Camelot Consortium. Indeed it could be said with its immense experience in the gambling and lottery industry in particular, to have provided the blueprint for the entire venture.[110] Forcing its complete withdrawal would almost certainly have spelt the collapse of the National Lottery.[111]

In determining to allow GTech to continue to act as a supplier of services to Camelot, John Stoker would have been only too aware of the damage to the Lottery that would have been wrought by GTech's complete withdrawal from operations. Nevertheless, in order to permit the continuing involvement of GTech as a supplier, the new Regulator sought a number of reassurances from the Company. These involved the demonstration of adequate systems to reduce the scope for impropriety (the key features of which had largely been in place since 1994) and included collective decision-making regarding the engagement of consultants and lobbyists, together with the adoption of a team-based approach to selling in order to help reduce the scope for maverick action by individuals; ending the practice of employing consultants for as long as GTech held the contract for a particular lottery, and instead employing them for specific periods of time and specific programmes of work once they had passed checks of propriety and good standing – all these steps were being and would continue to be supervised by a senior former FBI official as head of compliance.[112] Finally from March 1998 GTech agreed not to employ former lottery employees involved in the award of business to the Company until at least a year following the end of the relevant employment.[113] The Director General had also been satisfied by the prompt severance of Guy Snowden from the company, by the purposeful attempt of the Company's board to deal with the problems of the past, by their personal qualities and by their undertaking not to offer bribes or other improper inducements in the course of their business.[114] Mr Stoker concluded his deliberations by declaring his confidence in GTech systems designed (since 1994) to uphold the propriety of their operations, and by reminding those with an interest in the Lottery and of its need for high standards of governance and conduct, that GTech had not been indicted or convicted of wrongdoing by any court.[115]

The GTech episode seems to confirm the historical tendency for gambling and corruption never to be far apart from each other. Notwithstanding the distance in time, the débâcle, along with subsequent and related disclosures had a profound influence on the deliberations of the Regulator (The National Lottery Commission and its Commissioners) in reviewing the type and style of entity that will run the Lottery when the current Licence expires. This subject is returned to in Chapters 5 and 6. It is entirely possible that the outcome of the bribery case and the furore that greeted it merely confirmed the government in its belief that the model and regulatory arrangements that the previous administration had chosen for the Lottery were less than adequate. For the Labour Party had declared in its 1997 election manifesto: 'Because the Lottery is a monopoly to serve the public interest ... we will seek an efficient not-for-profit operator to ensure that the maximum sums go to Good Causes.'[116]

Once in power, the new Labour government confirmed that a wholly state-run system would be unlikely to provide the right incentives for efficiency, and that it therefore remained eager to harness the expertise of the private sector in such a way as to maximize the returns to the Good Causes while at the same time 'removing unnecessary profit margins'.[117] Certainly there had been (and continues to be) a feeling in the media and the country that the profits and bonuses of the directors of the Operator were excessive.[118] However, the problem for the government is in designing a model that is capable of delivering its stated objectives. The definition of 'unnecessary profits' is also an area potentially fraught with difficulty. A not-for-profit *modus operandi* may or may not help uphold the propriety of the Lottery by reducing if not eliminating the scope and incentive for skulduggery and questionable business practices. It is an altogether more questionable point as to whether any arrangements that might replace the profit motive will be more efficient in maximizing the returns to the Good Causes. Yet it is the Lottery's propriety as set out in the 1993 Act that is the overriding regulatory priority – above that of the returns that are generated for the beneficiaries. The issues that helped to determine the principles upon which the new Licence would be awarded is returned to in Chapters 5 and 6.

Perhaps as fundamental as any of the changes which have been introduced to the way in which the Lottery will be run after the expiry of the initial Section 5 Licence (September 2001) is the overhaul of the regulation of the Lottery which has come about in large part because of the outcome of the libel suit described earlier in this chapter. The potential risks of regulatory capture and the flaws associated with individual or personalized regulation were both exposed and brought to a head by the court action. While the removal of Peter Davis was felt by the government to be the correct response to the political needs of the moment, the measure did not in the government's view address the medium- to long-term regulatory requirements for the Lottery. It had arguably been the case that allowing the involvement of GTech in the Camelot consortium had been a serious mistake by the Director General which had damaged the Lottery's propriety; therefore the Director General had failed in one of his primary statutory duties. In light of these events and in order to strengthen the regulation of the Lottery, the government determined to replace the personalized regulatory model with a commission-based system of regulation (from April 1999). The ramifications of this 'root and branch' change in policy are assessed in Chapter 4.

2 PLAYER PROTECTION

The second primary duty of the Regulator under Section 4 (1) (b) of the 1993 Act is to protect the interests of the participants in any lottery that forms part of the National Lottery. That the venture is in the private as opposed to the public sector makes this task a particularly demanding one for the Regulator. The placing of the Lottery in the hands of a private operator effectively shifted the initial investment risk from public funds, and thereafter helps realize revenue ambitions with no obvious cost to the taxpayer.[119] However, unlike their state counterparts, privatized lotteries are likely to be less constrained in their advertising and other promotional activities, and will be prone in marginal cases where the players' interests favours restraint, to elect to exploit rather than withdraw from a lottery promotion.[120] Thus there is a pressing need for constant regulatory vigilance. The close association between the interests of Oflot and the Director General, on the one hand and the Operator Camelot, on the other brought into question just how effective in protecting the interests of players the National Lottery's regulatory regime would be. The same problem continues to apply to the new commission-based system that replaced the old model.

The Betting and Gaming Act 1960 established the principle that the provision of betting or gaming opportunities should only be permitted where they satisfied unstimulated demand.[121] The position was confirmed and extended by the Gaming Act 1968,[122] which also established the Gaming Board,[123] to *inter alia* oversee this 'social control' objective, and indeed by the Gaming Board itself in its 1993/94 annual report which stated that

> the promotion and stimulation of gambling necessary if the Lottery is to be a success is ... difficult to reconcile with the Government's established policy, under which the [Gaming] Board operates, that the demand for gambling should not be unduly stimulated'.[124]

With the introduction of the National Lottery this policy has been effectively if not formally abandoned, with the Gaming Board itself opining that the policy on unstimulated demand is looking 'increasingly threadbare'.[125] This abandonment relates not only to the introduction of the Lottery, but also to the liberalizing of and relaxing of controls over the gaming industry at large which has sought and received compensation from the government (in particular the Conservative administration, especially between 1994 and 1997) for the perceived impact of the freedoms given to the National Lottery.[126] The introduction of the Lottery, which is beyond the ambit of the Gaming Board's regulatory duties, has had a 'knock-on' or progressive effect that has served to undermine the very purpose (social control) for which the regime has a statutory mandate.[127] Indeed the Board has expressed concern 'that there is a 'ratchet' effect developing, with different sectors [of the gambling industry] vying for ways in which they can seek to match or better any concessions made to others.'[128] This phenomenon which might be justifiably termed a 'spillover' consequent upon the National Lottery's introduction is beyond the scope of these pages. However, the introduction of the Lottery, which is believed to have been the largest ever consumer product launch in the UK[129] with an advertising budget of some £40 million,[130] clearly represents the jettisoning of the principle that the demand for gaming or gambling products should not be stimulated.[131] Thus gambling policy as demonstrated most particularly by the introduction of the Lottery but also by the ensuing liberalization and deregulation measures may be said to have shifted from one of containment to one of revenue generation.

Apart from the arguments with regard to efficiency and the transfer of risk from the public purse, privatizing the Lottery may also be said to be politically adroit. By placing the undertaking in private hands the state distances itself from the operation and can thereby resist more easily the criticism that it is encouraging its citizens to gamble: maintaining that all it has done is to give individuals the right to choose how to spend their discretionary income.[132] The abandonment of containment or social control in favour of revenue generation, which finds its ultimate expression in the Lottery, coupled with the involvement of the private sector makes the requirements for a robust regulatory regime something of an exigent priority. The following lines assess the effectiveness of the regulatory structures and their implementation in delivering adequate player protection.

Under the (Section 5) Licence the Director General was required to approve Camelot's codes of practice for players and for advertising.[133] The Player Code of Practice (which includes the Code of Practice for Customer Relations and the Sales Code of Practice) required the Licensee to agree with the Director General certain standards. These relate *inter alia* to the handling of complaints, the provision of information regarding rules and procedures for claiming prizes, protecting the rights and privacy of winners and making available and displaying such information in every retail outlet.[134] In addition the Regulator sets performance standards for the Operator to meet regarding player protection, service and security. Each annual report of the Director General assessed Camelot's performance in these areas. The Licensee was also required to submit to the Director General for approval an Advertising Code of Practice which covered advertising and public relations.[135] This Code seeks to set standards having regard to the style and content of advertising and ticket design, including the avoidance of advertisements targeting those under the age of 16 or advertisements associated with tobacco, alcohol, pharmaceutical products, or other forms of betting and gaming.[136] This part of the Licence also makes provision for 'the presentation of information which describes or appears to describe the chances of winning, the nature of prizes or the cost of playing.'[137] The Advertising Code also specifies that advertisements should not present lotteries as an alternative to work (which is sometimes found in US lotteries)[138] or as a way out of financial difficulties, or seek to exploit people falling into any recognizable social categories.[139]

Since the launch of the Lottery the odds of winning each prize category and the likely amount of each prize have been outlined in a leaflet produced by Camelot entitled 'How to play', available at retail outlets.[140] Following the introduction of the Instants game in March 1995 similar information has been included on (Instants) Game Information leaflets and has also been made available from all retail outlets.[141] However in the annual reports for 1995/96 and 1996/97, the Director General recorded his disappointment at the lacklustre efforts made by Camelot and its retailers having regard to the adequate display and availability of these leaflets.[142] The Director General undertook that he and Oflot's Compliance Division would be striving to seek improvements from Camelot in this area.[143] This information defect clearly places the consumer at a disadvantage and may exacerbate the problem for players of unrealistic and ill-informed expectations of winning. This in turn may encourage excessive play (leading to negative externalities or spillovers) which the Regulator is statutorily obliged to prevent. This is addressed below. The regulatory response here is clearly to provide protection for the consumer by addressing information deficits through improving information flows.[144] Nevertheless the standards of player information are higher than is the case in most state lotteries around the world, and is more extensive than the player information provided by other lotteries in the UK.[145]

2.1 *Excessive Participation*

In addition to the measures to help protect players included in the Licence, the Secretary of State has issued Directions to the Regulator which are designed in large part to provide further layers of player protection. These Directions in the first instance empowered the Director General among other things to withhold licences to any games that in his opinion might encourage persons to participate excessively,[146] or not allow for sufficient controls to prevent persons under 16 from participating.[147] As well as being able to limit ticket prices the Directions also required the Regulator to limit the 'roll-over' of jackpots, and also not to issue licences for the promotion of any lotteries in which players could participate by means of Lottery machines which involve interaction with the participant,[148] and which are commonly found in North American lotteries.[149] These provisions continue to be in force.

The foregoing measures imply that in terms of player protection, on its own the provision of information to players has been deemed by those responsible for designing the Lottery's regulatory framework to be incomplete or less than adequate. As well as protecting vulnerable groups (for example under-16s) these Directions reflect an abiding historic concern *vis-à-vis* the adverse impact that gambling products can and have had on society at large. These steps also provide another tier of support and protection in areas where the dissemination of information is or could be unsatisfactory. All lotteries are to a lesser or greater extent guilty of elision, having regard in particular to the adequate communication of 'odds' to the player.[150] Nevertheless, it is possible to contend that vestiges of the long-standing and well-established regulatory policy which has traditionally sought to contain and allow for gambling only to meet 'unstimulated demand' continues to influence the Lottery's regulation and for good reason. These influences are paternalistic. Whether information flows are or are not sufficient there are some areas of social policy in which government will intervene, on the pretext that decision-makers in the marketplace will continue to make irrational and/or wrong decisions.[151] This is pure paternalism, and is predicated on the assumption that government knows better than the individual what he wants or what is good for him.[152] Elements of the regulation of the National Lottery as they relate to player protection may be said to be paternalistic.

While the term paternalism carries pejorative connotations, a strong case can be made for the licensing of activities (which is a form of paternalism) that can be addictive – such as alcohol consumption and gambling. Such paternalism will be reconciled with the government's need for revenues.[153] Nevertheless, policy-makers are likely to remain sceptical of consumer preferences which confer short-term satisfaction but can generate longer-term risks.[154] The National Lottery is a particularly apposite case. For long-odds games are renowned for having a high subjective utility.[155] Empirical evidence from psychologists demonstrates that people often underestimate personal risk ('it couldn't happen to me'), and tend to prefer current to deferred gratification, even if they know the latter will yield a greater benefit.[156] It follows from this that Lottery players are likely to overestimate their chances of winning.[157] It also confirms the aptness of the Lottery Operator's initial advertising theme 'It could be you'. The problem is compounded by the tendency of Lottery players to bet on numbers that have made few or no appearances in the bi-weekly draws – 'the gambler's fallacy' – and to bet on numbers that have a special significance for the player – 'the illusion of control'.[158] 'Participants in lotteries appear to be influenced more by the size of the monetary prizes than by the probabilities of winning.'[159] The need for strong regulatory measures to protect Lottery players is not merely a reflection of inadequate or flawed information flows, it is also a response to an unusual outcropping of 'bounded rationality' where the capacity of individuals to receive, store and process information is limited.[160] Lottery players are notorious for their tendency not to act in a fully informed or particularly intelligent manner.[161] Indeed the notion of the consumer *qua* lottery player as a rational risk averse actor is flawed. Rather than fitting the consumer into a traditional or classic continuous graphic representation predicated on risk aversion, lottery play challenges this and posits the idea that the individual may have a compartmentalized view of his or her life and finances, with different utility functions for different spheres of activity.[162] Having regard to the Lottery *per se* there is then evidently an inability (one might go so far as to say reluctance) on the part of some players to reason statistically,[163] a situation which was acknowledged by Oflot itself.[164]

While evidence consistently reveals that lottery play is a broad-based phenomenon and that most players play small amounts with regularity,[165] one of the potential consequences of the foregoing is the emergence of excessive participation among certain players. Some of the regulatory steps that have been taken to help reduce if not eliminate this problem and that are outlined above may be broadly stated to be based on the philosophy 'that to maximize welfare in the long-term it may be preferable for an external force to limit short-term desires.'[166] Yet in areas where this philosophy falls short, there is a need to correct for spillover costs. An appropriate regulatory response in such circumstances will find its justification on the ground that a product's price does not reflect certain major costs that its production imposes on society.[167] Such costs will relate in part to treatment or counselling for pathological or compulsive behaviour associated with National Lottery play. In the USA during 1998, 18 of the 38 states that were running lotteries made contributions to gamblers' assistance programmes or contributed towards research into compulsive gambling.[168] Since 1995 Camelot has been a significant funder of the charity GamCare (between 1995 and 1997, known as the UK Forum for Young People and Gambling).[169] Also in the USA during 1998, 20 of the lottery states were promoting in one form or another gambling-awareness campaigns based on a 'please play responsibly' theme; and 15 of these lotteries included a problem gambling 'hotline' number on lottery terminals, posters and on the lottery tickets themselves[170] (see Appendix II, p. 201). No similar measures were in place during the time of the Director Generals *vis-à-vis* the UK's Lottery. Yet such or similar steps could have represented an important additional tier of player protection. Cynically it may be argued that the failure to implement more vigorous social controls or measures reflects a pragmatic policy of acceptance of the negative consequences of gambling, as a cost of raising public revenues.[171]

If measures are to be taken, part of the problem relates to quantifying in some meaningful way the deleterious or harmful effects of excessive participation. Spillover cost rationale can be used for justifying the regulation of anything.[172] If the rationale is to be intellectually helpful it should be confined to instances where the spillover is large, fairly concrete and roughly monetizable.[173] The social costs that gambling imposes on the public policy process are notoriously difficult to quantify and measure;[174] however, a plausible case can be made for certain costs that are both attributable and to some extent, at least, quantifiable. Such costs might include increases to social services budgets (referred to above), loss of productivity at work, defaulting on debts, theft, and time incurred in apprehending, prosecuting and incarcerating addicts who have committed crimes to support their habit.[175] Information collected by Oflot on excessive Lottery play does not satisfy these criteria. In his reports for 1994/95 to 1998/99 inclusive the Director General recorded no evidence of excessive participation.[176] Yet during the term of his office as Regulator, Peter Davis was criticized for his lacklustre performance in finding out whether excessive participation was taking place.[177] A particular criticism centred on Oflot's tendency to research into behaviour and spending patterns of average or typical players rather than focusing on those players at risk from excessive play.[178] By way of mitigation it is fair to say that little substantive research had at this time been published anywhere in the world on the subject of lotteries and excessive or compulsive gambling.[179]

2.1.1 The Draw Game

There are two main types of game that comprise the National Lottery. The first, launched in November 1994 is a simple on-line lotto-type format initially played weekly (twice weekly since 5 February 1997) where the player chooses 6 numbers from a matrix of 49. The numbers the player successfully matches with those drawn (subject to a minimum of three numbers)[180] will determine the size of the prize(s) he or she will win or will share with other winners. The structural characteristics of the Draw or lotto-type game are not themselves a case for serious concern having regard to excessive participation. The odds of winning even the smallest prize (£10) of 1 in 57 are such that players are not presented with frequent minor prizes which might encourage them to play more or to chase larger losses.[181] The opportunities for spatial repetition are also restricted and regulated by the frequency of the draws, i.e. twice weekly. The characteristics are singularly distinguishable from the other National Lottery Instants game – an issue which is addressed in the following subsection.

In connection with the Draw game, initial concern was directed at the size of jackpots, which reached £42 million in January 1996.[182] This concern was most voluble among church groups anxious that very high prizes could encourage people to gamble beyond their means.[183] Indeed the Council of Churches for Britain and Ireland campaigned for a limit on jackpots of £1 million,[184] and the Opposition Labour Party recommended a limit of £5 million.[185] There is clearly a tension and potential conflict here between the maximization of revenue, on the one hand, which will be in part a function of the prize fund and the size of the jackpot, and the protection of players, on the other, who may be induced by high jackpots to spend beyond their means.[186] As well as the church groups, Gamblers Anonymous have also expressed concern over the impact of the Lottery.[187] Yet the debate can often generate more heat than light with none of the interested parties truly addressing the objective nature of games of chance. Typically, proponents of gambling will choose to stress the potential economic benefits that the gambling industry can produce, such as jobs, investment, economic development and enhanced tax or hypothecated revenues, whereas opponents underline the possible social costs, such as pathological gambling, crime, and other maladies.[188] Thus the issues highlighted will tend to promote the identity, mission and cultural values of the group involved, with the state advertising the benefits of the Lottery and minimizing the Lottery's negative consequences.[189] The implication is that

> gambling is not defined as dangerous to the public's welfare because it is or is not objectively determined to be dangerous, but rather because various aspects of the social construction of the reality of gambling are selectively emphasized to serve each group's interests and organizational goals.[190]

Conflict theory, which assumes neither a social consensus of common interests nor a single entity or process called 'society', is ideally suited to the study of these interactions.[191]

There are certain general conclusions about National Lottery participation that can be made with some safety. The UK had the second largest Draw lottery in the world in 1999 and fourth highest by annual per capita sales at $125[192] (c. £80 p.a.). These figures imply an average weekly spend on the Draw lottery in the region of £1.50. At first sight the incidence of excessive participation would not appear to be widespread. Research carried out by the Office of Population Censuses and Surveys in 1995 on behalf of Oflot revealed 62 per cent of 3585 people interviewed had participated in the Draw lottery in the past seven days, spending an average of £2.63 – a figure which varied little between different social groups.[193] With the introduction of the Midweek Draw in February 1997 overall weekly spending on the Draw lottery increased by 20 per cent.[194] Secondly, the importance of the size of jackpots in encouraging participation is confirmed by the increase in participation levels and the amount spent on the Draw lottery when the jackpot is rolled over from one draw to the next because there has been no winner of the top prize. On 6 January 1996 the jackpot which had been rolled over twice (the maximum permitted is three times)[195] stood at £42 million.[196] Participation rates increased from 62 per cent to 74 per cent and the average amount spent increased from £2.63 to £3.49.[197] During the year to March 1997 the jackpot was rolled over 8 times, in the following year 14 times,[198] and 13 times in both the year to March 1999 and the year to March 2000,[199] and 16 times in the year to March 2001.[200] Finally it is worth noting that while the record individual jackpot win is £17.9 million,[201] in the first two and a half years of the Lottery's life the average jackpot winning ticket value was £1.9 million, with the average win by an individual being £620,943 due to jackpots being shared between winning tickets and also to some players participating through syndicates.[202]

Other than demonstrating that excessive participation is not widespread, the foregoing does not provide clear or more precise evidence either quantitatively or qualitatively *vis-à-vis* the size and structural characteristics of the problem. Furthermore, such evidence as does exist is not conclusive. Research carried out by the London School of Economics in 1995 found that the poorest 10 per cent of society were spending 2.6 per cent of their income on Lottery tickets compared with 0.3 per cent for the richest 10 per cent.[203] In other words the poorest group were spending as a proportion of their income eight times as much as the richest group. This information of itself is not especially helpful as all expenditures on household goods and day-to-day living expenses will be regressive in that their purchase inevitably consumes a great percentage of the income of poor families as compared with rich ones.[204] In the case of the Lottery, richer households generally spend a little more than poorer ones, although as is the case with expenditure on most minor consumables, additional expenditure is not proportionate to the additional income.[205]

Two surveys carried out on behalf of Oflot by National Opinion Polls (NOP) in 1995 and in 1996 revealed that between 95 per cent and 97 per cent of the playing population spent no more than £5 per week on the Draw lottery,[206] and only about 1 per cent of players reported spending more than £10 a week.[207] However, within these (and other) statistics there are some important social findings which may give cause for concern. For example, 5 per cent of high spenders (those spending more than £10 per week) were found to earn under £4500 per annum with 22 per cent of high spenders earning under £9500 per year.[208] Furthermore 8 per cent of high spenders were also found to be on state benefits.[209] Of high spenders, 31 per cent left school at 16, and 25 per cent left at 15 – and these were the highest two categories.[210] These results were also supported by other research commissioned by Oflot in 1997 where it was discovered that households headed by someone who left full-time education at the age of 19 or later were twice as likely to be non-participating households when compared with those headed by someone who left full-time education at the age of 15 or 16.[211] The less well educated also tended, on average, to spend a little more than those who remained longer in full-time education.[212] The results of the 1998 survey carried out by NOP on behalf of Oflot and published by the National Lottery Commission revealed that households in which the respondent had completed full-time education at 15 were not only the most likely sub-group in this category to participate in the Draw lottery, but were also found to have spent the most.[213]

Finally, the concern expressed by church groups that high jackpots would encourage the poor to participate in the Lottery beyond their means receives some empirical support. Interviews carried out in January 1996 by NOP on 1797 people (with an overall success rate of 48 per cent) assessed the effect on spending habits of the £42 million jackpot:[214] 2 per cent of socio-economic groups C2, D and E spent £11 or more on the draw compared with 1 per cent in a normal non-roll-over week.[215] In the survey, the number of unemployed spending £11 or more in the double roll-over draw increased from zero to 3 per cent,[216] and the participation rate for those spending £11 or more and having left full-time education at 15 doubled from 1 per cent to 2 per cent.[217]

These figures do give rise for concern and suggest that a small although discernible element of the vulnerable in society, particularly those who have left full-time education comparatively early and who are from poorer socio-economic groups may be participating excessively in the Draw lottery. More encouragingly the 1998 Oflot-commissioned survey found that none of those in the lowest income group (under £4500 per annum) had spent more than £10 on the Draw lottery during the week 9–15 September.[218] During the period of the survey there was also a jackpot roll-over.[219] Nevertheless, it remains difficult to demonstrate qualitatively in any tangible or meaningful way what adverse social and familial effects excessive participation in the Lottery may lead to, although it is accepted that as well as causing damage to themselves and those close to them, a significant proportion of problem gamblers will also commit illegal acts to pursue their gambling.[220] Yet it is possible to advance that whatever these harmful results might be, the Lottery *per se* is not the culprit. Analysis of Family Expenditure Survey (FES) data for 1995/96 commissioned by Oflot showed that households which spent money on the National Lottery Draw were much more likely than households which did not play to spend money on other forms of gambling, and the amount they spent on other forms of gambling was on average greater than that spent by gamblers who did not play the Lottery.[221] Furthermore, the FES also showed a strong correlation between the number of Lottery tickets purchased and the likelihood of purchase and amount spent on tobacco and alcohol.[222] The more lottery tickets purchased the more likely the household was to have purchased tobacco and also alcohol.[223] Similarly the more the household spent on Draw tickets, the more it would spend on tobacco and on alcohol.[224]

The foregoing data imply that where a correlation between the Draw lottery and excessive participation can be discerned it may represent just one of a series of functionally similar lifestyle choices on the part of the individual that helps meet some sort of need fulfilment. In extremes and where by any objective criterion Lottery play is excessive and part of a pattern of other unhealthy lifestyle excesses, such as other forms of gambling and alcohol consumption, the term 'pathological' may be an appropriate description of such behaviour. Pathological gambling implies that gambling is a symptom and may be one of several alternative and functionally equivalent behavioural symptoms of an underlying disorder.[225] Pathological gambling is to be distinguished from 'compulsive' gambling, which calls attention to the set of activities rather than to the individual and as such is viewed as an activity that almost anyone could potentially become compulsive about.[226] On this basis it is arguably the case that the Draw game is not of itself designed and structured in such a way as to lead to excessive play. Indeed with only around one in a hundred players spending more than £10 per week on the Draw game the problems of excessive play associated with the game are not substantial. However, the research carried out by NOP on behalf of Oflot between July 1995 and October 1996 discovered that 8 per cent of those individual respondents (as opposed to 3 per cent of 'household' respondents included in the more recent 1998 survey)[227] who spent more than £10 on the most recent draw preceding interview were on state benefits, a percentage which when extrapolated amounts to some 33,000 people nationwide.[228] This suggests that while the problem may be small, it is not insignificant.

It is fair to conclude that for the Draw game the issue of excessive participation was not one of special concern for the Director General. This is influenced fundamentally by the fact that opportunities to play are limited by the frequency of the draws, i.e. twice weekly. This in turn inhibits the opportunities for excessive play. The importance of this link between opportunities to play, i.e. spatial repetition and excessive involvement is borne out by the Regulator's insistence when permitting the Midweek Draw that the Licence included the right to require changes in the game if evidence was forthcoming that players were encouraged to play excessively.[229] The Director General also expressed doubts over the Operator's plans to introduce a draw game (popular in the USA) called Keno.[230] This game played in social venues such as bars and clubs involves the player picking up to 10 numbers typically from a field of 80 with 20 winning numbers being displayed on a TV monitor sometimes as often as every five minutes.[231] The player matches the numbers he has selected to those appearing on the screen, and if a match occurs, he then claims his winnings.[232] In character, Keno as a repetitive and potentially addictive form of gambling is more akin to hard gambling.[233] Notwithstanding the games uncertain legal status the Regulator made it clear to the Operator that he did not regard Keno as an appropriate development for the Lottery, most especially due to concerns over the likelihood of its tendency to encourage excessive play.[234] While the Director General may be said to have flexed his muscles in this instance, the traditional Draw game did not require any intercession of note from the Regulator having regard to the incidence of excessive player participation. This has continued to be the case during the regime of the National Lottery Commissioners. 'It is far from being "hard" gambling and is unlikely to be seriously addictive to more than a very small minority of players.'[235]

2.1.2 The Instants or Scratch-card Games

Unlike the Draw game the Instants games do not utilize on-line computer facilities, and discovery of whether a particular ticket is a winning ticket can be determined immediately through scratching and removing latex panels on the card, rather than having to await the outcome of a twice-weekly draw as is the case in the on-line game. New games with new themes are introduced under Section 6 licences every few weeks, with names like 'Fast Cash', 'Money Spinner' 'UK Treasures' and 'Aces High'.[236] In contrast to the Draw game where the chance of winning a prize of some size is 1 in 57 (since June 1999, 1 in 33), between 1 in 5 and 1 in 6 of the Instants games cards pays out a prize typically of between £1 and £100,000.[237] They are not as popular as the Draw game (see Table 3, p. 71). Sales of UK Instants were the eighth highest in the world in 1999, by country, but ranked at only sixty-first in annual per capita terms – $16[238] (c. £10.00 p.a.). However, Instants games are structurally distinctive *vis-à-vis* the Draw game and pose a different set of regulatory challenges with regard to player protection and most especially with regard to the potential for excessive play.

Since the introduction of the Instants games in March 1995 there has been a chorus of objections from pressure groups and academics concerned that the characteristics of these games have more in common with 'hard' rather than 'soft' gambling. Indeed in May 1995 Gamblers Anonymous reported that 20 per cent of its increase in the flow of telephone calls were related to the National Lottery, with most of these calls being connected with problems associated with the newly introduced scratch-cards.[239] Furthermore, the introduction of the Instants or scratch-card games led to claims by the gaming machine sector (itself a widely recognized example of 'hard' gambling) of a fall in turnover of 11 per cent.[240] This would seem to lend some credence to those who have accused the scratch-cards of being like 'paper fruit machines' or 'paper gaming machines'.[241]

What are these structural characteristics of the Instants games that have given rise to concerns over their potential for encouraging addictive behaviour? The key factors relate to the linking of frequency of play with the outcome, and the payout intervals when winnings are due – a process known as 'operand conditioning', which establishes habits by rewarding behaviour.[242] High rates of participation will be reinforced through the intermittent presentation of monetary rewards. Short payout intervals of a few seconds together with ready access to comparatively cheap and uncomplicated opportunities for repeated and continuous gambling defines not only the Instants game but also games that are potentially addictive.[243] Rapid event frequency means the loss period is brief with little time or consideration given to affordability by the player, and winnings when forthcoming can be re-gambled at once.[244] The Instants games are arguably particularly attractive to those who cannot resist 'chasing their losses'.[245] One may go further and contend that the peculiar mechanics of game design are themselves deliberately structured in such a way as to encourage repeat play. This is supported by the inclusion of so called 'heartstoppers', i.e. tickets revealing two matching symbols where three are required, giving the impression to the player of having enjoyed a 'near miss'.[246] Oflot's view on this element of game design was that it would not encourage excessive play but rather would provide a little more excitement and thus enhance the players' entertainment.[247] Prominent experts in gambling psychology and behaviour have differed fundamentally from this rather sanguine and relaxed position on the matter, arguing that the inclusion of higher-than-chance frequency of near misses is likely to induce continued gambling.[248]

If one accepts the foregoing, then the Instants or scratch-card games are not an extension of the National Lottery, founded as it was on the Draw game, but are actually a completely separate and distinctive form of gambling. Having regard to these reservations it is questionable as to whether the Director General in prosecuting his statutory duties should have permitted the Instants concept to have formed part of the Lottery. In determining to allow Instants to be sold, the Director General argued that there had been a market for scratch-cards in the UK for some 20 years (typically sold in aid of local authorities, charities and sports clubs) that had not evinced a material problem associated with addictive gambling.[249] Although the Regulator had also made world-wide investigations, it would have been inappropriate for him to have derived comfort from the UK experience or to have used these findings as a predictor for the likely performance of National Lottery Instants. The National Lottery Instants games are heavily promoted, which was not the case for scratch-cards sold prior to the 1993 Act. More importantly the limit on top prizes for weekly lotteries prior to the National Lottery Act was £6,000,[250] compared with an unrestricted top prize for the National game.

In evaluating the problems of excessive participation it is helpful from the outset to make a clear distinction between pathological and compulsive gambling. It has been contended that the Draw game does not possess properties that are likely to encourage compulsive play and furthermore the game is unlikely to lead to excessive participation except in very extreme cases which may be described as pathological. In the case of the Instants game the structural characteristics are such that it has attracted much critical attention. Where excessive play is discovered, in the majority of cases it may arguably be more properly described as compulsive. From here it is necessary to try to quantify the size and nature of the problem. In doing so it is worth remarking that notwith-standing the great uneasiness with Instants as opposed to the Draw game among academics, psychologists and charities concerned with gambling addiction, there is arguably more comprehensive research data available for the on-line game.

From the height of its popularity in the summer of 1995 when 20 per cent of the adult population played Instants weekly,[251] the weekly figure had fallen by October 1996 to about 13 per cent,[252] and to only 6 per cent by September 1998.[253] Average weekly expenditure was (and remains) modest at £2.18 in January 1996, £1.71 in October 1996,[254] and £2.64 by September 1998.[255] But what evidence is there of excessive play? In broad terms almost no one buys scratch-cards who does not also buy Draw tickets; and those households that play in both Wednesday and Saturday draws, have been found to be twice as likely to have bought scratch-cards as those households who play only in the Saturday Draw.[256] Research carried out on behalf of Oflot by NOP on 13,054 adults between July 1995 and May 1996 discovered only 1 per cent of scratch-card players spending more than £10 a week.[257] Although no empirical work was undertaken having regard to the relationship between different gradations of spend-ing within income or social groupings, the research did disclose that 18 per cent of players had an annual income of less than £4500 (the lowest income group) and spent an average of £1.93 each week on scratch-cards.[258] While the amount spent was lower than for any other income class, this group only made up 8 per cent of the sample and was more likely to buy scratch-cards than any of the other groups by income. Furthermore, research carried out by NOP for the October 1996 survey revealed that 10 per cent of those with an annual income of under £4500 were spending £2.08 per week – an amount higher than for any other income group.[259] This survey also disclosed that 10 per cent of those on state benefits spent £1.99 on scratch-cards each week, a figure also higher than for any other 'socio-economic' group.[260] Finally, research carried out by NOP on behalf of Oflot in September 1998 on 1683 adults found that only 8 per cent of respondents were spending more than £5 a week on Instants.[261] The survey did not provide data of Instants participation by income or socio-economic group.

These results, which may be a cause for some concern, could not be described as alarming. Indeed the evidence reproduced above does not lend much support to those siren voices warning of the dangers of excessive participation whether compulsive or pathological in the Instants games. Work needs to be undertaken assessing the relationship between heavy purchasing of Instants cards and income and social class. This type of field study might yield more uncomfortable findings. Generally speak-ing, however, those vulnerable groups on low incomes and/or dependent on state benefits have been found in some NOP surveys to be most likely to purchase scratch-cards, and in some cases to be spending more not only proportionately but also absolutely on scratch-cards when compared with other socio-economic groups. As is the case with the Draw game, and also with scratch-card sales around the world, the popularity of the game declines as educational attainment rises.[262] Data from the October 1996 NOP survey showed that 13 per cent of those who left full-time education at the age of 16 played Instants games once a week or more, compared with only 3 per cent of those who left full-time education at age 19.[263]

For both the Draw and Instants games there is clearly an appeal and relatively high participation rate for those on low incomes and those who are comparatively less well educated. Although not a matter for the Regulator, if the Lottery is regarded as a fiscal instrument (a controversial proposition) as opposed to a consumer good then it is clearly regressive. It was the Director General's concern as it now is for the Commissioners to provide adequate player protection and to guard against excessive participation. While there is no room for complacency and the need for ongoing, longitudinal and more committed research into excessive Lottery play is a priority,[264] Oflot and both Director Generals arguably attained more acceptable standards in providing and monitoring player protection than could be said to be the case with regard to their (and more particularly the first Director General's) other primary duty – *viz.* guaranteeing the Lottery's propriety. Nevertheless, it remains a generally accepted rule that problems of excessive gambling and addiction are linked to the accessibility and acceptability of gambling, and that the legalization of gambling increases both.[265] The sheer size of the National Lottery will have had an impact, if an unquantifiable one, on this process. Taking both games together the UK National Lottery was the third largest in the world in 1999.[266] However, by the same measure it ranked only thirty-fourth in per capita sales.[267] Paul Bellringer, a director of the charity GamCare, does not consider the Lottery to be a major cause of problem gambling,[268] stating that

> its draw is not addictive in the way that fruit machines are ... Our national helpline gets 50 per cent of calls about slot machines, and only 2 per cent about problems with scratchcards and 1 per cent with the Lottery Draw.[269]

2.2 *Under-age Participation*

2.2.1 An Appropriate Age?

The Directions by the Secretary of State to the Director General included various supplementary provisions to help provide that the Regulator carried out his primary statutory duties of upholding the Lottery's propriety and protecting the interests of participants. Section 2 (1) (b) of the Directions to the Director General forbad the issue of licences for games that 'do not allow for sufficient controls to prevent persons who have not attained the age of 16 years from participating in such lotteries.'[270] Before assessing the performance of the Lottery's regulation in this area it is perhaps necessary to evaluate the appropriateness of and problems associated with setting a minimum age for participation. In Europe, the state lotteries of Norway, Sweden and Greece have no age restrictions, while the Danish Lottery does not recognize the legal status of sales over the value of £6 to persons younger than 16 – the German lottery Westdeutsche Lotterie GmbH imposes similar restrictions.[271] The national lotteries in Ireland, Belgium and Holland have an age limit of 18.[272] This is also the typical age limit for many of the state lotteries in the USA.[273]

In the UK, while there has been a long-standing debate as to whether 16 or 18 is the most appropriate minimum age for participation in the Lottery, there has not been any serious movement seeking to dispense with the requirement for there to be a minimum age. Church groups have signed a joint declaration calling for the age limit to be raised.[274] Yet it has not been church groups alone (many of whom have long-established moral objections to gambling)[275] that have argued in favour of an increase in the minimum age to 18. The leading psychiatrist and specialist in gambling addiction Dr E. Moran, who is also the chairman of the National Council of Gambling, together with the gambling support group GamCare have lobbied in favour of the minimum age being raised to 18.[276] Given that it is not easy for retailers to judge age reliably, and that many people under 16 look older and vice versa, it is not possible for staff selling tickets to be right every time.[277] Surprisingly and to its credit the Operator has also identified this problem and supports the idea of the minimum age limit being raised to 18.[278] Moreover the charity GamCare has argued that 'If the Lottery age limit is 16 that really means 13 and 14 year olds will be playing.'[279] The problem is further aggravated by the placing of Lottery tickets in retail premises next to or adjoining sweet counters.[280] There is some evidence to suggest that the difficulty of preventing under-age sales is less acute in larger retail outlets, where the Lottery ticket dispensers are more often located at the cigarette counter and where staff are more used to judging the age of customers.[281] Indeed research commissioned by Oflot and carried out by MORI on a sample of 1002, 12- to 15-year-olds between 2 June and 4 July 1997 revealed that the general success rate for attempted under-age purchasers was 56 per cent; yet the success rate for attempted purchases in large supermarkets was lower than for any other category at 45 per cent.[282]

Criticism has also been directed towards the inadequacy of the regulatory apparatus in respect of the advertising and promotion of the Lottery especially having regard to the protection of children. At the time of the launch of the Lottery the main promotional television advertisement had a Disney-like quality, including a small girl appearing at a window, entranced by the giant shadow of a rabbit in the sky.[283] The statement concerning the ban on children taking part in the Lottery appeared towards the end of the advertisement as a small and relatively indistinct caption in the lower half of the screen with no voice-over to reinforce the message.[284] The impression created is one that is attractive to children.[285]

Concern has also been expressed with respect to the Draw game, the results of which appear live twice weekly on television. The event is broadcast in advance of the 9 p.m. watershed (the time before which programmes are deemed to be suitable for children).[286] The show itself broadcast live by the BBC incorporates a large audience including a sizeable number of children who are encouraged to shout and clap.[287] Early evidence suggested that the programme was the third most popular television programme among all children and the second most popular among boys,[288] with 27 per cent of those between the ages of 4 and 15 watching,[289] and 38 per cent of 10- to 15-year-olds watching.[290] Evidence gathered during the summer of 1997 found that 84 per cent of 9774 respondents aged between 12 and 15 frequently watch the National Lottery live television show on Saturday, and 62 per cent frequently watch the equivalent Wednesday programme.[291] Between the summer of 1999 and the summer of 2000, in line with the general decline in Lottery play, of those 12- to 15-year-olds surveyed (9529 in 1999 and 11,581 in 2000) 38 per cent had watched the Saturday programme in 1999 in the week prior to interview, 28 per cent in 2000, and 25 per cent had viewed the midweek show the previous week in 1999, which had reduced to 19 per cent by 2000.[292] In both the 1999 and 2000 surveys regular gambling was more prevalent among viewers than among all young people, with 13 per cent of the whole sample having played the National Lottery in the week prior to interview, rising to 26 per cent of those having watched the midweek Draw and 23 per cent of those who watched the Saturday Draw.[293] The implication of the foregoing is that Camelot is introducing children and adolescents to the principles of gambling,[294] and as such is in breach of the Advertising Code of Practice which provides that:

No advertising should feature any characters, real or fictitious, who are likely for any reason to primarily appeal to or influence under 16 year olds. [And] no advertising should be designed or be likely to lead under 16 year olds to persuade or pressure their parents to participate in the National Lottery.[295]

The charity National Council on Gambling has lobbied Parliament maintaining that Camelot's advertising strategy not only contravenes its Advertising Code of Practice, but also is contrary to the spirit of the controlling legislation, and may even be in breach of it.[296] The charity (which keeps under review the promotion of gambling and its impact on the community and the family) has called for an end to the involvement of children in the advertisements for the Lottery, the screening of the draw after the 9 p.m. watershed, and the removal of children from the live audience at the time of the draw.[297] As well as being a leading campaigner for the minimum age limit for participation in the Lottery to be increased from 16 to 18, the Chairman of the National Council on Gambling has argued that the sale of Instants scratch-cards should be confined to licensed premises.[298] Not only has the charity been supported in its position by church groups, but it has also received the support of the influential Gaming Board for Great Britain.[299] The Gaming Board has been concerned that the Instants games have characteristics that have more in common with the harder end of gambling than the softer end, and the Board maintains that a common minimum age of 18 for all gambling would be a better policy choice.[300] In determining the most appropriate regulatory response to the minimum age, it is interesting to note that in the Parliamentary debates that addressed the National Lottery Bill, the idea was advanced that there might be one age limit for the Draw game and another for the Instants games.[301]

2.2.2 Enforcement

Whether or not 16 is an appropriate minimum age for participation in the Lottery is a moot point, yet the question remains as to whether the enforcement measures and policies themselves are appropriate and have been vigorously pursued. The responsibility for enforcing the age limit rests with the Operator.[302] In the opinion of the second Director General these arrangements are apposite since the Operator carries out sales of lottery tickets using retailers who are in legal terms its agents.[303] As Oflot did not itself have the power to institute prosecutions of retailers for under-age sales (the same applies to the National Lottery Commission), it fell in the first instance and to a large extent upon Camelot to carry out enforcement through the commercial sanction of terminating the retailer's contract.[304] This prospect is likely to have been viewed seriously by the retailer as average commission per retail outlet from the sale of National Lottery tickets reached £7700 in the year to 31 March 1998,[305] and from the commencement of the Lottery up to the end of March 2000 the average retailer had earned £41,000 in commission.[306] In the second instance, enforcement is applied by Trading Standards offices on an ad hoc basis and also by police forces – although they tend to afford under-age National Lottery ticket sales a low priority.[307]

The foregoing begs the further questions as to how successful the enforcement arrangements have been in deterring under-age play and secondly how to discover under-age play as and where it occurs. During the early part of 1996 a survey conducted in Merseyside by Trading Standards officers found that three 12-year-old boys and two girls aged 11 were able to purchase Lottery tickets in 10 out of 91 retail premises visited.[308] The findings were reported to both Camelot and Oflot.[309] Around the same time the Trading Standards department of Devon County Council carried out a similar study and found that attempts by children to make Lottery ticket purchases were successful on 12 out of 24 attempts.[310] In each case (and also in response to a report from Oxfordshire Trading Standards Services) Camelot wrote to all of the retailers concerned, reminding them that their contracts would be terminated if evidence was discovered that they had sold tickets to under-16s.[311] Despite Camelot mounting a surveillance exercise at each of the offending retailers no under-age sales were observed.[312]

In addition to the above, and more especially having regard to the findings from Oflot-commissioned research on under-age sales (the highlights of which are reproduced in the following section), the Director General expressed his disappointment with Camelot's efforts in trying to prevent under-age sales in his annual report for 1995/96.[313] It is worth remarking that it is in relation to such Licence breaches that the intermediate powers, including the ability to impose fines by Oflot on the Operator, would not only have been relevant and appropriate but also arguably very necessary. Yet there is evidence to suggest some improvement in the urgency and seriousness with which Camelot approached the problem following the Director General's report for 1996. Although the rules for National Lottery games stipulate that a purchase by an under-16-year-old is not a valid purchase, and so gives no entitlement to a prize,[314] in November 1996 Camelot successfully pursued an action in the High Court (at its own cost) against the mother of an under-16-year-old who had bought a £50,000 winning Instants National Lottery ticket on the mother's behalf.[315] The court found that persons under the age of 16 cannot purchase tickets or claim prizes, whether for themselves or on behalf of an adult.[316] In addition, in January 1997, the Operator launched a telephone 'hotline' for the public to report retailers they believed to have sold tickets to under-16s.[317] The scheme is supported by posters and terminal stickers in the retail outlets themselves,[318] though whether or not the retailers find wall space for the posters is another point. Oflot also required Camelot to produce detailed statistics on the volume and nature of calls to the dedicated line, and insisted that the Operator demonstrates what action it would be taking in response to each call.[319]

Between the launch of the Lottery and the spring of 1997 Camelot carried out four security operations across the country and spent 360 hours in surveillance of over 220 different retail premises.[320] Yet this represents considerably less than 1 per cent of the retail outlets selling Lottery products, which had reached 35,453 by March 1997.[321] However, from the early part of 1997 Camelot set up a further six test purchasing operations, with Trading Standards departments around the UK visiting 138 outlets between January and March of which only 7 sold tickets to the under-age test purchasers.[322] If this figure were to be reproduced nationally it would imply 1798 retail outlets were breaking the law by making under-age sales. Moreover research commissioned by Oflot and carried out on 9774 12- to 15-year-olds in June/July 1997 revealed that 6.5 per cent of respondents had made an illegal under-age purchase (as distinct from a purchase by an adult on behalf of a child which is legal) in the week prior to interview.[323]

In 1998 the Operator sent actors over the age of 16, but who looked younger, to try to buy Lottery tickets in 209 outlets – 28 per cent of the retailers sold tickets to them.[324] The delinquent retailers were then trained not to repeat the 'misselling'; yet a third of these retailers were again found to have sold tickets to 'under-age' players.[325] Although welcoming the steps Camelot had put in place, the new Director General in his annual report for 1997/98 averred:

> I am not satisfied that Camelot is doing as much as it should [with respect to under-age sales] . . . I would like to see a clear commitment to continuous improvement and a stronger better-resourced programme of detection, along with evidence that those who do sell to underage young people are indeed having their terminals removed.[326]

In addition the Director General requested that Camelot should produce a plan stating how it intended to reduce under-age sales, together with proposed arrangements to monitor progress against a rolling research programme commissioned by Oflot.[327] The Regulator's concern would seem to be well placed as Camelot had withdrawn the terminals of only 91 retailers for under-age sales or failure to rigorously implement reasonable safeguards between the launch of the Lottery and November 2000.[328]

As a result of the foregoing findings and the promptings of the Director

General, Camelot introduced Operation Child as part of a so called 'Project 16' campaign involving a rolling programme from April 1999 (after the era of personalized regulation) of some 5000 annual test purchase visits.[329] The Operator resolved as part of the campaign that for a third offence the retailer's contract would be terminated.[330] Perhaps a more appropriate measure might have been to have adopted a 'no second chance' policy as obtains in the Dutch Lottery.[331] Nevertheless, evidence gathered from research authorized by the National Lottery Commission during the summer of 1999 suggests Camelot's 'Project 16' campaign may have had some success. In fieldwork carried out on a sample of 9529 12- to 15-year-olds between 7 June and 23 July 1999 it was found that 7 per cent of those surveyed had made illegal purchases of National Lottery products (in 1997 the figure had been 6.5 per cent).[332] However, these results should be seen in the context of an overall increase in under-age Lottery purchases (including legal purchases where an adult buys the Lottery ticket on behalf of the child) from 13.5 per cent in 1997 to 17.7 per cent in 1999.[333] In other words illegal under-age sales as a proportion of total under-age sales (i.e. including legal purchases) fell from 48 per cent in 1997 to 39.5 per cent in 1999 – a decline of some 17.7 per cent. Yet there remains no room for complacency as over 40 per cent of 12- to 15-year-olds interviewed (14.3 per cent of the sample attempted an illegal purchase) were not refused because they were under 16, and this rose to 60 per cent for those aged 14 or 15.[334] Furthermore in the research carried out during the summer of 2000, above referred to, overall purchases of National Lottery tickets by 12- to 15-year olds had fallen to 13.2 per cent, but this fall was influenced principally by a reduction in legal purchases to 7.1 per cent (1999 10.5 per cent).[335] Illegal sales fell from 7 per cent to 6 per cent.[336] Clearly Operation Child has yet to make a significant impact on reducing illegal sales. Indeed of those 12- to 15-year-olds attempting illegal purchases in 2000 – during the whole week prior to interview 55 per cent were not refused on the grounds of age for the Draw game (1999 45 per cent) and 55 per cent were not refused for the Thunderball game (48 per cent 1999).[337] The results suggest that purchasers identify a retailer who is willing to sell to them regularly, and thereby manage to avoid refused purchases.[338] In the absence of a government-endorsed proof-of-age scheme, which has been mooted in certain quarters,[339] the problem is likely to continue.[340] Camelot's own findings from the Operation Child programme (involving attempted purchases by young people over 16 but who look younger) found some cause for cheer with 77 per cent of retailers refusing to sell tickets in 1999/2000, rising to 88 per cent of retailers in 2000/2001.[341] Operation Child's annual test purchase visits will increase to 10,000 during the second licence term.[342]

2.2.3 The Demographic Characteristics of Under-age Play

The previous section sought to assess the effectiveness of enforcement policies as they relate to under-age Lottery play. This section seeks to quantify the problem. Within the first year of the Lottery's life there was already some evidence intimating that under-age participation was likely to be more than a marginal problem. Dr Emanuel Moran carried out a study towards the end of 1995 at a mixed-sex comprehensive school where he found that out of 187 children, 114 (61 per cent) had purchased Lottery tickets.[343] Conclusions drawn from these results should be treated with caution owing to the small sample size. However, shortly after the launch of the Lottery, Oflot commissioned the visiting senior research fellow at Plymouth University, Dr Sue Fisher, to analyse data gathered by John Balding's health-related behaviour questionnaire at the University of Exeter.[344] The initial survey carried out between May and July 1995 involving 1762 children (12- to 15-year-olds) drawn from 12 schools in the north-east, east and south-west of England,[345] was subsequently followed by further and larger surveys. Some of the key findings of these reports are reproduced below.

In the first Oflot-commissioned survey, 22 per cent of the young people surveyed had spent their own money on the National Lottery in the seven days prior to interview.[346] The most active subset was found to be boys aged 14 to 15, 29 per cent of whom had played the Lottery.[347] The Report revealed that 69 per cent of under-age Lottery participants lived with both natural parents compared with 75 per cent for non-participants; and that young people having access to their own money were more likely to be players, with 31 per cent of participants having received more than £10 from paid work in the week prior to interview compared with only 15 per cent of non-participants.[348] The Report did not address the issue of amount spent by under-age players. Finally, this first or preliminary study indicated a clustering of risk behaviours, with 23 per cent of under-age National Lottery participants having also spent their own money on arcade gambling (fruit machines) in the week prior to interview compared with only 6 per cent of non-participants; 38 per cent of under-age players had also purchased alcohol compared with 17 per cent of non-participants; and 25 per cent of under-age players were found to have spent money on cigarettes in the previous week compared with only 13 per cent of non-participants.[349]

While this preliminary study disclosed some interesting and, from the Regulator's point of view, worrying findings, the sample size was considered to have been too small to have provided reliable information.[350] A second preliminary survey was carried out between May and December 1995 on a larger sample of 6786 people (including the 1762 children interviewed for the first survey) drawn from 44 schools in Cornwall, Cumbria, Devon, Essex, Lancashire, the West Midlands and Yorkshire.[351] This study replicated the earlier work and found that 18 per cent of children had spent their own money on the National Lottery in the week prior to interview, with boys aged between 14 and 15 being the most likely participators at 26 per cent.[352] The survey also confirmed some of the findings from the first report, with 21 per cent of under-age participants receiving more than £10 from paid work in the week prior to interview compared with only 9 per cent of non-participants.[353] In addition 18 per cent of participants had spent their own money on arcade gambling (fruit machines) in the previous week compared with 4 per cent of non-participants; 32 per cent of participants had purchased alcohol in the past week compared with 13 per cent of non-participants, and 22 per cent of participants had spent money on cigarettes in the last seven days compared with 11 per cent of non-participants.[354]

The second preliminary survey showed a general reduction in expenditure on marginal or illegal products, yet this difference was not attributed to the unreliability of the small sample of the first study. Rather, the authors of the report concluded that the higher figures from the first survey were the result of it having been carried out in the summer months when more paid work is available for young people and that because the second survey had been carried out partly during the autumn and winter months when less paid work was available, this helped to explain a fall in income that was only partially compensated for by an increase in pocket money.[355] This is important as there is a direct association between income and under-age participation. Secondly, the first sample gathered data from children in their final term in each year for 12- to 15-year-olds and the second sample gathered the majority of data from children in their first term in these years.[356] This is also important as it has been demonstrated from the above findings that older children are most likely to be involved in under-age Lottery participation. The authors also conceded the possibility that young people might be losing their taste for National Lottery products or could be unable to buy them because of greater vigilance on the part of retailers.[357]

Between February and July 1996, a third survey produced from an initial sample of 7200 children drawn from 48 schools situated in 8 different regions found that 15 per cent of those surveyed had spent their own money on the Lottery in the week prior to interview.[358] For the first time this study sought to distinguish between children who had asked an adult to purchase a lottery ticket on their behalf (a legal transaction) and children who had made purchases themselves (an illegal transaction).[359] Of the 15 per cent who had spent their own money on the Lottery 9 per cent reported legal transactions, and 6 per cent had made illegal transactions; while respondents demonstrated little preference for Draw tickets compared with Instants, with 5 per cent making illegal transactions on Draw tickets in the week prior to interview compared with 4 per cent for Instants – 6 per cent had spent their own money on both.[360] Again, as had been the case in the first two reports, 14- to 15-year-old boys were the most likely to have spent their own money on Lottery tickets, with 21 per cent having made purchases, 11 per cent of which were illegal.[361] Although little difference was found in the survey having regard to the number of respondents purchasing Draw or Instants tickets, regular Instants players were most likely to be involved in a cluster of potentially addictive behaviours, with 33 per cent of this group being regular smokers, compared with 14 per cent of other children, 44 per cent having consumed alcohol on three or more days in the past seven compared with 11 per cent of other children, 35 per cent having experimented with illegal drugs, compared with 19 per cent of other children and 46 per cent having played fruit machines at least weekly compared with 6 per cent of other children.[362]

On a prima-facie basis these findings may well have provided both Regulator and Operator with some cause for optimism with under-age play having fallen in each of the three surveys, and with only 6 per cent of children making illegal transactions. Indeed Camelot was eager to announce these encouraging results and claim some responsibility for the fall.[363] Yet it must remain a cause for concern that children are gambling with the approval and assistance of their families and parents, especially having regard to the effect this might have in encouraging potentially addictive behaviour. Furthermore, the third report carried some disturbing data. It revealed that 3 per cent of children interviewed were playing the Instants game twice a week or more, with 9 per cent of this group having spent more than £10 in the week prior to interview.[364] Perhaps more worrying still is the fact that 3 per cent of all those interviewed admitted experiencing withdrawal symptoms in trying to cut down their play on Instants (19 per cent of regular players experienced this) and 4.2 per cent admitted spending more than they planned on Instants (41 per cent of regular players experienced this).[365] In addition 2.7 per cent of all surveyed admitted to having stolen from their families to play the Instants game (24 per cent of regular players admitted to this) and 1.1 per cent had stolen from outside the family in order to play (compared with 14 per cent of regular players).[366] These spillovers or externalities are manifestly negative.

During the summer of 1997 a further survey involving some 9774 interviewees aged 12 to 15 revealed that 47 per cent had gambled on the Instants game and 40 per cent on the Draw game at some stage.[367] There was a decline to 13 per cent in the number who had played in the week prior to interview (5 per cent Draw, 4 per cent Instants, 4 per cent both) from the 15 per cent uncovered in the study carried out between February and July 1996, although this was entirely due to a fall in legal transactions (where the money is handed over in the shop by an adult on behalf of the child).[368] As in earlier surveys older children and those with access to personal incomes, whether from paid work or from pocket money, were most likely to have gambled on the Lottery in the week prior to interview.[369] The percentage of 12- to 13-year-olds found to have spent their own money on the Lottery was 9 per cent (29 per cent of these children reporting illegal transactions) compared with 19 per cent of 14- to 15-year-olds (60 per cent of whom reported illegal transactions).[370] Of the children who received personal incomes of more than £5 a week 17 per cent had spent money on the Lottery in the week prior to interview compared with 7 per cent of the other children.[371] It is also significant that of those children reporting illegal/under-age purchases in the week prior to interview, 64 per cent had purchased Instants scratch-cards compared with 46 per cent who had purchased Draw tickets.[372]

These findings from the 1997 survey are of themselves disturbing. However, the survey also found that 3 per cent of the young people interviewed had spent £10 or more in the week prior to interview on Instants, which was also the percentage of respondents who had spent £10 or more on the Draw game in the previous week.[373] Interestingly and by way of comparison 5 per cent of children interviewed had spent £10 or more in the previous week on scratch-cards unconnected with the National Lottery.[374] The survey also identified 5 per cent of the children interviewed as problem gamblers, with 17 per cent of this group having a particular problem with the Instants game.[375] The research did not identify the Draw game as a discrete and offending category in relation to problem gambling. Although 46 per cent of problem gamblers had spent their money on the Draw game in the week before interview, only 5 per cent of problem gamblers had spent more than £5 on the Draw game compared with 36 per cent of problem gamblers who had played the Instants game, and 8 per cent of problem gamblers who had spent more than £5 on Instants products in the previous week.[376]

A further survey carried out on 9529 12- to 15-year-olds between 7 June and 23 July 1999 (and after the era of personalized regulation) showed that gambling activity among young people had increased since 1997, with a third of those interviewed having spent their money (either legally or illegally) on gambling in the week prior to interview, with fruit machines being the most popular game (a quarter of those interviewed having played this game).[377] The research also confirmed many of the findings of the 1997 survey including the tendency for Lottery players, whether social gamblers or problem gamblers to be male, older and to have access to their own income.[378] However, past week play had increased to 17.7 per cent of those surveyed in 1999 compared with 13.5 per cent of those who had been included in the 1997 survey.[379] This increase was made up principally of that proportion playing Instants which had increased significantly (11.6 per cent in 1999 vis-à-vis 7.9 per cent in 1997).[380] This is of itself troublesome as the dynamics of the Instants game are known to be more likely than the Draw game to give rise to excessive or problem gambling. Although the percentage of 12- to 15-year-olds that had a problem with gambling on Instants fell from 2.2 per cent in 1997 to 1.7 per cent in 1999, 2 per cent of players had spent more than £20 in the past week on Instants (1 per cent in 1997).[381] Surprisingly, the number of 12- to 15-year-olds spending more than £20 on the Draw game in the week prior to interview had increased from 1 per cent to 3 per cent between 1997 and 1999 and of particular concern is the fact that 5 per cent of those interviewed had spent in excess of £20 in the last week on the Thunderball game (introduced in June 1999).[382] The findings from the summer 2000 survey referred to earlier, as well as revealing an overall fall in under-age participation in the National Lottery from 17.7 per cent in 1999 to 13.2 per cent, also confirmed much of the qualitative work carried out the previous summer. A point of concern however, in spite of the overall fall in participation levels, is the increase in the number of children spending large amounts on National Lottery products. 6 per cent of those interviewed and who had spent their own money in the past week bought in excess of £40 worth of Thunderball tickets (7 per cent over £20).[383] The number of children spending over £20 of their own money on Instants also increased during the twelve months from 2 per cent to 3 per cent.[384]

The impact of under-age Lottery play is both immediate and long-term. It had been estimated in 1990 – before the introduction of the National Lottery – that children and young people accounted for around a quarter of all new members of Gamblers Anonymous in the UK.[385] The arrival of the Lottery will not have helped to reduce this statistic, and is likely to have increased it. The longer-term effects of under-age play is a further cause of concern as retrospective research studies have shown that the majority of male pathological gamblers started gambling in their teens.[386] Parental influence should also not be underestimated as research has demonstrated that children who gamble are more likely than other children to come from home backgrounds where at least one parent is a regular gambler.[387] Indeed the research carried out in the summer of 1997 and referred to above found that a parent or step-parent of 57 per cent of young problem gamblers aged 12 to 15 had participated in the Instants game in the week prior to interview, compared with just 27 per cent for other children.[388] Moreover, in the 1999 survey over 40 per cent of the children interviewed felt their parents approved or did not mind if they played National Lottery games, (43 per cent Instants, 41 per cent Draw).[389] These percentages had reduced to 38 per cent for the Instants games and 37 per cent for the Draw game in the 2000 survey.[390] While some of the verifiable percentages for all those included in the surveys above are small, in absolute numerical terms when extrapolated they are not.

In addressing the problem of under-age Lottery play Paul Bellringer, a director of the gambling support group GamCare, stated: 'It is quite devastating. First they use up all their own money, then they steal from the family and finally they steal from the outside. They will often start absenting from school and become isolated from their friends.'[391] These are clearly difficult and worrisome statistics for the Regulator and the Operator to address. Children steal for purposes other than to play the Lottery but in this case they are stealing for a state-promoted and -regulated purpose.[392] This piece on under-age play has been included as a subsection of 'Player Protection'; however, children under the age of 16 should not be players at all. Notwithstanding the Operator's efforts it would appear that in the vicinity of 7 per cent of children manage to make Lottery ticket purchases. From the Regulator's position this is too high, and John Stoker when Director General called on Camelot to redouble its efforts to bring about a continuous improvement in this area.[393] Whether or not adults should be allowed to purchase tickets on behalf of a child, which is currently the case, is a moot point. This was outside the remit of the Director General and Oflot, and remains beyond the scope of the Commissioners and the National Lottery Commission. If the problem were to be addressed it would be a matter for Parliament or the courts. With the potential for longer-term difficulties that have been shown to be associated with gambling in the young it is an issue requiring serious consideration. Indeed it should be reiterated that there is a substantial body of research indicating that the onset of gambling addiction occurs during the adolescent or teen period.[394] Yet if adults are buying tickets on behalf of children one might argue that some control is being exercised and is to be preferred to children making independent and illegal purchases. If the right to purchase tickets by an adult on behalf of a child were to be made unlawful this might result in an outcropping of under-age Lottery ticket purchases or attempted purchases, placing even greater strains on the need for retailer vigilance. Nevertheless, the problem of under-age sales of Lottery products during and since the time of both Director Generals is clearly less than satisfactory, and represents unequivocally a negative spillover directly attributable to the National Lottery. This is an area where the absence of the power to fine impeded the Director Generals' ability to prosecute with vigour their primary statutory duties. The position of Director General only enjoyed this regulatory option between 10 July 1998[395] and 31 March 1999 when the position of Director General was replaced by a team of five Lottery Commissioners. During the time when the second Director General enjoyed the authority to impose fines for under-age transgressions, no financial penalties were exacted from the Operator.[396] During the first two years of its life the National Lottery Commission also did not impose any fines on the Operator.

3 MAXIMIZING THE PROCEEDS

3.1 *The Bid Structure*

The secondary responsibility of the Regulator (and the Secretary of State) is to do his best to secure that the net proceeds of the National Lottery are as great as possible. By net proceeds, the Act refers to the funds applied equally through the Distribution Fund initially to the five Good Causes of the Arts, Charity, Heritage, Sport and the Millennium Commission. The National Lottery Act of 1998 created a new category, *viz.* the New Opportunities Fund for expenditures connected with health, education and the environment.[397] In assessing the success of the Director Generals in their efforts to maximize the flow of funds to the Distribution Fund, the starting point is most certainly the bidding process for the award of the Licence.

In their submissions for the award of the Licence, applicants were required to specify the proportion of ticket sales income which would be committed to prize money and the Distribution Fund, over a range of revenue scenarios up to and beyond their principal business forecast, in the expectation that economies of scale would enable the applicants to offer higher percentages to the Fund as the overall size of the Lottery increased.[398] In this way it would benefit from any unexpected success enjoyed by the Lottery. In relation to the information required in the applicants' submissions outlined at Appendix I on pages 199–200, the Director General set up a series of tasks. Tasks N to Q were designed specifically to determine which of the applicants would be most likely to meet the statutory objective of maximizing the contribution to the Distribution Fund.[399] These tasks were especially complex involving some 14,600 calculations.[400] Camelot won the bid as it offered the greatest contribution to the Good Causes over a wide (but not all) range of revenue scenarios, and retained the lowest percentage of turnover to cover its operating costs and profit.[401] The contest for the award of the Licence was a remarkably close one, suggesting that, within the framework set by the relevant legislation, the process produced the best possible result for the Distribution Fund.[402]

Table 1, on page 67, shows the allocation of ticket sales revenues over the period of the Licence based on the forecast included in Camelot's winning bid. Lottery duty is set at 12 per cent under the Finance Act 1993, and is the first charge against the proceeds of the Lottery, after which the Licence provides that the net revenue is apportioned initially between the Target Prize Fund and the Distribution Fund with the balance being retained by the Operator to meet its costs (including retailer commission) and ultimately to derive its profit.[403] The complexity of the Licence is such that there are no less than 48 different percentages governing how much the Operator pays to Good Causes, and the revenue bands are themselves subject to adjustment for inflation.[404] As Table 1 demonstrates under the ticket sales payment columns, revenue payable to the Distribution Fund depends on total revenues and the year. Revenue applied to the Good Causes through the Fund is generally higher in later years both in monetary terms and also as a proportion of total income.

Table 2, on page 70, demonstrates that revenues passed to the Distribution Fund are also higher for higher tranches of total income in each year. The percentages at Table 2 are commitments under the Licence; they illustrate that the greater the success of the Lottery the greater is the amount not only in absolute terms but also in percentage terms that is passed to the NLDF. These increases in percentages are made at the expense of that proportion retained by the Operator.[405] For example, in the financial year 1997/98, of the first £0.8 billion of Lottery ticket sales, Camelot retained 11 per cent and 22.3 per cent was passed to the NLDF.[406] The share of ticket sales income moves through a series of six bands in each case, with the NLDF share increasing at the expense of the Operator.[407] In 1998 when sales reached £3.9 billion, for each incremental increase in sales thereafter the Operator retained 1.6 per cent and 31.7 per cent was passed to the NLDF.[408]

3.2 The Outcome

If one compares the allocation of revenues contained in the Operator's forecast at Table 1 with the actual allocation of Lottery revenues in Table 3, on page 71, then it is evident that Camelot's contribution to the NLDF is higher than forecast both in absolute and percentage terms. This is a reflection of the outstanding success of the Lottery, with sales since the launch in November 1994 and up to the end of March 2001 being nearly 10 per cent ahead of forecast, and with the contribution to the NLDF being over 21 per cent ahead of forecast. This again confirms the principle enshrined in the Licence that the Good Causes receive a greater proportion of any unanticipated success.

In the same way the income retained by the Operator is reduced as the Lottery grows. Comparing Tables 1 and 3 (Camelot's retention in Table 1 includes retailer commission) it appears that the Operator's retention for 1995 and 1996 is higher than forecast, notwithstanding the fact that revenues are greater than forecast. This is in large measure a function of the prize target which has fallen short of that contained in the forecast. The effect of this has been for the Operator to pay over to the NLDF a sum equal to the Prize Target Shortfall in the July following the financial year to which the shortfall relates.[409] Thus the shortfall for the four and a half months to March 1995 of £18 million is added to the payments applied to the NLDF at the expense of the Operator's retention monies in the following year. Similarly the shortfall for 1996 of £135 million is included in the figures for 1997, the shortfall for 1997 of £122 million is carried forward and included in the figures for 1998, the amount of £100 million for 1998 is included in the results for 1999, and £88 million is provided by the Regulator for 1999 and included in the results for 2000. Finally, a shortfall of £91 million for 2000 is carried forward and provided for the FY ending March 2001.[410] The impact of this is for the Operator's retention to be inflated in the first two periods, which are abnormal owing to the effect of the shortened first accounting year. The outcomes for subsequent years in terms of retention percentages as exhibited at Table 3 (including retailer commissions) are closer to those forecasted and included at Table 1.

3.3 *The Retailer*

An important reason behind Camelot winning the Licence relates to its plans for an extensive on-line retail network compared with the other bidders.[411] Nearly 10,000 retailers were selling National Lottery tickets at the launch in November 1994,[412] exceeding the minimum number of on-line retail outlets stipulated in the Licence of 9225.[413] By February 1996 Camelot estimated that 90 per cent of players lived or worked within 2 miles of a National Lottery retailer.[414] Nevertheless, even though by the end of March 1996 the on-line retailer network had reached 20,283, and thus exceeded the minimum required of 19,260 in the Licence (but not the targeted figure of 21,400), Instants-only retailers stood at 9424 which was below the minimum requirement of 10,800 (and the target of 12,000).[415] For this Licence breach the Operator was censured by the Director General who, in the absence of the ability to impose financial penalties on Camelot, considered (but did not implement) an application for a court order to compel compliance.[416] By March 1997 Camelot had increased the number

Table 1 Allocation of ticket sales revenues over time (based on Camelot's forecast sales)

Year ending 31 March	Forecast sales (gross)	Duty		Target prize total		Ticket sales payment		Camelot's retention (including retailer commission)	
	£m	£m	%	£m	%	£m	%	£m	%
14/11/94–31/03/95	850.0	102.0	12.0	401.2	47.2	220.3	25.9	126.5	14.9
1996	2950.0	354.0	12.0	1494.3	50.7	719.0	24.4	382.7	13.0
1997	4160.0	499.2	12.0	2099.8	50.5	1098.8	26.4	462.2	11.1
1998	5075.0	609.0	12.0	2517.0	49.6	1432.3	28.2	516.7	10.2
1999	5212.0	625.4	12.0	2583.2	49.6	1497.0	28.7	506.4	9.7
2000	5350.0	642.0	12.0	2669.9	49.9	1522.3	28.5	515.8	9.6
2001	5485.0	658.2	12.0	2737.3	49.9	1564.7	28.5	524.8	9.6
01/04/01–30/09/01	2810.0	337.2	12.0	1401.6	49.9	805.9	28.7	265.3	9.4
Total	**31892.0**	**3827.0**	**12.0**	**15904.3**	**49.9**	**8860.3**	**27.8**	**3300.4**	**10.3**

Note: The Licence application envisaged Camelot's retention reducing by approximately one-third over the life of the Licence, with the National Lottery Distribution Fund being the main beneficiary through increases in the ticket sales payment.

Source: National Audit Office analysis of data taken from Camelot's Section 5 Licence application and from the Section 5 Licence, cited by the Comptroller and Auditor General, *Payments to the National Lottery Distribution Fund H.C. 678 Session 1995–96* (National Audit Office, HMSO, London, 23/07/96), p. 61, fig. A2.

of on-line Lottery retailers to 24,578 and the number of Instants-only retailers to 10,875.[417] This compares with a minimum requirement as outlined in the Licence of 24,300 on-line retailers (target 27,000) and 10,800 Instants-only retailers (target 12,000).[418] The number of on-line retailers is still short of the total of 27,000 proposed by Camelot in its winning bid to run the Lottery.[419] This is worthy of note owing to the 'particular import-ance' attached to the size of the proposed on-line retail network by the Director General in his decision to award the Licence to Camelot.[420] Nevertheless, the Company has committed itself to maintain 1000 termin-als as a community service even though the terminals cannot be justified on any profitability basis.[421]

3.4 Developing the Product

The drive to maximize revenues to be applied to the 'Good Causes' demands constant product innovation. As has already been shown the design of the on-line National Lottery game is such that when jackpot prizes are not won, that proportion of the prize fund that would have been allocated to the jackpot can be carried over to three further draws. From the launch of the on-line Lottery in November 1994 up to the end of March 2001 there had been over 60 single roll-overs and 5 double roll-overs.[422] Each single roll-over has typically resulted in additional sales of between 15 and 20 per cent.[423] The four double roll-overs have increased sales by between 54 and 148 per cent.[424] 'From this it is clear that big prizes sell more tickets which in turn raise more money for Good Causes.'[425] Indeed in a bid to drive up sales Camelot has introduced a number of so-called 'Superdraws' in which the Operator guarantees minimum jackpots of anywhere between £5 million and £25 million.[426] In the year to March 1999 the Operator promoted seven 'Superdraws',[427] and in the following 12 months a further eight, including a roll-over Super-draw,[428] and in the year to March 2001 seven 'Superdraws'.[429]

The introduction of the Instants product in March 1995 was designed to compete in an already established marketplace. Charities and local authorities had been selling instant scratch-cards since the 1975 Lotteries Act,[430] and in an effort to create a 'level playing field' the National Lottery etc Act 1993 increased the permitted size of such lotteries.[431] As National Lottery on-line sales increased from £3694 million in the financial year ending March 1996 (the first full accounting year for which tickets were being sold) to £3846 million for the following year, it is safe to conclude that the Instants game was competing in a different market and not cannibalizing the sales of the on-line game.[432] With sales in excess of £1.5 billion in the first 12 months, National Lottery Instants established a dominant position with a share in excess of 90 per cent of the total scratch-card market.[433] Weekly sales of National Lottery Instants peaked at £44 million during 1995 but had fallen to just £10.5 million by FY 2001.[434] Table 3 confirms the fall-off of Instants sales both in absolute terms and as a proportion of total Lottery sales.[435] By the year ending March 1999 National Lottery Instants sales may have represented around 80 per cent of the total scratch-cards market.[436] In an effort to try and improve the sales of Instants, Camelot introduced a television programme *The National Lottery Big Ticket* on BBC1 in March 1998.[437] The results were, however, disappointing, and the promotion was swiftly withdrawn; but not before the Broadcasting Complaints Commission had received complaints that the programme was undesirable, particularly with regard to young people, and especially as it was being shown before the '9.00 p.m. watershed'.[438] The Commission agreed with the complaints and concluded that the programme glamorized gambling and should not have been shown during family viewing time.[439] This is an area where the Director General could and should have taken a stronger lead. The Operator required the approval of the Director General to launch all new games. In allowing 'the National Lottery Big Ticket' game to proceed the Regulator arguably fell short in delivering on one of his primary duties of preventing underage sales.[440] The same argument would conclude that Camelot was also in breach of its Licence commitments.[441]

Table 3 demonstrates one of the problems experienced by almost all lotteries – *viz.* player apathy or player fatigue.[442] The second full year of the Lottery's life saw a slump in sales. 'Experience has shown that lottery players need constant prodding: first year lottery sales always boom, but then players tire of the novelty and sales can fall.'[443] This underlines the constant need for lottery products, and in particular instant lotteries which have short life cycles, to be revamped.[444] Between March 1995 and March 1999, 57 Instants games were introduced.[445] The fall in National Lottery revenues in 1997 owing to the decline in popularity of the Instants brand was reversed in 1998 following the addition in February 1997 of the Midweek Draw to support the on-line game.[446] The introduction of the midweek game has increased total weekly sales by around £15 million.[447] It is also possible that the year on year decline in Instants sales may be reversed in 2001–2002. In January 2001 the first Instants game involving non-cash prizes was launched.[448] 'The Cars and Cash' game has become the fastest selling Instants game since 1997.[449] This together with the launch in June 2001 of the first Instants game guaranteeing a £1 million top prize (of which there are 5)[450] should result in a pick-up in Instants sales for the first time since FY 1995/96.

The National Lottery is almost always referred to as a monopoly; however, it is not a pure monopoly. More accurately the Lottery should be styled a partial monopoly operating in an imperfect market which is

Table 2 Commitments to the National Lottery Distribution Fund (NLDF)

Tranche boundary (ticket sales)	Year end 31 March 1995	Year end 31 March 1996	Year end 31 March 1997	Year end 31 March 1998	Year end 31 March 1999	Year end 31 March 2000	Year end 31 March 2001	Six months to 30 Sept. 2001
Up to £750 million	25.79%	20.66%	21.01%	22.26%	23.27%	22.92%	22.92%	23.12%
£750–£1500 million	26.80%	21.66%	22.01%	23.26%	24.27%	23.92%	23.93%	24.12%
£1500–£2000 million	29.55%	24.41%	24.76%	26.01%	27.02%	26.67%	26.67%	26.88%
£2000–£2500 million	32.05%	28.60%	28.78%	29.66%	29.69%	29.35%	29.35%	29.37%
£2500–£3500 million	33.80%	30.35%	30.53%	31.41%	31.44%	31.10%	31.10%	31.13%
Greater than above	34.05%	30.60%	30.77%	31.65%	31.69%	31.35%	31.35%	31.37%

Note: The greater the success of the National Lottery, the more money will pass to the Good Causes via the National Lottery Distribution Fund, and the lower the proportion retained by Camelot.

Source: Oflot, The National Lottery: preferred applicant announced (press release) (Oflot, London, 25/05/94).

Table 3 Allocation of Lottery proceeds since launch

Year ending 31 March	Actual sales £m	Duty £m	Duty %	Prizes (claimed) £m	Prizes (claimed) %	Ticket sales payment and other to NLDF[a] £m	Ticket sales payment and other to NLDF[a] %	Retailer commission[b] £m	Retailer commission[b] %	Camelot retention (to cover costs and profits) £m	Camelot retention (to cover costs and profits) %
14/11/94–31/03/95	1191 (on-Line 97.2%)	143	12	544	45.7	312	26.2	61	5.1	131	11.0
1996	5217 (on-Line 70.8%)	626	12	2470	47.3	1454	27.9	265	5.1	402	7.7
1997	4723 (on-Line 81.4%)	567	12	2208	46.7	1444	30.6	242	5.1	264	5.6
1998	5514 (on-Line 85.5%)	662	12	2561	46.4	1753	31.8	282	5.1	259	4.7
1999	5228 (on-Line 86.7%)	627	12	2423	46.3	1671	31.9	265	5.1	252	4.8
2000	5094 (on-Line 89.0%)	611	12	2383	46.8	1581	31.0	258	5.1	267	5.2
2001	4983 (on-Line 89.0%)	598	12	2342	47.0	1551	31.1	253	5.1	246	4.9
01/04/01–30/09/01											

[a] Payments to the National Lottery Distribution Fund include ticket sales payments, unclaimed prizes, Prize Target Shortfall, ancillary activity income and interest from trust accounts. Oflot and the National Lottery Commission include the figure for the Prize Target Shortfall in the year it is paid, i.e. in the July following the end of the previous financial year. The shortfall for the four and a half months to March 1995 was £18 million, and is included in the following year's contribution to the NLDF. The shortfall in 1995/96 was £135 million and is similarly carried forward. (This has the effect of inflating Camelot's retention for 1995/96.) Camelot's accounts, being on an accruals basis, recognize payments to the Prize Target Shortfall when they arise, rather than when they are paid.

[b] Retailer commission of 5 per cent is enhanced by a further 1 per cent commission on prizes paid out between £10 and £200. Memorandum submitted by Camelot Group plc to National Heritage Commission.

Sources: Annual reports of Oflot and the NLC; Director General of the Lottery, *Annual Report 1997/98*, p. 8, app. A (Stationery Office, London, 09/07/98; Camelot, Memorandum, Supplementary submitted to National Heritage Commission, *Minutes of Evidence H.C. 240 iii Session 1995–96* (HMSO, London, 29/02/96), p. 46.

monopolistically competitive. For the Lottery competes in a market with other near substitutes in the form of consumer products and more specifically gambling products. Additionally the National Lottery etc. Act 1993 allows for suppliers other than the head or main Licensee, Camelot, to promote individual games[451] through the creation of a two-tiered rather than a unitary licensing system. The main Section 5 Licence is granted to run the Lottery, and individual games are then promoted under Section 6 licences which can be awarded to more than one supplier.[452] However, no such Section 6 licences will be granted unless the supplier is contractually bound to the main Section 5 Licence-holder, Camelot[453] (which remains liable for the funds generated). Even if the applicant satisfies the Regulator that it meets the statutory requirements, the Section 5 Licensee can veto the proposals and prevent the supplier from providing games, which it will do if the proposed game falls short of the head Licensee's own revenue forecasts.[454] The first Director General, during his time in office, made it clear that while he was keen to see independent Section 6 licensees involved he had no statutory duty to promote competition or to promote a level playing field.[455] Furthermore, he concluded that Camelot's economies of scale and low marginal costs made it very difficult for an outside supplier to deliver a competitive product.[456]

Nevertheless, in May 1997 the first Section 6 Licence was awarded to a body other than Camelot.[457] This innovation was a further response to the disappointing results for the year to March 1997. The Licence was awarded (with the necessary agreement and cooperation of Camelot) to Vernons Lotteries Ltd to promote an On-line lottery based on a football theme.[458] The new game was projected to provide up to £200 million in additional benefit to the Good Causes over the life of the initial licence.[459] However, this proved to be too optimistic, and the product was withdrawn in May 1999 following disappointing sales figures.[460] The Vernons game had only raised just over £5 million for the Good Causes.[461] This failure encouraged the Regulator to examine ways (in formulating the new Licence) to facilitate more readily the provision of games by organizations other than the main Licence holder.[462] Finally, the disappointing fall in Lottery sales for the year ending March 1999 (see Table 3) saw the introduction in the following June of the 'Thunderball' game. This game is essentially a redesign of the main on-Line Draw Lottery and pays out £5 for matching two numbered balls in the draw including the prescribed 'Thunderball'. The game guarantees a win of £5,000 for matching five balls, with a chance of increasing this amount up to £250,000 (depending on the number of winners) if one of the balls is also a 'Thunderball'.[463] Up to the end of March 2000, the game had sustained a level of sales at around £4 million per week.[464]

3.5 Balancing the Maximizing of Revenue with Player Protection

One of the concerns of those who have criticized the Lottery's regulatory apparatus is the inherent potential for conflict implicit in the Regulator's statutory remit. The Regulator's primary duty is to uphold the propriety of the Lottery and to protect the interests of players. However, it is not always immediately obvious as to whether proposals for game development and innovation submitted by the Operator in the interests of maximizing revenues will also serve the players' interests. This judgement was an important part of the Director General's rôle; it remains so for the National Lottery Commission, and its Commissioners. Directions issued by the Secretary of State do not allow the licensing of games which in the estimation of the Regulator would encourage persons to participate excessively.[465]Thus, as has already been referred to, the first Director General turned down the Operator's request to introduce Keno, a game popular in the USA, which involves a high frequency of draws (perhaps 5, 10 or 20 minutes apart) and allows players to choose from a selection of odds.[466] The Directions also limited to three the number of jackpot roll-overs,[467] limited the price of tickets and forbade the licensing of games in which persons participate by means of interactive lottery machines.[468] Interactive lottery machines – so-called video lottery terminals (VLTs) – which are in effect gaming machines, are common in North America and have allegedly been responsible for triggering a rash of social problems.[469]

It remains within the gift of the Secretary of State to modify or relax these Directions. There is a real concern that if there is a decline in ticket sales the Secretary of State and the government will come under pressure to relax controls designed to provide player protection.[470] Concern was also voiced during the parliamentary debates prior to the introduction of the Lottery that the on-line game, with its major prize draw, should not be promoted more frequently than once a week.[471] Indeed Condition 9 of the Operator's Section 6 Licence which authorizes the on-line game, privides that the Lottery shall be drawn weekly and, in addition, with the Regulator's consent, on a further six occasions in any one year.[472] In light of the declining sales during 1996/97 (see Table 3) the Director General agreed to a variation in the Licence permitting the introduction of the Midweek Draw.[473] Although it was not necessary for a formal Direction to be issued by the Secretary of State to the Director General, the Secretary of State would have known of the proposed change in advance and could have intervened to prevent the variation had he considered such a course of action appropriate.[474] The ongoing and continuous decline in the sale of Instants tickets[475] would have influenced the Director General's decision to allow the introduction of *The National Lottery Big Ticket* television spectacular in 1998 (referred to above), but this only attracted the criticism of the Broadcasting Complaints Commission, and did not improve the fortunes of the Instants product. This again highlights the difficulties for the Regulator in balancing primary regulatory duties with the secondary promotional function. This issue is addressed further in Chapter 4.

3.6 *Ancillary Income*

While the vast majority of income that is applied to the Distribution Fund comes weekly from ticket sales there are a number of other sources of income that help to 'top up' and thereby maximize the contribution to the Good Causes. The most significant sources of income not to come directly from ticket sales relates to revenues generated by the so-called 'Prize Target Shortfall'. If less than the target percentage is paid in prizes, Camelot pays the shortfall to the Good Causes by 28 July following the year end.[476] From the launch of the Lottery up to the end of March 2001 £546 million had been paid over to the NLDF in this way.[477] Camelot agreed with the Director General to pay over from the end of March 1997 the interest (which the Operator had previously retained) earned on these monies.[478] This is expected to have amounted to a further £20 million over the remainder of the first Licence period.[479]

The second largest source of revenue applied to the Distribution Fund and not received directly from ticket sales is income from unclaimed prizes. Between 2 and 3 per cent of the value of prizes in each draw is never claimed and this money passes to the NLDF (with interest) 180 days after each draw.[480] From the launch of the Lottery up to March 2001 the extra income from this source passed to the NLDF (each week)[481] amounted to £381 million.[482] The Distribution Fund also enjoys any investment income earned on the Players' Trust (which is responsible for paying out prizes to players) after all other obligations have been met.[483] Between the launch and the end of March 2001 the total received from this source had reached £29 million.[484] The Section 5 Licence also requires Camelot to maintain in an Escrow account a balance equal to 2.5 per cent of the value of the previous year's ticket sales, less £40 million.[485] Monies on this account can be invested as the Secretary of State sees fit, with the income generated from such investments accruing to the Distribution Fund.[486] Although no payments have been made from this source, the balance of funds reverts to the Fund on termination of the Licence for whatever reason including the effluxion of time.[487]

Finally, income is also raised through the Operator's activities that do not relate directly to revenue derived from ticket sales. The most important source of funds to come from ancillary trading is that which is derived from the BBC in respect of the sale of broadcasting rights for the twice-weekly on-line Lottery Draw. In 1995 Camelot agreed to broadcast the Lottery Draw on the BBC for three years for a fee of £1.65 million.[488] Half of this fee is paid over by Camelot to the Distribution Fund.[489] The contract with the BBC has also been extended.[490] During the financial year 1995/96 Camelot established a separate internal division of the company – National Lottery Enterprises – to focus on harnessing revenue-generating opportunities outside core activities associated with running the Lottery.[491] The division has entered into agreements and marketing partnerships giving third parties the right to use the National Lottery brand under licence.[492] Additionally Camelot sells products such as key rings, fridge magnets, wallets and T-shirts which bear the National Lottery's logo.[493] The Good Causes enjoy 50 per cent of the net revenue generated by the foregoing ancillary activities,[494] and the amounts payable to the Distribution Fund are checked by the Regulator's Compliance Division.[495] Camelot commissioned the National Lottery merchandise in 1995/96 without the final consent of the Director General.[496] This Licence breach could be the type where the Commission might wish to consider imposing a fine on the Operator, a power extended to the Lottery's Regulator by Section 2 of the National Lottery Act 1998, which provides that all such fines be passed to the Distribution Fund.[497] Ancillary activity income which is passed to the Fund quarterly[498] amounted to £3 million between the launch of the Lottery and the end of March 2001.[499]

3.7 Gauging the Lottery's Success

The National Lottery has been an outstanding success if one compares the forecast sales (included in Table 1) and contribution to the Distribution Fund with the outcome (see Table 3). It is worth reiterating that from the start of the Lottery up to the end of March 2001 actual sales exceeded forecast sales by nearly 10 per cent and the contribution to the NLDF was more than a fifth ahead of that figure included within Camelot's forecast.[500] The popularity of the Lottery is perhaps well illustrated by the fact that more people played in the first double roll-over Lottery game (in January 1996)[501] than voted in the 1992 general election.[502] National Lottery ticket sales have been estimated to be almost 3 per cent of all retail sales and 1 per cent of total consumer expenditure.[503] Moreover, the delay in the payments made by the Distribution Fund to the Good Causes has had the impact of reducing the public sector borrowing requirement by up to £1.75 billion a year.[504] As payments made out of the Fund build up to match payments paid into it, this has been calculated to be the equivalent of around 0.1 per cent of GDP.[505]

While the raising of funds for the Good Causes has comfortably exceeded the Operator's forecasts, this has led to the criticism in some quarters that the targets set for Camelot proved to be far too low, and that the profits made by the company have been too easily earned.[506] Critics of the Lottery have further suggested that Camelot has exploited its position as a monopoly or quasi-monopoly so as to generate excessive profits.[507] The reasoning and implications behind such fault-finding is to question whether the profit seeking private entity model is the most appropriate or efficient way of running the Lottery. It should be remembered that this incipient reservation regarding the association of a for-profit organization with the Lottery lay behind the structuring of the UK Lotteries bid headed by Richard Branson which had pledged all profits to charity.

The debate as to whether the Lottery should be organized as a public or private or not-for-profit entity is an enduring polemic. However, the following points should be borne in mind. The launch of the National Lottery was an entirely new venture with no ready or reliable method to confidently estimate likely demand. Camelot's projections were based on international precedent, econometric modelling of spending power and trends in the UK, and projections as to likely levels of consumer participation.[508] Even those who had some experience of lotteries from around the world, had little idea of what could be expected from the UK version.[509] This is reflected in the bidding process with the revenue forecasts over the course of the Licence period (from all final bidders) ranging from £14.1 billion to £31.6 billion.[510] The bid process was designed to ensure *ceteris paribus* that the Licence would be awarded to the applicant who would be most likely to contribute the greatest amount to the Good Causes while retaining the lowest proportion of turnover to cover operating costs and profit. Furthermore, as Table 2 demonstrates the more successful the Lottery, the greater is the proportion passed to the Distribution Fund at the expense of that which is retained by the Operator. It is estimated that Camelot will pass over five times the amount that it retains to cover running costs and profit to the Fund over the period of the Licence.[511]

By placing the operation and promotion of the Lottery with a commercial organization the government effectively transferred the risk associated with the venture and all its attendant uncertainty from the public to the private sector. In the period up to the end of March 1995 Camelot invested £200 million in the Lottery, comprising £100 million operating costs.[512] This investment was funded by a combination of £50 million shareholders equity,[513] loans from the Royal Bank of Scotland and net income from the first period of sales.[514] Critics of the Lottery and of the profits made by the Operator have argued that in the bid Camelot claimed it would not make a profit in the first three years,[515] an accusation denied by Camelot who claim that even in the bid submission the consortium envisaged making a profit in the first year.[516] Camelot's initial intentions had been to write off the start-up costs for the launch which amounted to £30 million, over three years.[517] However, the success of the first four and a half months of trading up to the end of March 1995 allowed Camelot to charge all the start-up costs to the profit and loss account for the period and still make a pre-tax profit of £10.8 million.[518] Moreover, Camelot had originally planned to pay a dividend to its shareholders in the third year;[519] yet the unexpected success of the Lottery allowed it to pay a dividend of £18.4 million in the second year.[520] In similar vein Camelot, whose shareholders receive their return through dividends, did not expect to recover their initial investment of £50 million and £10 million bid costs until 'approaching the millennium'.[521] Cumulative dividends paid to the end of March 1998 had already reached £63.4 million.[522]

In large regulated industries it is not easy at the best of times to assess whether out-performance is the result of greater efficiency, changing market conditions, or market defects producing monopoly profits.[523] In the case of the National Lottery the difficulty is compounded as there is no useful recent UK based historical precedent or point of reference to aid the process. Even though cumulative pre-tax profits from the launch of the Lottery up to the end of March 2001 amounted to just over 1.34 per cent of turnover (post-tax profits for the same period were 0.90 per cent of turnover),[524] there has been an unease voiced in the media and elsewhere with regard to the absolute profits, dividends and bonuses paid to directors. There is a feeling in certain quarters which ignores the rôle of the profit motive in improving efficiencies that these amounts should also be paid to the Good Causes. This is a position with which the Labour government has also expressed some sympathy,[525] and has informed the bidding process and the thinking behind the terms on which the new Licence has been awarded. This is addressed in Chapter 5.

Yet by international standards the UK Lottery is remarkably efficient. It certainly benefits from the economies of scale that follow from being one of the largest lotteries in the world. The lottery operating expenses in many states typically average 15 per cent,[526] while the UK Lottery's expenses including costs, retailer commissions and profits are considerably lower – at around 10 per cent (for years ending 31 March 1998 to 31 March 2000).[527] Independent research has demonstrated that the surplus generated by the UK Lottery (comprising payments to the Good Causes and Lottery Duty) is both the highest amount and the highest proportion of turnover generated by any major lottery in the world.[528] Table 4 demonstrates the success of the Lottery in generating funds for the Good Causes and the government in the form of taxes (including Lottery Duty, corporation tax and irrecoverable VAT).[529]

By international standards, and irrespective of the discrepancy between the Operator's forecast and the outcome, the UK Lottery is efficient.

Table 4   Net income generation of top 10 lotteries in 1997* (%)

Rank	Lottery organization	Country	Net income as a percentage of total sales
1	UK National Lottery	UK	44.3
2	Caixa Economica	Brazil	43.8
3	Pennsylvania Lottery	USA	40.8
4	New Jersey Lottery	USA	40.7
5	Westdeutsche Lottery	Germany	40.5
6	Oy veikkaus	Finland	40.0
7	Dai-Ichi Kangyo Bank	Japan	39.8
8	S Toto-Loto (Stuggart)	Germany	39.6
9	Florida Lottery	USA	39.2
10	New York Lottery	USA	38.5

* Year ends will differ.

Source: T. La Fleur 1998, cited by Camelot Group plc, *Lottery Briefing Issue*, no. 9 (Camelot, Watford, summer 1998)

Whether altering the fundamentals of the regulatory architecture or seeking to change the running of the Lottery, from a private entity model to a not-for-profit entity, would serve to enhance the maximization of revenues to be passed to the Good Causes is a moot point. Indeed the success of the Lottery has been such that Camelot has upgraded its forecast for the contribution to Good Causes over the period of the Licence from just under £9 billion[530] to £10 billion.[531] It is entirely possible that the outcome will even exceed this revised forecast, as it is already estimated that the contribution to the Distribution Fund will exceed 30 per cent of turnover over the term of the Licence.[532] If interest on monies held in the Fund is included, the final figure could be as much as £11 billion.[533] Figure 1 projects a turnover for the Lottery over the duration of the Licence of £35 billion (against a forecast of £31.9 billion).[534] This projection if demanding is not unrealistic and is informed by the results as outlined at Table 3. These figures suggest that the operational arrangements appertaining to the Lottery in terms of revenue maximization have worked well, although since a peak in 1998, sales have been slightly weaker, implying the need for a revamping of the Lottery's game portfolio. In light of the foregoing it is not unreasonable to posit that in overseeing the Lottery, the Director

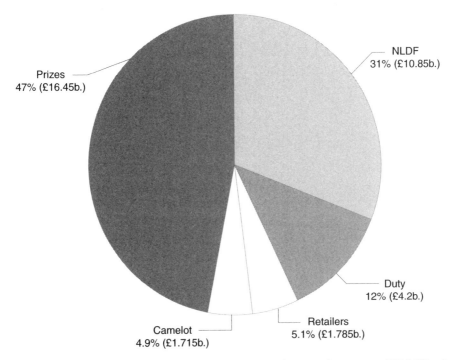

Figure 1 Possible outcome over seven-year licence (turnover £35 billion)

Generals were most successful (during their regime which ended in March 1999) in meeting the secondary statutory duty of maximizing the funds for Good Causes when compared with either of the Regulator's two primary duties of ensuring the propriety of the Lottery and the protection of the players. In determining therefore, what the design or model for the operation of the Lottery should be after the expiry of the initial seven-year licence period, with regard to the generation of revenue at least, the government and the National Lottery Commission and its Commissioners will have been well advised to reflect carefully on any modification to the Lottery's operational structures.

CHAPTER 4

REGULATORY DESIGN: PROBLEMS AND CONFLICTS

Chapter 3 assessed the regulation of the Lottery during the time of the Director Generals. In so doing it evaluated the project in the context of the Regulator's primary duties of guaranteeing propriety and protecting the interests of players, alongside the secondary responsibility of maximizing the funds to be applied to the Good Causes. In other words, the chapter measured the Lottery's regulation against the criteria of the enabling legislation. The assessment also correlated closely with those classic regulatory issues and theoretical constructs as set out in Chapters 1 and 2 – particularly having regard to the problems of balancing responsibilities, the use of discretion, the interpretation of duties, the particular challenges of new regulatory frameworks and the peculiar difficulties of personalized regulatory regimes. The following lines provide a critical appraisal of the Lottery's regulatory design. This chapter addresses the extent of the powers invested in the rôle of Director General, the inherent conflicts in relation to the Regulator's duties, the implication of this with regard to principal/agent relations and the uncertain status of the Lottery's regulation within the polity.

4.1 *Regulatory Powers and Their Application*

The tendency for regulatory commissions and agencies to be passive towards the public interest is a problem of ethics and morality as well as administrative method.[1] The life-cycle theory of regulation posits that all social institutions are subject to inertia and loss of vitality over time, as procedural patterns tend to become sanctified as unalterable guides for bureaucratic conduct and accepted behaviour.[2] However, the Director General of the Lottery was criticized for his perceived inertia very shortly after the regulatory process commenced and was advised by the PAC to 'adopt a more proactive approach, promoting more the public interest and using his personal energy and the power of his legal status to that end.'[3] Evidence suggests that the first Director General took a highly normalized if somewhat restricted stance *vis-à-vis* his duties. He regarded himself quite properly as a 'Creature of Statute' with his powers set out and limited by the National Lottery Act.[4] Controversy associated with the regulatory process centred around the degree of discretion that the Director General was prepared to exercise or crucially believed he was able to exercise within the limitations of his statutory brief. The first Director General's style of regulation was likened in some quarters to that of an auditor – being reactive rather than proactive and as such was indicative of his training as a chartered accountant.[5] This section assesses the extent of the Director General's powers and his willingness to use them.

Parliament decided that the UK was to have a National Lottery and that it would be run under licence by a private operator; once these principles had been enshrined in legislation, the Director General and his advisors thereafter played a key rôle in designing and putting in place the regulatory architecture. 'It was a very important part of my rôle to set that framework,' he stated.[6] The Director General was in some respects invested with more power than comparable director generals of other regulated offices in that he was able to make unilateral changes to the Operator's Licence.[7] However, this power was qualified and limited by the 1993 Act, as the Regulator could not vary the Operator's Licence in any way which would require the Licensee to transfer any property or rights.[8] In other words the Director General did not have the legal power to impose on the Operator any change in the financial arrangements.[9] In this way it can be argued that the Director General actually enjoyed less power than the regulators of the privatized utilities who may intervene to control the level of profits of the firms under their charge.[10]

There is little doubt that a serious weakness in the drafting of the 1993 Act remained the inability of the Regulator to impose financial penalties on the Operator for Licence breaches. This omission was subsequently rectified in the National Lottery Act 1998.[11] However, it is not unreasonable to contend that one of the reasons for the first Director General's apparently lacklustre regulatory style is to be found in the fact that the enforcement option of fining was not available to him. Indeed he opined:

> The Director General can seek a court order requiring compliance with licence terms and can report breaches publicly. In the last resort he can suspend or revoke a licence. There appears, however, to be a gap in the intermediate range of regulatory weapons to be deployed when necessary. Most commercial operations recognise the importance of an economic imperative and Camelot is no different in this respect.[12]

The Director General was also prepared to cite incidences where he would have liked to have had the power to impose fines on the Operator. These included failures by Camelot to meet its Licence commitments having regard to the number of retailers dispensing Lottery tickets, and the submission by Camelot to the Director General of inaccurate data on the subject.[13] Indeed this failure by Camelot to meet its Licence commitments regarding retailer numbers can be seen as an archetypal or classic justification of the need for regulation (and appropriate regulatory instruments). The concern of the Regulator with providing a universal service to players[14] is likely to be at odds with the Operator's priority of delivering profits and returns to its shareholders. In other words, the Operator is likely to be less eager to install Lottery terminals in marginal areas where the costs of trading are higher and prospects for sales and profit are lower.

Had the first Director General been invested with the power to fine the Operator, it may have provided him with the ideal instrument with which to have demonstrated his regulatory credentials, and to have taken and to have been seen to have taken a more proactive and vigorous approach to his duties. The Director General's eagerness to obtain this added regulatory weapon is demonstrated by his requests to his sponsoring governmental department for legislation giving him the authority to impose fines on Camelot to be promulgated.[15] These powers were not extended to the first Director General during his tenure in office. The absence of these powers may also have contributed to the impression that the Director General was more concerned with avoiding conflict with the Operator than in providing effective and robust regulation. With a little more foresight the ability to impose fines could have been included in the enabling legislation, which the Director General was not responsible for formulating.[16] It is not possible to establish whether or not this question arose during the initial discussions that took place with regard to regulatory design, as the information is not in the public domain. Nevertheless, this is an area where the Director General would have benefited from the support of a sponsoring government department willing to accede to requests that were not only reasonable but wholly necessary.

The attitude of a regulator or commission to their enforcement responsibilities affects the entire regulatory programme;[17] for unless an agency demonstrates a capacity to enforce its regulations, it will be more honoured in the breach than the observance.[18] Yet an agency also requires the instruments to carry out effective enforcement strategies. Thus, in the judgement of the first Director General the defects in the regulatory design for the Lottery left only a limited number of intermediate regulatory measures at his disposal with which to effectively discharge his duties. This feature in turn played an important part in influencing the style of regulation, and he became over-reliant on persuasion and publicity in his supervision of Camelot. Moreover, he recognized the limits of such an approach.[19] Even in those areas in which the Director General believed he had authority there were flaws. The Operator's failure to meet its Licence commitments regarding the number of retailers vending Lottery tickets led him to take legal advice

> about whether I could go to court and ask the court to give me an order requiring them to put it right and requiring them to compensate the good causes, and I was advised that I would not get such an order.[20]

The style of regulation that defined the National Lottery between the commencement of operations in November 1994 and the introduction of the 1998 Lottery Act could arguably be described as one of compliance rather than deterrence. This may or may not have been the outcome of deliberate government policy. Broadly, if somewhat crudely, regulatory enforcement strategies can be said to fall into two camps – *viz.* compliance or deterrence. These categories are not mutually exclusive. It is one of the tasks for the regulator where he enjoys the flexibility to be able to adapt to and identify those circumstances where one approach is likely to be the most effective.[21] Many enforcement agencies will provide mixed strategies of control, combining compliance and deterrent policies.[22] While both compliance and deterrence systems of enforcement are geared towards preventing violations, compliance is essentially premonitory, attending to conditions that induce conformity or prevent harm, whereas deterrence is postmonitory, reacting to violations that have already occurred.[23] Although penalties may be employed in either system, they are integral only to deterrence systems where they are presumed to have a causal effect, the principle of which is to prevent future violations; compliance systems by contrast either reward or withhold imposing penalties to induce compliance.[24] In the case of the National Lottery the award of the Licence to the Operator, with the ultimate threat of revocation, can be seen as a compliance measure. By contrast the threat by the government to impose a fine on Camelot equivalent to £10 million per week for failure to meet the start date for commencement,[25] is clearly an example of regulatory deterrence.

While it has been argued that regulatory systems often combine compliance and deterrence strategies, it is also possible to say that one system is likely to be the more appropriate response for the majority of regulatory problems having regard to the special characteristics of the regulated industry or firm in question. Deterrence systems are generally most suitable when the occurrence of events in time and space are difficult to predict and when their causes are imperfectly understood so that specific preventative measures cannot be taken.[26] It follows that the more predictable any violation, or the greater the certainty that a particular intervention will prevent violations, the more likely the agency will resort to compliance strategies.[27] It may well have been the case that those responsible for putting in place the regulatory structures for the Lottery, believed the project, based as it is on a licensing principle, to be best adapted to a system of compliance. The award of the Licence to run the Lottery was contingent upon the Operator accepting its obligations to conform to agreed standards of behaviour prior to launching the undertaking. The Licence itself can be seen as a conditional reward or at least as conditionally related to rewards – so long as one conforms or complies, one is licensed to be rewarded.[28]

In practice the initial arrangements for the Lottery demonstrated both compliance and deterrence features, although the underlying regulatory ethos of these arrangements was one of compliance. Bearing in mind the limits of the Director General's authority as laid down in the 1993 Act, the first Director General, Peter Davis, adopted a policy when and where appropriate of 'negotiated compliance'. This is where an attempt is made to settle on a negotiated solution through bargaining.[29] Peter Davis took up this position most visibly and following promptings from the PAC,[30] and the National Heritage Committee,[31] with respect to Camelot benefiting at the expense of the Distribution Fund in connection with interest earned on the Prize Target Shortfall. The Director General was forced into a position of negotiation, as he was unable to alter a condition of the Licence that would have had an adverse financial impact on the Operator. Furthermore, Camelot was unwilling to take one element of the Licence and discuss it in isolation; it was only prepared to discuss the interest earned on the Prize Target Shortfall providing it could also negotiate other terms of the Licence.[32] The Director General's annual report for 1996/97 recorded that Camelot had agreed to pay over to the Distribution Fund interest earned on the Prize Target Shortfall from 31 March 1997; a figure estimated to be worth in excess of £20 million over the remainder of the Licence period.[33] The report was silent on what concessions had to be made to Camelot in order to secure its willingness to comply with the Director General's request. It is possible that by surrendering payments to which it was contractually entitled, Camelot may have made a commercial judgement, believing that it had generated good will, which might improve its prospects of continuing to be involved in the Lottery after the expiry of the initial Licence either as a supplier or operator.[34] This theory seems entirely plausible as both Camelot and the Director General had come under considerable political pressure from the Secretary of State for National Heritage, the NAO and the PAC to ensure the Distribution Fund benefited from the interest earned on the Prize Target Shortfall.[35] The gesture may also have been designed to act as a sop to mollify the press and public outrage at the levels of bonus the Camelot directors had awarded themselves for the year to March 1997.[36] Nevertheless, the difficulties associated with the workings of the Prize Target Shortfall can be seen as one of those instances where there can be said to be a benefit of public ownership, where government can impose desirable adjustments to the firm in light of unforseen circumstances, while it must bargain with a private firm,[37] and/or introduce new legislation.[38]

While it is possible to contend that a considerable element of bargaining must characterize the enforcement of regulations,[39] there are dangers in this process. A regulatory system based on compliance theory and more particularly one prosecuted on the principles of negotiated compliance affords the regulator considerable scope for discretion. However, the problem with discretion when exercised on a case-by-case basis is that it creates opportunities for both parties to game-the-system.[40] Gaming-the-system occurs when regulation is operated in a discretionary way which provides each party with an incentive to behave strategically to obtain an advantage or avoid loss.[41] This issue of company and agency costs associated with such a mode of behaviour and the dead-weight losses they represent is a cause for real concern. Resources are consumed both directly and indirectly as the industry attempts to take advantage of the regulatory system, and the scene is set for regulation potentially fraught with strategic negotiations and inefficiency brought about by industry chiefs trying to outwit the regulator.[42]

It is possible that the regulatory powers extended to the Director General of the National Lottery by the 1993 Act were perhaps more restrictive in practice than had been envisaged at the time these powers were put in place, and unwittingly the Lottery's regulation became over-reliant on compliance strategies – both voluntary and negotiated. In the absence of a robust set of regulatory instruments and in particular with the Director General unable to impose fines on Camelot, the Operator will almost certainly have been tempted to behave tactically. Given that the regulator will avoid taking legal action at each failure to comply with regulatory requests, the firm will be likely to fail to implement all requested changes.[43] There is no outstanding or irrefutable evidence demonstrating that Camelot has been guilty of such selective non-compliance. However, the Operator's failure to meet its Licence commitments in 1996 having regard to the required minimum number of retail outlets may well represent a case in point. Not only did Camelot fail to meet its Licence obligations, but it also provided the Regulator with misleading information on the subject. This Licence failure (regarded by the Director General as serious)[44] is unlikely to have been a mere oversight as Camelot also approached the Director General to reduce the number of retail outlets specified in the Licence.[45] The Director General did not accede to the request.[46] It is worth reiterating that had the Director General been empowered to impose financial penalties on Camelot in relation to Licence breaches, it is likely that he would have used them on this occasion.[47] A further area in which the Operator's efforts might have demonstrated more alacrity is in relation to under-age sales. As highlighted in Chapter 3 the problem of under-age sales is both sizeable and persistent, and both Director Generals expressed disappointment with Camelot's efforts in this area.[48] The serious prospect of regulatory intervention might have resulted in greater efforts by the Operator. Instead the Director Generals became heavily dependent on their powers of persuasion, and on publicizing their frustration in the annual reports. In this matter the regulation of the Lottery came to be overly reliant 'on Camelot to persuade people to stop buying its products, an approach with limited chances of success.'[49]

4.2 *Conflicts of Interest*

It has been argued above that the National Lottery etc. Act 1993 invested the rôle of Director General of the National Lottery with inadequate powers, or powers that were unlikely to consistently deliver effective or satisfactory regulatory outcomes. The 1998 Lottery Act sought to address these shortcomings. That the initial powers extended to the office of Director General lacked force may have given the impression, or may even have resulted in the relationship between Regulator and Regulatee becoming too intimate. Moreover, two key aspects of the Lottery's regulatory design as defined in the 1993 Act contained features liable to compromise the integrity and independence of the Director General.

The first of these areas where potential for conflicts of interest to arise can be found relates to the Director General's duty not only to regulate the Lottery but also to select the private sector licensee responsible for running the venture. It has been suggested that the notion of the same person choosing the Operator and then assessing the performance of that Operator is seriously flawed.[50] Those, including the National Heritage Committee[51] who have advanced the case for the appointment of the Lottery Operator and its subsequent regulation to be carried out by different agencies, have done so in order that 'the person or people choosing the Operator are not closely involved with regulating it [as] they would have a vested interest in defending their own decision.'[52] Notwithstanding the cogency of this argument, the Secretary of State rejected the opportunity provided by the 1998 Lottery Act of splitting the selecting and operating regulatory functions, maintaining that with the ongoing need to award Section 6 licences, the question would continually arise as to whether the original selection body or the ongoing monitoring body would be best placed to make those determinations.[53] While this is a valid point, a strong case can still be made for the main Section 5 Licence holder to be chosen by a different agency than the one charged with its regulation. Nevertheless, the Secretary of State resolved not to make this distinction, arguing that the information gathered at the decision-making stage, informs the regulatory process throughout the course of the Licence.[54]

The other aspect of the Lottery's regulation that may give rise to too close an association between the Regulator and the Operator, relates to the balance struck by the Director General having regard to his enforcement or regulatory responsibilities apropos his promotional rôle. It has been posited in some quarters, if a little unfairly, that from the commencement of his duties, the first Director General was guilty of positive (as opposed to normative) characteristics in carrying out his regulatory function. In particular, criticism was directed at the Director General's elevation of his secondary duty of maximizing the proceeds to be applied to the Good Causes to a status ranking alongside his primary duties of ensuring the Lottery's propriety, and the protection of participants.[55] From Camelot's position, the maximizing of the income passed to the Distribution Fund is clearly a priority, as this is a function of, as well as a demonstration of, the Operator's success in increasing the size of turnover; and the higher the turnover of the Lottery the higher are the profits retained by the Licensee. In this context it is possible to argue that managers working in the public sector would be more likely to choose the socially optimal level of output for a given level of cost, whereas private managers/operators will not, since they seek monopoly profits.[56] The decision as to where the socially optimal level of output (ticket sales) lies is a decision for the Regulator. It has been argued above that it is entirely appropriate for the Regulator to seek to balance his responsibilities, and that to give any one of his obligations absolute or unqualified precedence over the others would in all probability be counter-productive. Nevertheless this assessment does beg the further question as to the appropriateness of the balances and judgements arrived at by the Regulator.

It is worth reiterating the inherent and invidious difficulties associated with regulation which combines both social and economic functions. The Lottery *per se* is in place not to provide a gambling service to the public, but as a means of raising funds to be applied to defined (if somewhat broad) objectives designed to improve the quality of life for the nation. However, this justification and primary purpose for the Lottery remains only a secondary objective or responsibility for the Regulator. The delivery of the Lottery's primary or ultimate objective is met by way of economic instruments including the bidding process. As outlined earlier in the work, economic regulation, while not always entirely precise at least provides the regulatory agency with some sort of framework, is more likely to be rule-based and of itself is likely to provide more prescribed opportunities for regulatory discretion. Having regard to the Lottery, these economic instruments are connected to and allied closely with the Regulator's secondary and promotional function.

Combining social with economic regulation (whether personalized or commission based), makes it far harder for the agency to be an effective and acceptable economic regulator.[57] The Director General's primary duties were social, and essentially regulatory – rather than promotional. The Director General had the power to give what weight he chose to any duty laid down in the Act. Like many other UK regulators, he had the discretion, indeed the responsibility, to preserve or elevate any non-economic aspects of the regulatory process, and to interpret widely his duties, which were themselves set out in abstract terms.[58] The same is true of the Commission. The implication of investing any regulator with this breadth of discretion is that regulators can always find justifications for any of their decisions. This degree of freedom is problematic for 'the effect of having many standards . . . is virtually the same as having none at all.'[59]

Such a lack of standards and the concomitant implications for the use of discretion can result in a departure on the part of regulators from normative behaviour (which is itself difficult to identify and agree upon) as the agency is tempted to engage in a wide range of political or social policy-making of its own initiative.[60] Furthermore, where discretion exists regulators are liable to come under pressure from different groups and constituencies eager for regulatory outcomes and the exercising of regulatory discretion to serve their own social and/or political goals. Indeed this point in particular can be seen as a defining feature of the regulatory process during the time that the National Lottery's first Director General held office.

A policy response to these difficulties might be to design economic instruments, in the Lottery's case not only to meet the Regulator's promotional brief of maximizing funds for the Good Causes, but also to deliver the social and primary goals of propriety and in particular, player protection. This is easier said than done. But if regulation can be oriented so as to allow the Regulator to consider his objectives in relation to any divergence between private (Operator) and social (player-related) costs or benefits purely in economic terms, and leave to others the political or social judgements,[61] then the rôle of the Regulator is less likely to attract controversy and become politicized. This goal may be highly desirable but is it realistic and practicable? The problem of quantifying negative spillovers in a way that is monetizable has already been alluded to. Nevertheless, investing the Regulator with the power to impose fines at least allows for an attempt to associate negative externalities with penalties. It would be simplistic and reductive to suggest that this association is likely to be a matter of precise science; indeed it will still involve a degree of discretion on the part of the Regulator. Yet the implication is that the tenor of the Lottery's regulation has the capacity to achieve a more equitable and sustainable balance by moving from a system not over-reliant on compliance and the rôle of discretion in addressing the problem of social costs, to one that is more predictable, incorporating the threat of penalties (fines) as a means of deterring the Operator from miscreant behaviour, for example in the area of under-age sales. This in turn carries with it the potential to make less fraught the conflicts of interest between the Regulator's promotional and regulatory functions; although it may lead to a more confrontational and legalistic relationship between Regulator and Regulatee. This problem of finding the right balance between discretionary and rule-based models of regulation is enduring, and is arguably made more difficult in personalized regulatory regimes.

> Only the select and most enlightened individuals can be entrusted with . . . a use of their discretion. . . . If a regulatory system can be designed so as to secure and retain able, even outstanding, regulators, then the nature of regulatory offences is such as to make this the best solution; but it may be better that a bad or indifferent regulator be shackled within the cage of law despite the understood shortcomings of a legalistic [rule-based] regulatory process.[62]

With the foregoing in mind and given the limitations of the regulatory instruments made available to the Director Generals, a defence can be mounted having regard to their primary duty of protecting the interests of players. Yet it is clearly an area fraught with difficulty; especially when set against the Director General's secondary and promotional rôle of maximizing the funds to be passed to the Good Causes. It has been advanced earlier that the security of the Lottery, while not perfect, has been in most if not all respects satisfactory where the protection of players is concerned. Furthermore, as it exists evidence of excessive play has demonstrated the problem to be small, though not insignificant, and arguably within realistic and tolerable parameters.

> One fact that might be useful in this regard is the current position of the UK lottery as one with the third largest turnover with the 34th in ranking per capita spend; and, on that I would place some degree of reassurance that the regulatory and commercial . . . duties have gone well together in the past, both with our predecessors and the Commission.[63]

However, it is in the area of under-age participation that player protection has proven to be unsatisfactory. During the time of the Director Generals, it is arguably the case that this shortcoming had less to do with the abilities or effectiveness of the Director Generals *per se* than it had to do with the limits and scope of the powers conferred on their office. It is then possible to defend the performance of the individual Director Generals in meeting one of their primary duties, *viz.* the protection of players' interests. Had their office enjoyed more appropriate and more flexible powers (including the ability to fine), it is likely that the regulation and prevention of under-age sales in particular could have been handled more effectively. Thus the problems encountered by the National Lottery in this area can be viewed as less to do with any inherent conflict of interest between the Director General's regulatory and promotional functions, than the consequence of the Director General not being given an appropriate range of regulatory instruments with which to formulate and then prosecute enforcement policies.

It is in connection with the other primary duty of upholding the propriety of the Lottery that more serious regulatory failings and potential conflicts can be identified. Indeed it is in relation to the matter of the Lottery's propriety *per se* that brings into sharp relief the problems associated with the same body selecting the Lottery Operator and then supervising its ongoing delivery of services. Arguably this area of difficulty is itself exacerbated where regulation is personalized rather than commission-based. The rôle of GTech in the Camelot Consortium and the controversy associated with the Company's participation which is outlined above, severely undermined and damaged the Lottery's standing. In so doing the GTech saga exposed weaknesses and limitations in the National Lottery's regulatory design.

As events transpired it became apparent that from the very outset the first Director General had not been sufficiently rigorous in establishing standards and criteria that would assist him in his enquiries as to the 'fit and proper' status of the Lottery Operator. Notwithstanding the reservations held by the Director General regarding GTech, he allowed the Company to participate in the Camelot Consortium.[64] It is difficult to defend this decision, and it provides powerful evidence to support the position of those who accused the Director General of elevating his secondary responsibility of maximizing the proceeds of the Lottery to a position ranking alongside his primary charges – in this case the upholding of the Lottery's propriety. Furthermore, it is entirely plausible to advance the hypothesis that a regulatory commission would have been less inclined to have arrived at such a controversial determination. The risk that the first Director General was prepared to take in accepting GTech's rôle in the winning Consortium was at best a calculated gamble and at worst a decision both ill-conceived and eccentric. There is no guarantee that a commission would not have also permitted GTech's involvement, but with the internal checks and balances which characterize the commission model it is arguably the case that it is less likely that the members of a commission would have reached the same conclusions on this important matter as those arrived at by the Director General. Whatever the nature of the entity chosen to regulate the Lottery, that this same body should be given the responsibility of selecting the Operator and then monitoring its performance is potentially invidious and raises pertinent questions regarding the credibility and independence of the regulatory agency.

4.3 Regulatory Capture

The public interest theory of regulation posits that the ultimate goal of regulation is to pursue some conception of the general good (which is itself difficult to define). However, regulatory processes can also be seen as taking place in an environment in which special interests compete for the right to use government power for narrow or private advantage.[65] This section assesses the Lottery in the context of the 'positive' political-economy model also known variously as capture theory, economic theory or the government-services theory of regulation.

When a regulatory agency is established, its real and potential capacities will contrast sharply with those of the regulated body(ies).[66] It lacks administrative experience, its policy and objectives are vague and uninformed, its legal powers are unclear and untested, and its relations with Parliament and the Executive are uncertain.[67] The National Lottery etc. Act 1993 outlined the goals of regulatory policy in general terms and afforded the Director General a degree of latitude and discretion in meeting those goals. Under such conditions an agency left to its own devices and which is also likely to have a smaller machinery and resources to draw on than the commercial regulatee is liable to be guided by the dominant interest of the regulated industry in its formulation of the public interest.[68] This discrepancy in size is notable having regard to Oflot and the multinational public companies which comprise the National Lottery Operator. Given also the superior resources of the regulated industry vis-à-vis those of consumer groups, who are also largely dispersed and uncoordinated, there is a danger that the Regulator and the regulatory process will veer towards the industry's interests.[69]

During the time that the Director Generals were in office, it was suggested by some that the involvement of citizens' juries set up to involve the public in key decisions about the Lottery would be a way of countering the problem of capture.[70] This concept (more firmly established in the USA and in Germany through the Plannungszelles is found in relation to agriculture, town planning and environmental issues),[71] involves small groups of citizens, selected to represent a cross-section of the general public and meeting on a regular basis to help build a public consensus about how the National Lottery should serve the public interest.[72] A national citizens' jury taking soundings from sub-groups in the regions could place popular pressure on the organizers of the Lottery (i.e. government, Regulator, Operator and distribution bodies) to respond to its recommendations.[73] During the mid-1990s, while in Opposition, the Labour Party developed (but did not introduce once in power) a not dissimilar concept for the Lottery involving citizens working alongside the Director General but with separate priorities and duties.[74] Although the foregoing ideas are comparatively underdeveloped in the UK, drawing people into the political process represents a potentially effective antidote to the problems of capture and indeed paternalism, through the encouragement of more participatory and pluralistic democracy. It should not be forgotten that the danger of capture is all the greater when there is just one firm and not a group of competing entities for the agency to regulate. Furthermore, capture is more likely still when the regulator is an individual rather than a commission. Indeed part of the rationale within the 1998 Lottery Act for the creation of a Lottery Commission to replace the single regulator system was in order to reduce the risk of 'regulatory capture' – on the basis that it is more difficult to 'capture' a commission than an individual.[75] The Act requires the Commissioners to elect from among their number a chairman, rotating the post on a yearly basis,[76] to avoid the risk of concentrating too much power in one individual.[77]

The proceeding argument holds that it is fallacious to suppose that the privilege of private monopoly can be harmonized with the public interest by the imposition of regulation.[78] Critics of the regulatory process have argued that regulation originated as a system of social restraint designed primarily, or at least ostensibly, to protect consumers from the exploitation of monopolists, but has in fact become a device to protect the property and interests of those same monopolists.[79] Such institutional decadence sometimes referred to as public choice theory has resulted in public utility status becoming the haven of refuge for all aspiring monopolists who find it too difficult, costly or precarious to secure and maintain monopoly by private action alone.[80] The Operator of the National Lottery is not a public utility but it is the near monopoly supplier of a universally available product and as such may not unreasonably be styled a quasi- or close relative of the public utility. The Lottery is also endowed with a number of characteristics normally associated with a public or social good.[81] It is undeniably the case that from the Lottery Operator's point of view, regulation has been an excellent mechanism for eliminating or at least minimizing competition within the industry and for preventing direct entry. And a single regulator is more easy to influence and cajole than a hundred thrusting, hungry businessmen.[82]

A firm that discovers a way to benefit from regulation has a tremendous stake in perpetuating the regulatory mechanism.[83] A particular benefit for an industry like gambling that has historically been plagued by scandals, is that regulation can come to be regarded by that industry as an economical way of winning the respect and esteem of the public.[84] Though as the evidence from the National Lottery demonstrates regulation of itself is no guarantee that scandals associated with the industry in question will be eliminated. Nevertheless, while the regulation of gambling in general and the National Lottery in particular is of the utmost importance having regard to the sector's long history of misconduct,[85] it also confers a legitimacy on those operating in this field. Such considerations will inform the relationship between the regulator and the regulatee and in particular the strategic thinking of the regulated body(ies) in any dealings and negotiations with the regulator.

From the Operator of the National Lottery's perspective there are then clear and cogent arguments for the skilful management of the regulatory process. Yet the same could also be said of almost any regulated undertaking; and the managing of relations by a commercial entity with its regulatory agency is not intrinsically designed nor will it inevitably lead to capture (unless one accepts the thesis of the more radical proponents of capture theory who maintain that capture is inevitable and systemic to regulation). However, in connection with the Lottery *per se* the common purpose of the Regulator and the Operator serves to increase the likelihood of capture. Thus the promotional duties of the Director General and Oflot (and since April 1999 the Lottery Commission and its Commissioners), while being secondary to the regulatory function, carry with them the potential for inviting too close an association between the Regulator and Regulatee. Indeed the Secretary of State in evidence to the National Heritage Committee confirmed the sympathetic aspects of the Director General's and Oflot's relationship with Camelot, without conceding or alluding to the presence for any inherent conflicts of interest in the arrangement: 'Oflot differs from other regulators in that, in addition to protecting the interests of players, it is required to maximise the proceeds. This gives rise to "a degree of common interest" with Camelot.'[86]

Critics of the Lottery's regulation seek to distinguish the regime not only from those governing the utilities and other suppliers of public goods and services, but also from those governing other modes of commercial gambling.[87] The implications of these criticisms is that the public interest is not being adequately protected, as the identity of interest between Regulator and supplier is more apparent than between Regulator and consumer. Whether or not the regulator shares a common purpose with the regulated entity, the regulator will wish to avoid drastic adverse consequences to an enterprise as a result of any enforcement policies, and in this way the regulator may consider tailoring his actions to the commercial circumstances of the company.[88] The danger of the regulator allowing the regulated body too much latitude and of allying himself too closely with the commercial interests of the company is clearly greater where, as in the case of the National Lottery, there is a common or shared purpose. The problem is further exacerbated where the regulator is afforded high levels of discretion in prosecuting his statutory mandate. There is thus a case for the Agency responsible for the National Lottery's regulation to have no promotional function whatsoever, and to carry out solely the primary duties of player protection and upholding the project's propriety.

The regulatory process is then one which will tend to give rise to the conditions whereby private or special interests (in particular the regulated body) will try to manipulate government or an agent of the government for their own narrow advantage. It has been argued that the initial regulatory structures of the National Lottery contained inherent design flaws that made it especially vulnerable or susceptible to conflicts of interest and indeed capture. This begs the further question as to what evidence can be uncovered that might imply the capture by the Operator of the Lottery's Regulator? This point is without doubt most meaningfully addressed to the Lottery's regulation during the time the first Director General was in office. In attempting to answer the question it should be stressed that it is not always clear or easy to distinguish regulatory style or competence from incidences of what might be advertent or inadvertent capture. This is to some extent a matter of semantics and will depend on the strictness of the criteria that are established and by which the presence, absence or degree of capture can in some substantive way be evaluated.

From the very outset the independence of the Lottery's Regulator was subject to scrutiny and critical attention. In some ways this situation was aggravated by the Director General's judgements *per se* rather than by any perceived or apparent conflicts of interest inherent in his office. As referred to earlier, between the award of the Licence to Camelot and the commencement of trading, the Director General made a series of internal flights within the US to visit a number of State lotteries. These flights were taken in GTech aircraft and at GTech's expense.[89] In so doing the Regulator had compromised his independence for which he was censured by the Secretary of State and the PAC.[90] There was not at this stage, nor indeed at any stage during the term of the first Director General, any suggestion that the Regulator was abusing or seeking to profit personally from his rôle. Yet once the Lottery was under way the Regulator's style and approach to his duties were soon the subject of adverse comment. Critics were concerned that the Director General was operating a hands-off approach,[91] and argued that a more proactive policy would promote more effectively the public interest.[92] This issue of the Director General's non-interventionist style may or may not have made the likelihood of capture greater, but it is certainly likely to have created the impression, no matter how misleading, of the Regulator enjoying too cosy a relationship with the Operator. More worrying still and indeed more damaging to the Director General's credibility was the PACs' assessment of the Regulator's success in defending the public interest: 'The Committee are not surprised that developments have taken place since the launch of the lottery and that unforeseen matters have arisen, but we note that those we examined all seem to have worked to Camelot's advantage.'[93]

It appears that a central and recurring problem for the Director General was a fundamental difference in his interpretation of the scope of the powers that he enjoyed or believed he enjoyed under the 1993 Lottery Act, and the determination and assessment made of these powers by key members of the polity. A good case in point relates to the problem with the Prize Target Shortfall whereby under the terms of the Licence, interest earned from holding the Annual Prize Shortfall – worth some £6 million per annum (before the principal sum was passed to the Distribution Fund)[94] – accrued to Camelot. This is despite the fact that the shortfall reflects the extent to which Camelot failed to meet its Section 5 Licence Prize Target.

While accepting that the prize shortfall arrangements were not working as expected, the Director General maintained that he was reviewing them, but was unable to change those arrangements without the Operator's consent,[95] as the 1993 Act prevented him from altering any conditions of the Licence that might impact adversely on the finances of the Operator.[96] He added that the annual target is designed to encourage the Operator to manage its business over the medium term in such a way as to maximize its own revenues and hence the revenues of the Distribution Fund[97] . The Director General further remarked that if Camelot agreed to pay interest on the shortfall to the Fund it would be given a greater incentive to meet the prize payment target by paying more money to players which could produce a worse result for the Fund than simply receiving the shortfall.[98]

Both the PAC,[99] and the National Heritage Committee,[100] were unhappy with the Director General's assessment and handling of the Prize Target Shortfall. The Director General's position was all the more uncomfortable as he was not only responsible for the Lottery's regulation, but had also played a prominent rôle in designing the regulatory architecture in the form of the Licence.[101] As the Director General himself conceded, it 'is I who set most of the rules.'[102] This placed the Director General in the unenviable position of having to defend a set of regulatory instruments, including the Prize Target Shortfall, which he had been in large measure responsible for formulating and which were proving to be unsatisfactory in practice. The PAC asked the Director General why he had not included a claw back provision in the Licence,[103] and was unimpressed with his response that including a claw back would have reduced the amount included in the bids that was to be passed to the Good Causes, as all the applicants knew that they had to plan on the basis that there would be no prize shortfall.[104] Furthermore, the PAC was of the opinion that the Director General's legal powers allowed him to insist on Camelot passing the interest earned on the shortfall to the Distribution Fund, as the Invitation to Apply had made it clear that the applicants' business plan should be consistent with the Prize Target totals as specified in their applications.[105]

This fundamental difference in the interpretation of the range of the powers of the Director General by the Director General, on the one hand, and by the PAC and the National Heritage Committee, on the other, served to undermine the authority of the Regulator. Clearly the Prize Target was not working as had been intended, but in the Director General's defence had he sought to alter the terms of the Licence unilaterally then it is entirely possible that his decision would have been challenged in the courts by the Operator. The PAC clearly regarded the Prize Target Shortfall mechanism as a Licence defect. In its eagerness to see the problem rectified, the Committee was in fundamental disagreement with the Regulator having regard to the determination of scope and extent of the Director General's authority to alter the conditions of the Licence. The Committee was also unhappy that interest in excess of £800,000 a year was accruing (and continues to accrue)[106] to the Operator in a series of bank accounts established by Camelot for a players' trust designed to provide protection for players' money.[107] The PAC did not accept the Director General's argument that he could not press for the transfer to the Distribution Fund of interest on these accounts without negotiating the rest of the Operator's Licence, arguing that interest earned on the Players Trust Account was not referred to in Camelot's bid.[108] Finally, the Operator was earning (and continues to earn)[109] interest in the region of £420,000 a year on ticket sales monies received from multiple retailers on a Monday and held by Camelot in a Retailers' Collection Account until being passed over to the Players Trust Account each Wednesday.[110] The PAC was also unhappy with this and remained particularly concerned with the Director General's view that he did not think it was part of his rôle to know the level of interest Camelot was earning in this way, as he regarded it as the Operator's entitlement as part of a package of cash flow.[111]

Much of the foregoing could reasonably be advanced as evidence of a regulatory style lacking vigour and firm leadership. Indeed the Regulator's reluctance to challenge the Operator in areas which would have involved a transfer of benefit to the Distribution Fund at the expense of Camelot, arguably exposes the Regulator to accusations of having aligned himself too closely with the Operator and even of having become a victim of regulatory capture. Certainly the PAC was reluctant to accept the Director General's assessment of the limitations of his freedom of action as laid down in the 1993 Act. Yet that the Director General had a limited or restricted view of his rôle can be viewed both as a strength and weakness.

> I am a creature of stature: I am told that I am not a natural person. I exist only as a creature of the National Lottery Act and my powers are defined in that Act and that is the limit of what I can do.[112]

This literal if rather unimaginative and mechanistic view of his office is likely to have been closely linked to the Director General's desire to avoid the controversy which would have undoubtedly been associated with any legal wranglings with the Operator, and which in turn could have damaged the Lottery's reputation. The PAC's view that Camelot was benefiting from its operations in a way not anticipated at the time of the bid, and as such should sacrifice these benefits to the Distribution Fund may have sounded reasonable and fair, but these same arguments were in truth of dubious legal validity. The Director General, while being exposed to sustained pressure from the PAC (and elsewhere) and while undoubtedly having some sympathy with the points raised, was bound to be reluctant to compromise his position by acting in a way which might have been *ultra vires* and vulnerable to legal challenge by the Operator.

In his eagerness to maintain the smooth running of the Lottery the first Director General developed a regulatory style less like that of a policeman and more like that of a manager of an industry. His business background will have informed his relations with the Operator and may have given rise to a degree of empathy, buttressed by a common interest of delivering a successful National Lottery. In this way it could be adduced that the Director General, with the best of motives, tailored his actions to the commercial circumstances of the company. If one accepts this proposition, then the Director General's preference for a regulatory style of 'negotiated compliance' can be seen as much a reflection of temperament and personality as it is a measured response to the limitations of the Regulator's authority as laid down in the 1993 Act.

The first Director General's approach to his duties attracted much criticism for being hands-off and not adequately proactive or vigorous. This style was in part a natural expression or outcropping of the Regulator's own character, which he himself described as 'careful and cautious', and as such manifests one of the inherent difficulties of personalized regulatory models. Regulatory agencies operate in the storm centres of politics where intense pressures can be and often are magnified by the media. This feature is all the more poignant where the point of attention is focused on the individual. 'Regulators can be tempted to embark on a course of social engineering, or to tinker with operational matters in response to short-term political and media pressures.'[113]

It is not unusual for regulators to come under considerable pressure during the regulatory period if firms declare high profits.[114] However, if the profit level is not an explicit target of regulation (which it is not in the case of the National Lottery) then tightening restraint in response to higher profits involves reneging on the relevant bargain.[115] The Director General resisted the hue and cry of both the media and the key members of the polity to make changes to or fundamentally re-evaluate his interpretation of the Lottery's regulatory framework. In the Regulator's defence he consistently maintained that he was not legally competent to alter the terms of the Licence in any way which would have involved the transfer of a financial benefit away from the Operator (without the Operator's consent). While it is possible to have some sympathy with this line of defence, it remains the case that the Director General played a leading part in designing the Licence which contained the fine details, financial and otherwise, with which the Operator would have to comply. However, that these conditions were established in connection with an entirely new and untested venture provides further mitigating evidence in support of the Director General.

It is less easy to defend the Director General's performance in his duty to implement and guarantee compliance standards. As noted earlier the PAC was 'deeply dissatisfied' and with justification[116] at the Director General's failure to execute 11 out of 21 compliance programmes monitoring Camelot's Licence obligations a full year after the launch of the Lottery, covering such important areas as draw procedures, the protection of players' interests and security arrangements.[117] The PAC was unmoved by the Director General's reassurances that decisions on priority and frequency of programmes had been based on risk assessment and that he had met his requirements.[118] In the Director General's defence he was willing in some circumstances to respond positively to suggestions for improving his practices – accepting the NAO's recommendations for amending and refining his verification procedures for certain types of money payments.[119] Nevertheless, the foregoing issue of guaranteeing compliance is unambiguously one of regulatory style and indeed competency and cannot be attributed to any limitations imposed on the Regulator by the 1993 Act.

From the above it is evident that regulatory commissions or agencies can lack clearly defined standards and policies. In the case of the Lottery one of the Director General's tasks was therefore to interpret statutory arrangements, but the 'inevitable consequence of the failure to provide definite statements of statutory policy is that broad discretion makes a politician out of the Regulator.'[120] Members of the polity, pressure groups and the media – the so called 'external theatres of judgement' – were in a number of respects dissatisfied with the rôle of the Lottery's Regulator, and as they saw it his reluctance to engage in the wider social and political process. Their frustrations were addressed to what was perceived to be the personal shortcomings of the Regulator and his passive or reactive style of regulation. The Director General clearly did not accept that he enjoyed as much freedom of movement under the Act as others believed he had. The Regulator was either not prepared, did not consider it appropriate or was temperamentally unsuited to play the rôle of politician, and this may have ironically contributed to his difficulties.

The capacity to fine would have provided the Director General with a stick with which to discipline the Operator, and equally importantly an opportunity to demonstrate a more resolute and uncompromising regulatory style. In the absence of such authority the Director General became too heavily reliant on his powers of persuasion to bring the Lottery Operator to heel. Thus in terms of the effective regulation of the Operator, the range of practical and meaningful options allowing the Regulator the exercise of real discretion were in truth limited. Nevertheless, there were without doubt key areas of the Licence where the Director General with the benefit of hindsight would have liked to have included terms that would in practice favour the Operator less. Yet the inherent conflicts of interest in a system where the same individual or agency designs or helps to design the regulatory structures, and chooses and then regulates the entity charged with running the Lottery also carried with it the potential to compromise the position of the Director General and may have made him vulnerable to capture (as indeed did his promotional function). These conflicts played a part in ending the first Director General's tenure in office. Whether or not the Director General fell victim to capture by the Operator is a moot point. To suggest that the Regulator had been subverted or suborned by pressure, influence or bribery by Camelot away from his statutory enforcement goals (a crude definition of capture theory) would be too simplistic and probably inaccurate, although the possibility cannot entirely be discounted, as discussions and negotiations between Regulator and Regulatee were carried out in private, and not in the public domain. At a subtler level, however, where 'capture' embraces a preference on the part of the Regulator to avoid confrontation with the body(ies) in its charge and to opt for settled procedures,[121] for example negotiated compliance, there is a more substantive case to answer. The Regulator's preference for preserving the status quo[122] and for what might appear to be a disproportionate interest in the health of the Operator (due in part to a commonality of interest), manifesting itself in a reluctance to introduce changes that would impact adversely on the Operator,[123] is also a cause for some concern. Thus it can be seen that the dangers of regulatory capture may occur in ways that are not only subtle but also oblique and often difficult to identify, let alone reach a concensus on.

4.4 *Accountability and Access*

As the foregoing demonstrates an absence of unequivocal rules and guidelines can serve to undermine the delivery of good regulation. This state of affairs creates uncertainty which in turn can result in controversy and arguably confers on the regulator too great a degree of discretion in areas where discretion is perhaps least appropriate. This can have the effect of politicizing the whole regulatory process. The UK system of personalized regulation which emerged during the 1980s is perhaps especially vulnerable to these types of problems. However, such difficulties do not confine themselves only to matters of regulatory design, the rôle of rules versus discretion, or the allocation of responsibilities between government and politicians on the one hand and the regulator on the other. Questions also arise having regard to the accountability of regulatory agencies and the adequacy of those mechanisms that exist to help ensure their accountability not just to the relevant minister but also to key members of the polity.

As referred to earlier, the discussions and negotiations that take place in the UK between the regulator and industry leaders do not have to be made public, nor do they have to involve other affected parties. These and other key aspects of regulation in the UK have been criticized for lacking transparency. Indeed those who would condemn the personalized system of regulation have gone so far as to claim that it threatens the rule of law and the overall legitimacy of regulation in the UK, describing the agencies as constitutional anomalies falling somewhere between the legislative, executive and judiciary.[124] In short, the personalized system of regulation coupled with arguably a weak system of accountability[125] has been the subject of a good deal of attention, much of it censorious.

In connection with the National Lottery, fundamental differences of opinion between the first Director General, on the one hand, and the PAC, on the other, revealed serious fault-lines in the workings of the polity. These differences related to the accountability of the Regulator, and in particular the degree of access the PAC believed it and the NAO should be afforded to facilitate the effective monitoring of the regulatory function. The PAC (which is independent of government) exists *inter alia* to examine the accounts showing the appropriation of the sums granted by Parliament to meet the public expenditure, and of such other accounts laid before Parliament as the Committee may think fit.[126] The NAO headed by the Comptroller and Auditor General, is also independent of government and exists to examine and report to Parliament on the economy, efficiency and effectiveness of public agencies (and government departments) and is thus primarily concerned with financial accountability.[127] These accountability mechanisms represent an important if rather narrowly defined check on regulators who are themselves not civil servants and therefore have no formal Parliamentary status.[128] On occasions, however, these two watchdogs seem to stray beyond the narrow confines of their jurisdiction into questions of substantive accountability.[129] With regard to the Select Committees like the PAC made up of politicians, it is easy to see how the system might be hijacked by partisan members intent on influencing regulatory outcomes.[130] Indeed this is one of the ways in which the regulatory process is susceptible to politicization. In the case of the Lottery, the differences that existed between the Director General and the PAC were certainly of a substantive nature, and were the product of a less than emphatic set of guidelines on matters appertaining to access and accountability. Nevertheless, it is noteworthy that among the members of the PAC the most vehement critics of the Regulator were also members of opposition parties.[131]

The matters of disputation related to three critical areas. In the first instance the Director General in making his 'fit and proper' enquiries (Task G in his duty of evaluating the applications to run the Lottery) disagreed with the PAC in respect of the amount of information he believed it was necessary or appropriate for him to disclose to the Committee. The Director General had sought and received declarations completed by individuals, companies and UK and overseas agencies in respect of third parties associated with the different applications to run the Lottery;[132] however, much of the information had only been secured by the Director General in response to his preparedness to enter into confidentiality undertakings.[133] The PAC took issue with the Director General and in particular with regard to the rôle of GTech in the winning bid.[134] The Committee was concerned with criminal cases in the USA in which senior officers of GTech had been indicted or called as witnesses, and as such it wished to have sight of any reports from enforcement agencies relating to those matters that were in the possession of the Director General.[135] The Regulator while being prepared to share the information with the PAC in private session was not prepared to agree to have the details published (even though the Committee retain the power to publish findings taken in private session).[136] Peter Davis did not share the information with the Committee averring that to breach the confidentiality undertakings could prejudice cooperation and the availability of information and thus undermine the Director General's ability to carry out his functions in the future.[137] In further defence of the Director General's position it is worth noting that the FBI, while being prepared to let the Director General name the Agency as a source of information, remained insistent that the Regulator should maintain the confidentiality of the information that it had provided to him.[138]

A further area of contention arose between the Regulator, on the one hand, and both the PAC and NAO, on the other, and related to formal undertakings given by the Director General at the time of publication of the Invitation to Apply for a Section 5 Licence that he would not divulge information from applications to third parties without the applicant's consent.[139] The Director General contended that while he appreciated the need for transparency in public affairs he felt it was essential to encourage a high quality and a fully comprehensive set of applications, and that by giving confidentiality undertakings he believed he would be more likely to achieve this.[140] The PAC disagreed, arguing that those applying for public sector contracts and licences must recognize that Parliament has a right to information to provide assurances that contracts and licences are properly issued without impropriety and that they represent best value for money.[141] In his deliberations with the Comptroller and Auditor General the Director General maintained that breaking the undertaking would be injurious to his personal integrity and could also erode confidence in the Regulator, not only of the business community within which the Lottery worked but also of those companies that might wish to bid for a licence in the future.[142] Notwithstanding the Regulator's entreaties, the Comptroller and Auditor General published the information and was supported in his decision by the PAC.[143]

The third and final area of controversy having regard to issues of access and accountability was the most serious and was only remedied by the enactment of new law, *viz.* the National Lottery Act 1998. In this case the Director General was at variance with both the PAC and NAO in relation to the access the NAO should have to the records and accounts of the Operator. The PAC was eager for the Director General to facilitate the access of the Comptroller and Auditor General and the NAO to the primary business records held by Camelot, especially those relating to the financial control of lottery activities.[144] The Director General insisted that it would be quite improper for him to exercise his powers under the 1993 National Lottery Act in order to allow the Comptroller and Auditor General to exercise his functions.[145] The Director General cited legal advice from the Treasury solicitor which sought to emphasize that the National Audit Act 1983 did not confer any right on the Comptroller and Auditor General to have access to Camelot or its accounts or records[146] (as Camelot is a private company and not a public body). Furthermore, the Treasury solicitor confirmed Peter Davis's position that the National Lottery etc. Act 1993 did not provide the Director General with any mandate to facilitate the exercise of functions of some other person(s), such as the NAO.[147]

The PAC remained concerned that while the 1983 National Audit Act authorized the Comptroller and Auditor General, and NAO to have access to the Director General's records it did not permit their access to the records retained by Camelot. The concern of the PAC was summarized by Alan Williams, 'if you [the Director General] are dilatory or unimaginative in the information you require from Camelot, the Comptroller and Audit General is automatically precluded from information which you do not regard as important.'[148] In other words, under these conditions the Comptroller and Auditor General and the NAO were only able to satisfy themselves that all payments 'recorded' as due to the Distribution Fund had been made punctually and in full; they were not able to express an opinion on whether the sums recorded as due were in fact correct.[149] The PAC's uneasiness was heightened by the fact that there had been areas brought to its attention where the Director General's efforts had in the Committee's opinion been less than satisfactory.[150] Subsequent annual reports of the Comptroller and Auditor General[151] (from and including Session 1995–96) certifying the payments made to the Distribution Fund, carried the rider

> I am not required to attest to the adequacy of the Director General's procedures or his Statement of Assurance. Moreover, since I do not have access to the Lottery Operator, Camelot, I cannot assess independently whether the Director General's procedures have sufficient regard to the rules and controls in Camelot's systems.[152]

The PAC's misgivings regarding the above had been such that within the first year of the Lottery's activities the Committee recommended to the government that the Department of National Heritage and the Director General should make arrangements to provide the Comptroller and Auditor General with access to Camelot's records as they related to the financial control of the Lottery.[153] In a Treasury minute dated 4 October 1995 the government rejected the PAC's recommendation although for a different reason from that which would be given by the Director General to the PAC in November 1996.[154] While the Director General maintained that he had no statutory authority to facilitate the access of the Comptroller and Auditor General to the records of Camelot, the Treasury minute upheld the case for the status quo. The minute averred that the policy stated in relation to Camelot was long established, that the existing arrangements were adequate and that it was not appropriate or necessary to alter them in order to provide the Comptroller and Auditor General with access to the Operator's records.[155] Notwithstanding the government's stated position the NAO contacted Camelot in November 1995 to seek access to its records.[156] Camelot declined the request and added that it was subject to close regulation by the Director General to whom the NAO's enquiries would be more properly addressed.[157] The Operator also stressed that it was very open in its reporting procedures and followed all the best practices as recommended by the Cadbury and Greenbury committees, even though as a non-quoted company it was not obliged to do so.[158]

The foregoing problems which stemmed from a lack of clear principles and unequivocal guidelines in the structures of accountability became something of a running sore during the first Director General's time in office. It is perhaps unsurprising, bearing in mind the Lottery was an entirely new venture requiring primary enabling legislation that there would be areas of the regulatory process requiring reform and adjustment in the light of experience. That the Director General was not legally competent to facilitate Parliamentary accountability by securing the access of the Comptroller and Auditor General to the records of Camelot was in the assessment of the PAC a particularly unsatisfactory state of affairs. This omission served to limit the scope of the work undertaken by the Comptroller and Auditor General and his office in evaluating the economy, efficiency and effectiveness of the Lottery. In the absence of unambiguous rules or directions there is no sound reasoning to intelligently suggest that a regulatory commission would have been able to manage the position any more adeptly or to have been able to be any more facilitating to the Comptroller and Auditor General. The National Lottery Act 1998 not only replaced the Director General with a Lottery Commission from 1 April 1999, but also and at the same time allowed the Comptroller and Auditor General and the NAO, unfettered access to the records of the Section 5 Licensee.[159]

4.5 *Summary of Findings*

Putting in place the appropriate structures for the regulation of the Lottery in the UK has undoubtedly represented a very special and distinct set of challenges. In order to be politically acceptable, the legislation of gambling must be linked to one or more 'higher purposes'.[160] Unlike other forms of gambling there has always been a clear political and social purpose for lotteries.[161] Governments legitimize gambling by linking it to a variety of 'good causes', but often in the absence of any consideration of what social consequences the resulting expansion of the industry might have.[162] For to legalize gambling ventures and supervise their orderly conduct is bound to bring about a higher volume of gambling.[163] It is for this reason that the Gaming Board for Great Britain, which is responsible for the regulation of the various segments of the gambling industry other than the National Lottery, has called for an independent review body to be set up to seek a comprehensive approach to the regulation of all the gambling and lottery industries.[164] Indeed, the Board, along with key elements of the gambling industry, including Camelot itself, have made the case for there being a single regulator for all forms of gambling.[165] It is disappointing therefore that an independent Gaming Review body reporting to the Minister for Culture Media and Sport in the summer of 2001, excluded the National Lottery from its deliberations.[166] The Culture, Media and Sport Committee has recommended that the issue should be considered by the body that will review the selection process for the operation of the lottery from 2009.[167]

By sponsoring and placing the National Lottery in the private sector through a licensing system, the government, while not operating the undertaking, has unequivocally legitimised gambling. 'Sociologically speaking, licensing in the gaming business constitutes a formal affirmation of non-deviance. One cannot participate in it without being investigated, reviewed and found acceptable.'[168] By licensing the Lottery to a commercial entity the theoretical advantage to the government is that it can expect to reap the dividend of efficiency associated with the private market and, by not being directly involved in the operation, it can manage to side-step the conflict between government's rôle as a public representative, on the one hand, and a potentially uneasy rôle as a promoter and operator of gambling services, on the other. The government has been criticized for applying up to a third of Lottery Good Causes revenue to its own programmes[169] and thus abandoning the principle of additionality, i.e. that Lottery funds should be additional to and not a substitution for government funding. However, controversy about the regulation of the Lottery, to which the foregoing testifies, has largely focused not on the government (except in cases of government interference, such as that relating to Camelot's directors' bonuses) but on the performance of both Regulator and Operator and the nature of the relationship between the two.

This book sets out the major regulatory issues that marked the life of the National Lottery during the time the Director Generals were in office (25 October 1993[170] – 31 March 1999[171]). In so doing, the work addresses the nature of, and problems associated with, personalized models of regulation. The replacement from April 1999 of the Director General with five Lottery Commissioners represents a clear rejection by the government of the concept of personalized regulation – at least as far as the Lottery is concerned. However, in examining and criticizing those areas of the Lottery's regulation that proved to be controversial and in some cases poorly designed it is important to separate the more general criticisms from those that can be attributed to the rôle of the Director Generals *per se*.

There is no international precedent to draw on with regard to the design and format chosen for the Lottery. As stated from the outset the fact that it was placed in the private as opposed to the state sector is a reflection of the philosophy of privatization that defined the Conservative governments' 18 years in power (1979–97). Thus key elements of the project's regulation had grown up in connection with the public utilities, following their privatization during the 1980s and were borrowed and grafted on to the National Lottery *'faute de mieux'*. Furthermore, one of the inherent problems associated with long-term franchises is that it is not possible to draw up a complete contingent contract allowing for every possible eventuality.[172] As an entirely new venture and with the above in mind it is of little surprise that once under way there would be areas of the Lottery's regulation that would inevitably need to be reassessed, irrespective of whether the venture was regulated by an individual or a commission.

In broad terms there are areas of the Lottery's regulation during the Director Generals' tenure that were found to be less than satisfactory but that would in all likelihood have been so whether the regulatory body had been an individual or a commission. A case can be made in support of the Regulator's rôle of helping to design the Lottery's regulatory framework in the form of the Licence. However, the agency responsible is also likely to feel the need to justify or defend the workings of this critical part of the Lottery once it commences operations. Similarly, a regulatory agency that is given the duty of selecting the Lottery Operator and then monitoring and regulating it, will also be prone to defending the choice of Operator if questions or misgivings arise having regard to the various aspects of the commercial entities performance. Finally, there is an inherent tension or dissonance within an agency which has conflicting or potentially conflicting terms of reference. In the case of the National Lottery this has been demonstrated apropos the Director Generals' potentially contradictory responsibilities for both the Lottery's regulation and its promotion. For while regulation may (or may not) restrain as effectively as competition can, it is of essence a restrictive instrument and is not designed to do the promotional job as effectively as competition.[173]

The foregoing issues could all be said to have impinged to a greater or lesser extent on the functioning of the Lottery's regulation under the Director Generals. These aspects of the 1993 Act are not matters that are likely to have been any less tendentious had the Lottery's regulation been carried out by a team of commissioners rather than an individual. Notwithstanding some of the criticisms voiced by certain interest groups and members of the polity with regard to the Lottery's regulatory design, the 1998 Act did not address any of the potentials for conflict that are listed above. However, in the context of those areas with which this book is concerned, apart from replacing the position of Director General with five Lottery Commissioners, the 1998 Act introduced two further fundamental regulatory changes. From 10 July 1998,[174] the Regulator was invested with the power to fine the Operator.[175] The Act also facilitated from 1 April 1999 the access of the Comptroller and Auditor General to the records of the Operator.[176] Had these two measures been included in the legislation that established the National Lottery then the rôle of Director General would have at once carried more authority and would have been less vulnerable to certain criticisms and particularly those raised by the PAC and NAO. Criticisms that served to discredit and degrade the status of the Regulator, and the regulatory process. From the Operator's point of view, however, it should not be forgotten that the extension of the power to impose fines by the Regulator was introduced during the mid-term of the Licence. There are problems with this in terms of fairness and equity. For the Licence was applied for under one set of conditions, which have been altered halfway through, thus altering the risks the Operator faces.[177] Furthermore, the danger of the government making such policy changes will increase the potential costs of the Operator. The threat of such expropriations can reduce the efficiency of private production, creates uncertainty about future profitability, can undermine incentives for profit-seeking, creates incentives for rent-seeking, and distorts the implicit factor prices for the firm.[178]

While the measures included in the 1998 Act would certainly have bolstered the position of Director General, there remain other areas of equal importance that are also problematic. The enabling legislation for the National Lottery sought to make the Secretary of State responsible for all policy matters, including making Regulations, issuing Directions to the Director General, dealing in particular with matters that the latter should take into account in deciding whether or not to grant licences as well as the conditions that the licences should contain.[179] However in regulation there is often no clear line of demarcation between policy and its implementation.[180] In the case of the Lottery the Director General played a leading part in designing the Section 5 Licence. He was also instigative in setting targets for the Operator to meet, including prize targets and retail network targets. One might contend that the act of target-setting is itself a matter of policy.[181] Furthermore, and in common with other instances of personalized regulation in the UK, once the Lottery commenced operations, the Regulator not only acted as policeman, but also as law maker (having regard to the power to negotiate modifications to licence terms, i.e. make new law), and judge.[182]

At first sight it would appear that the office of the Director General was invested with rule-making and discretionary powers. Indeed it can be argued that the 1993 Act turned out in practice to be underinclusive and vague in a number of respects, the by-product of which was to confer inadvertently on the Director General a function relying too heavily on the use of discretion and interpretation. In this way the National Lottery's regulation was vulnerable to and indeed became politicized. The first Director General in particular attracted criticism for his restrictive or highly normative style of regulation. The powers he was believed to possess and his apparent reluctance to use them, coupled with his unwillingness to engage in the wider political process frustrated and aroused the ire of the polity and the media. However, in defence of the Director General, the scope of these powers (themselves the subject of contention) were on closer inspection far less substantial than they gave the appearance of being. The effect of this verisimilitude was to raise unrealistic expectations of the Director General. Perhaps most crucially of all, it was the absence of the ability to fine and an over-reliance on his powers of moral suasion which restricted the rôle of Director General and his ability to prosecute enforcement policies that would have been and would clearly have been seen to have been more vigorous.

Whatever the weaknesses of the 1993 Act that may have hindered the delivery of good regulation, it is also unavoidably the case that personalized regulatory designs and their success or failure will inevitably be influenced by the individual qualities and characteristics of the incumbent regulator. This form of regulation is therefore to some extent likely to be idiosyncratic, and is always prone in the absence of appropriate checks and balances to arrive at determinations which may appear to be capricious or eccentric. It is advanced in defence of personalized models that if individual regulators can develop a style that is consistent and predictable and by so doing can create a stable environment, then this has the potential to deliver satisfactory regulatory outcomes. However, this defence does not accede to the fallibility of personalized regulation in terms of the very particular lapses and errors of judgement to which individuals are prone. Neither does it address the real problems of 'capture' that individual regulators are most especially exposed to. Finally, real problems of consistency can arise in connection with personalized regulatory models when one regulator is replaced by another. This will inevitably alter regulatory decisions and policy more than (by way of comparison) replacing one judge by another will alter legal judgments, just because of that defensible middle ground of discretion.[183] Even equally able regulators may strike a different balance between the interests of parties and give different weights to various criteria, not because of any change in the law or government policy, but because they have the freedom to do so.[184] In the Lottery's case the second Director General, John Stoker, sought a much lower profile than his predecessor, and acted to some extent as a stopgap or temporary expedient. His preoccupation was most certainly to restore the credibility of the Lottery and its regulation, and to avoid the controversy that had engulfed Peter Davis, while holding the reins (between 9 February 1998 and 31 March 1999) in readiness for the assignment of his powers to the Lottery Commissioners and their Commission.

It is difficult to assess with absolute confidence whether the decision to replace the position of Director General with a panel of five Commissioners was a reaction (or over-reaction) to the perceived failings of the first Director General, or a more considered decision based on a mature and dispassionate assessment of the inherent defects of personalized regulation *per se*. The difficulties of finding an appropriate balance between the regulatory charges of guaranteeing the Lottery's propriety, protecting the interests of players and maximizing the funds raised for the Good Causes as outlined in Chapter 3 is an invidious task whether the Regulator is a Director General or a commission. This task is arguably made more difficult still with the arrival of a new government that will almost inevitably shift in one way or another the terms of reference for the Regulator. Nevertheless, there were undoubtedly serious errors of judgement that marked the first Director General's time in office. The least defensible of these errors relates to the risk the Director General was prepared to take in allowing GTech to participate in the Camelot Consortium. No unqualified guarantee can be given that a commission would not also have allowed GTech to join the Consortium. However, it is unlikely that all the members of a commission would have taken up such a sanguine position on this matter, especially having regard to the nature of the information about GTech to which they would and to which the Director General did have access. While it is too early to assess fully the Lottery's regulation under the Commissioners *vis-à-vis* the Director Generals, it is certainly the case that the new model will profit from some of the difficult and uncomfortable lessons learnt during the tenure of the first Director General. Indeed, as has been demonstrated, some of the difficulties referred to above have been addressed in the 1998 National Lottery Act. Nevertheless, it remains the case that many if not all of the conflicts and problematic balances that influenced the course and style of regulation under the Director Generals will continue to be prominent issues with which the Lottery Commissioners will also have to engage.

CHAPTER 5

THE NATIONAL LOTTERY COMMISSION AND THE NEW LICENCE

5.1 *The National Lottery Commission*

The introduction from April 1999 of the five Lottery Commissioners and National Lottery Commission (a non-departmental public body) in place of the Director General and the Office of the National Lottery (a non-ministerial government department) ended a period of nearly five and a half years of personalized regulation.[1] This period had been marked by a steady flow of criticism, particularly between the commencement of the sale of Lottery tickets in November 1994 and the resignation of the first Director General on 9 February 1998. Much of the criticism from a number of different interest groups with both a formal and informal concern in matters appertaining to the Lottery had been voluble and highly personalized. By depersonalizing the regulatory process, not only will over-reliance on a single decision-maker be done away with, but so too (it is no doubt hoped) will the blurring of policy by personality, which can itself be aggravated by the tendency for regulatory issues in personalized models to be fought out in an atmosphere of 'High Noon'.[2]

The five newly appointed Lottery Commissioners boasted a breadth of experience covering the voluntary sector, business, regulation, politics and consumer protection.[3] None of them, however, had participated in running a large business.[4] Nevertheless, this broad base of expertise and know-how is held out as one of the advantages of commission based regulation. Yet, as outlined earlier, there are question marks against the capacity of such models to deliver consistent regulation. Furthermore, it is also possible to advance that the new regulatory system chosen for the Lottery may in some ways be less accountable than the one it replaced. The day-to-day operational issues previously discharged by the Director General are now carried out by a Chief Executive who is accountable to the Lottery Commissioners;[5] however, the regulatory (and arguably the strategic) function formerly carried out by the Director General is now performed by the Commissioners.[6] The Commissioners are ultimately accountable to the Secretary of State.

While the splitting of day-to-day operational and regulatory responsibilities may carry advantages by clarifying and making more transparent the distinction between these two aspects of the regulatory process, this construct may also pose new questions having regard to accountability and the locus of responsibility. The separation of powers arguably creates a further layer of regulation; and while the Lottery's regulation is in the final analysis clearly a matter for the Commissioners, the potential difficulty of pinpointing accountability within a commission has already been alluded to. To some extent this may be aggravated by the requirement of the Commissioners to elect from among their number a chairman, rotating the post on a yearly basis.[7] The rotation, however, avoids the risk of concentrating too much power in one individual,[8] as is prone to occur in most US commissions, where over time the chairman tends to dominate.[9] Accountability problems may also obtain between the Commissioners and the Chief Executive where the distinctions between regulatory and operational issues may not be clear-cut. The new regulatory arrangements invest a degree of authority in the Chief Executive under a 'scheme of delegation' whereby and for example new game licences are granted by him unless the game design contains novel or innovative features which would automatically require the approval of the Commissioners.[10] In practice, however, there will inevitably be a process of learning as to where the Commission's powers end and the Commissioners' begin. In turn the Commissioners will have to grapple, as did the Director Generals before them, with the hoary and enduring problem of determining where the line should be drawn between regulation for which it is responsible, and what should more properly by styled 'government' policy. Policy changes should be expressed in terms of Directions issued to the Commissioners by the Secretary of State.[11] But as has been demonstrated earlier, this definition may be too restrictive and of limited value in evaluating and identifying the rôle of policy within the regulatory process. Thus while the outlook for regulation as it has been re-designed will certainly be less personalized (and perhaps less accountable) there is no certainty that it will be less vulnerable to politicization, and the difficulties of agreeing the essential nature and boundaries of principal/agent relations.

The paradigm selected for the National Lottery's commission-based regulation can be seen as something of a classic British compromise for a peculiarly British institution. The introduction of a Lottery Commission influenced as it was by US regulatory practices stopped short of embracing all the defining characteristics of these alternative yet long-established systems of regulation. The American system has traditionally favoured a more open procedural format than has been found in the UK involving access by different interest groups to the regulatory process through the forum of public hearings. Although this style of regulation is slower and more expensive,[12] it is held out by its advocates to be altogether more accountable and transparent than its UK counterpart.[13] Critics of UK regulatory practice have long-held and oft-repeated misgivings with regard to what has been called 'the more secretive British framework',[14] of closed procedures, where the regulator and his counterpart in the regulated company arrive at a mutually agreeable determination of just where the public interest lies.[15] The implicit criticism clearly being that such a *modus operandi* deprives the regulator's decisions of the credibility that only an open system can confer.[16]

According to the Secretary of State, part of the rationale behind the introduction of the 1998 National Lottery Act and the replacement of the office of Director General with five Lottery Commissioners has been to restore public confidence in the Lottery, and to advance the interests of transparency and democracy.[17] While the full and unrestricted access of the NAO to the records of the Operator which is facilitated by the 1998 Act represents an important step in making the Lottery's workings more transparent, the Act did not open up further or address directly this aspect of the relationship between Regulator and Regulatee. For example, the minutes of the monthly (sometimes as frequently as fortnightly) meetings of the Lottery Commissioners remain confidential.[18] This elision will undoubtedly be seen as a fudge by some, including those who would support the adoption of US regulatory practices in the UK,[19] and by those who would champion the rights of the consumer.[20] Alternatively, the failure to embrace the US regulatory model in its entirety may be seen as an intelligent and conscious decision designed to avoid the heavily legalistic and litigious nature[21] of a system that seeks to give all affected parties access to the regulatory process.[22]

Next to the introduction of the Lottery Commission and Lottery Commissioners, the ability of the Regulator to impose fines on the Operator is from the regulatory standpoint the other single most important feature of the 1998 Act. The authority was conferred on the office of Director General between 10 July 1998[23] and 31 March 1999. Looking forward, and over the longer term, this extra regulatory deterrent and the extent of its deployment has the capacity to influence fundamentally the regulatory style of the Commissioners and the nature of their relationship, not only with the Operator but also with the Commission. In deciding whether it is appropriate to impose a fine, the issues the Regulator may take into account will include whether the Operator has infringed key principles of the relevant licences, whether it has brought the Lottery into disrepute, the extent to which the Operator has derived a financial advantage from a licence contravention, whether the default was deliberate or the result of negligence and to what extent the offence was part of a pattern of similar past contraventions.[24] In deciding to impose a fine the Regulator will also have regard to the financial position of the Licensee.[25] The capacity to fine as a result of licence breaches allows sums lost to the Good Causes to be recovered and paid over to the Distribution Fund.[26]

This extension of power to the Director General in the first instance and thereafter to the Lottery Commissioners raises a number of pertinent regulatory issues. Importantly, in connection with fining *per se*, the 1998 Act invests the Regulator with the authority to exercise discretion in this new and potentially sensitive area. The Commissioners are not required to impose a penalty for all licence breaches, and may consider representations from the Operator when a breach has occurred as to whether on reflection the imposition of a financial penalty is appropriate.[27] The Operator also retains the right of appeal.[28] When the ability to fine was first introduced, the Regulator (the second Director General) confirmed that the types of contraventions where a financial penalty might be the most appropriate regulatory response would include failure by the Operator to meet its Licence obligations for the minimum number of retail outlets selling Lottery products (as had occurred during the first two quarters of 1996) and failure by the Operator to comply with the Player Code of Practice, having regard in particular to the prohibition of sales to persons under the age of 16.[29] The scope for discretion does not just confine itself to whether or not a fine should be imposed on the Operator, but also provides the Commissioners with the power to determine the size of the levy. However, the Act does not equip the Regulator with a tariff or formula to provide direction or guidance having regard to the size of fines. As the 1998 Lottery Bill passed through Parliament there was some pressure for a tariff to be included to help ensure that public opinion could not result in political influence being placed on the Regulator to make the fines extremely punitive.[30] This proposal was rejected as unworkable.[31] Bearing in mind the difficulty of anticipating an array of hypothetical infractions by the Licensee the non-inclusion of a tariff would not seem to be inappropriate. During the second Director General's tenure no financial penalties were exacted from the Operator.[32]

There is little doubt that the sanction of fining has been put in place to act as a deterrent.[33] It is the Commissioners who decide whether to fine the Operator and at what rate.[34] The discretion the Commissioners enjoy and the manner in which they exercise that discretion will have an important bearing on the regulatory process. In some ways the Commissioners may be said to have been invested with more tangible scope to arrive at decisions than had been the case during the personalized regulatory regime of the Director Generals. With regard to fining in particular, the latitude the Commissioners have been given has the potential to cause a very basic alteration in the relations between Regulator and Regulatee, one which has the capacity to become at once more confrontational and tactical. If the Commissioners adopt a hard line and take up the position that the Operator should comply with all regulations, and should be punished for any failing, then the style of the Lottery's regulation will shift from one which during the period of the Director Generals was characterized by negotiated or voluntary compliance to one of enforced compliance, (sometimes referred to as the penalty model). The danger of such a model is that it can tend to lead to overinclusiveness, ranking trivial offences equally with larger ones and thereby fails to allocate enforcement resources rationally.[35] Such a strategy would also serve to undermine any good will or spirit of cooperation that may exist between the Commission and its Commissioners and the Operator. By contrast, if the Regulator is too lenient with the Operator then the effectiveness of the deterrent will lose a measure of the force that it might otherwise have.

The implications of the above is that the relationship between Operator and Regulator is likely to be influenced at least to some extent by strategic manoeuvring. To suggest that the Operator is merely an 'amoral calculator' would be a contention at once naïve and guilty of reductionism. Indeed the case for Camelot's rôle in society being that of a 'Corporate citizen' has already been made.[36] Yet the firm is quintessentially an economic entity, and as such its willingness to comply with agency directives will be influenced inversely by the costs involved.[37] Large increases in costs (fines) will be likely to lead the firm to appeal and/or lobby for modifications to the arrangements, while small levies may be accepted on the grounds that the effort involved in fighting them will not be warranted either by expectations of a successful outcome,[38] or by the costs involved. The issue of fining has then the potential to influence in a very fundamental sense the course and tone of the regulatory process. During the first two years of its life the National Lottery Commission had imposed no fines on the Operator.

The problems associated with the rôle of discretion in regulation are likely to be as extant for the Lottery Commissioners as they were under the preceding personalized regime. The working arrangements for the Commission will also be likely to come under close scrutiny. In particular, the delineation of responsibilities between the Commissioners and the Chief Executive will require monitoring, and is likely to be the focus of critical attention. The new model will also have to demonstrate a protean quality as it will need to be flexible and responsive to the new challenges it will face in a way that the personalized model (but only partly as a result of the shortcomings of the 1993 Act) was incapable of. For good regulation is not fixed or static, rather it should be defined and evaluated in terms of process. It needs to possess an organic and dynamic quality which not only seeks to protect, but which can also respond intelligently to changes and shifts in society's overall goals and emerging or new priorities. In the final analysis the success of the new regime in identifying and serving the public interest will inevitably be a function of the quality of its decisions and the response to these decisions of an array of key constituencies or so called 'external theatres of judgement', the views of which played such a pivotal part in ending the personalized era of regulation.

5.1.2 Policy Considerations for the Next Licence

The stated position of the Labour Party, both when in Opposition and nearly one year after the Lottery had commenced trading, was that 'when the current contract for the operation of the National Lottery comes to an end, the new Section 5 Licence should be on a not-for-profit basis.'[39] The rationale behind this statement was that the level of profits the Lottery Operator had earned during this time were considered by the Opposition to be excessive.[40] Furthermore, the Labour Party advanced the notion (in 1996) that an effective cap on profits should be considered if a competitive not-for-profit organization were not to be found.[41] Labour's belief in Opposition that there was a growing feeling in the country for the Lottery to be reconstituted to serve the public interest rather than the narrow interests of the Operator's shareholders[42] found its expression once in government in the form of a White Paper entitled 'The People's Lottery'.[43] The White Paper considered four models for the new Licence, including a single company made up of a consortium of suppliers (the current arrangement), a holding company contracting out individual services, a multi-purpose company, able to use the Lottery network for other activities and an organization where the distribution of profits is not to shareholders but to employees and the Good Causes.[44]

In July 1999, the National Lottery Commission announced the basis for granting the next main Lottery Licence.[45] The Commission declared that the preferred bidder would be announced by the end of June 2000 (all bids to be received by February 2000), and that it welcomed both not-for-profit and other bids.[46] The responsibility for deciding whether the new operator would be a commercial or not-for-profit entity was to be determined by the Commissioners.[47] In this way the government avoided or sidestepped direct responsibility for the contentious idea which it had championed of replacing the current commercial arrangements with an alternative not-for-profit model. The Regulator also confirmed that subject to safeguards regarding propriety and player protection, the ultimate criterion for awarding the Licence would be the ability of the applicant to raise the greatest sums for the Distribution Fund.[48] The Commission rejected the option included in the White Paper of a multi-purpose body, insisting that all bidders be single-purpose bodies.[49] However, it did confirm in its announcement that as there were few companies offering technology services for large on-line lotteries, suppliers of such services would be permitted to participate in more than one bid.[50]

While the Regulator confirmed that not-for-profit bids were welcome and would be considered for the new Licence, the announcement did not articulate any policy preference for not-for-profit bidders *vis-à-vis* out-and-out commercial entities. However, the 'Statement of main principles' and the subsequent Invitation to Apply established that the award of the Licence would be based not only on ticket sales ('primary contributions'), but also, whether from not-for-profit bodies or others, on proposals for contributions to the Distribution Fund from surpluses gained from running the Lottery ('secondary contributions').[51] It should not be forgotten in this context that a not-for-profit organization is not barred from earning a profit.[52] Many such organizations produce an annual accounting surplus, but are prohibited from distributing the profits.[53] Self-evidently one of the advantages held out by proponents of the not-for-profit model is that profits/surpluses can be distributed to the Distribution Fund, and would not have to be divided with shareholders.

It would appear in connection with the foregoing that lessons have clearly been learnt from the first licensing period. In the new Licence, the Operator's retention will be a function of the amount it raises for the Good Causes, rather than sales as obtains in the current Licence.[54] Under the revised arrangements a significant part of the Licensee's retentions will be calculated on the proceeds of the Lottery, net of prizes, Lottery Duty, and a separate sales-related retention for the Licensee.[55] The sales-related element will be based on those of the Licensee's external costs that are directly proportional to sales.[56] These arrangements will avoid the situation in which, in certain circumstances, the Licensee can under the present Licence have an incentive to increase its retentions by increasing sales without the Distribution Fund benefiting,[57] by for example increasing the proportion of sales allocated to prizes at the expense of that assigned to the Good Causes.[58] In addition to the reconstitution of the Lottery's 'primary contributions', the Commission in recognition of the fact that public perception of the Lottery can be affected by the amount of surpluses retained by the Operator (in the Invitation to Apply) encouraged applicants to make 'secondary contributions' to the Fund from profits or surpluses.[59] The welcoming of not-for-profit bidders was also unquestionably a policy response to the controversy that dogged the Lottery during the first Licence, whereby the Operator was deemed by some to have made excessive profits. This was reiterated in the Invitation to Apply which held that 'there is a widespread view, which the NLC shares, that retentions by the Licensee should be lower under the next Licence.'[60] However, the fact that profit-seeking enterprises were not precluded from applying for the new Licence is a recognition of the success achieved by Camelot in generating funds for the Good Causes. The concept of the Distribution Fund benefiting from 'secondary contributions' can be seen as an attempt to assuage those who have criticized the Lottery's 'excessive' profits, while not rejecting entirely the rôle of the profit motive in delivering a successful National Lottery.

The initial Licence has also yielded other lessons which informed the Commission's 'Statement of main principles'.[61] The volume of Lottery sales generated has demonstrated the size of the market that exists, the corollary of which is that the risks faced by the Operator are more easy to assess than was the case when the undertaking was launched. The implication of this is that the Commission based its Invitation to Apply for the new Licence more in terms of the outcomes that bidders should deliver.[62] Notwithstanding the protestations by the incumbent Operator for a more lengthy licence period, the Commission confirmed that the Licence would be granted for a further seven years.[63] The Commission evidently determined that this time frame is sufficiently long to obtain a reasonable return on investment, which would in turn attract a sufficient number of bids, while not being so long as to enable the Operator to acquire and exploit monopolistic power.[64] Furthermore, the length of the Licence term combined with the lessons learnt during the period of the first Licence will have influenced any adjustments to regulatory design. For short-term contracts can be more specific and thus easier to enforce, while longer-term contracts (like that for the Lottery) need to be more flexible (as has been demonstrated in the course of this book) so that both agency and franchisee can adapt to changing circumstances.[65] While the controversy over the size of the Operator's profits is addressed by the not-for-profit and 'secondary contributions' options, the 'Statement of main principles' and ensuing Invitation to Apply also uphold the importance of transparency over the factors determining salaries and bonuses to guard against levels of remuneration that are excessive in relation to the responsibilities and performance of management.[66] It is noteworthy that Camelot announced that should it secure the new Licence, then director's remuneration and bonuses would be significantly lower than during the initial Licence term (for example the Chief Executive's pay package would be cut by one-third).[67] In addition Camelot undertook to reduce profits retained from 1 per cent to 0.5 per cent.[68]

Bidders were also required to explain fully how they intended to prevent under-age and excessive play and to set out the steps they would take to deal with such problems if they occur.[69] However, the Commission, in something of a departure, demonstrated a willingness to consider new and more aggressive product developments including fast-draw Keno and video lottery terminals.[70] These types of games which had been specifically forbidden during the tenure of the Director Generals,[71] are closer in design and character to some of the 'harder' constituents of the gambling industry. Moreover, from February 2000, the Secretary of State withdrew the restriction of three roll-overs on the Draw Lottery, and devolved the responsibility for determining the limit on roll-overs to the National Lottery Commission and its Commissioners.[72] In response, the Commission declared that bidders for the next Licence could submit plans for games involving more than three roll-overs.[73] Finally, the Commission declared that it expected the successful applicant to welcome third parties as independent Section 6 Licensees, and also that it expected all bidders to set out how they intended to encourage proposals by third parties, and the basis on which they anticipated reaching agreements with those making them.[74]

5.1.3 The Incumbent Operator and Its Challenger

If (as in the case of the National Lottery Commission) the regulator is unable to commit to a multi-period policy regarding regulation, then the regulatee(s) must form expectations about which policies will be adopted in the future.[75] The firm will anticipate the policy the regulator will adopt given what it learns about the firm during the previous period(s).[76] Camelot certainly learnt from the difficulties it experienced during the first half of the initial Licence term in the areas of propriety (for example the GTech imbroglio, the level and justification of bonus payments and profit levels) and also issues connected with player protection (for example under-age sales). It is instructive in this context that in its bid to secure the new Licence, Camelot pledged to reduce directors' bonuses, and the level of profit in relation to turnover.[77] Moreover, as outlined earlier Camelot went to some lengths to enhance its reputation as a corporate citizen during the second half of the Licence although with limited success. In 1999 research commissioned by Camelot found that only 47 per cent of adults believed the Company to be trustworthy.[78] In addition to the foregoing steps Camelot partnered the Post Office (subsequently renamed Consignia) in its bid for the next term.[79] This was both strategically and tactically astute as some 16 per cent of Lottery ticket sales are sold through around 10,000 post offices, and the government welcomed Consignia's involvement as a demonstration not only of the new powers and freedoms that it has conferred on them,[80] but also as a model of New Labour Public–Private Partnership.[81]

Notwithstanding the controversies that beset the Operator during the early part of the Licence, Camelot in conjunction with Consignia was widely acknowledged as the leading contender for the new Licence.[82] By the deadline for the submission of bids (29 February 2000), only three were forthcoming, *viz.* Camelot, The People's Lottery headed by Sir Richard Branson, and an application from an unidentified charity consortium,[83] which was subsequently withdrawn.[84] Branson's bid through the vehicle of The People's Lottery Ltd, promised that all of the profits would be applied to the Good Causes through the Distribution Fund.[85] Suppliers were not shareholders in The People's Lottery, so there would be no profit-sharing among suppliers as is the case currently.[86] However, it is to be fairly assumed that suppliers would have expected to derive profits on the services they were to provide to the company. In addition the company was a wholly owned subsidiary of the People's Lottery Holding Company Ltd – which was a company limited by guarantee.[87] Both Camelot and The People's Lottery forecast a sum of £15 billion for Good Causes over the next Licence.[88] To be able to achieve this ambitious target, both organizations included plans to introduce more aggressive gambling formats, including Lottery play via mobile telephones, interactive television and the Internet.[89] These developments will clearly involve the Regulator having to make difficult ongoing judgements in setting player protection against the generation of funds for the Distribution Fund.[90]

Whatever its constitutional make-up, it should be noted that a newcomer is likely to be placed at a disadvantage *vis-à-vis* the incumbent, having regard to the latter's experience of the business and its market, and knowledge of the agency and its processes.[91] To counterbalance this, the incumbent is at the disadvantage of other bidders knowing more about its performance than it does about them.[92] However, there is evidence that agencies tend to prefer the status quo by routinely renewing the franchises of established operators, or at least requiring newcomers to make a particularly powerful case, implying the possible capture of the regulator by the incumbent,[93] regulatory apathy or risk averse behaviour by the regulator. In addition many regulated industries (including the Lottery) are characterized by high levels of sunk costs which are irreversible and more or less industry specific.[94] If the life of the capital does not coincide with the life of the contract (it does not in the case of the Lottery), then when the contract expires but the existing Operator is not the preferred bidder, one policy option would be for the surviving capital to be sold to the new provider at a 'fair market value'.[95] This task can be complex and expensive to perform.[96]

The existing Section 5 Licence does not impose any requirements on

Camelot to transfer assets to a new operator or to assist a new operator in other ways at the expiry of Camelot's Licence period.[97] This omission will be remedied in the new Licence to ensure the Operator is obliged to cooperate in the event of a transfer at the end of the next Licence period.[98] Nevertheless, while it may or may not be the case that much of the Operator's existing equipment will be of an advanced age and written down, it was the view of the first Director General that if Camelot were not to win the next Licence, there would be good economic reason for it to seek to recover the value of whatever assets were left by coming to a sensible arrangement with the new operator.[99] Furthermore, although it was not obliged to, Camelot assured the Commission that it would cooperate fully in planning and supporting the transition if another operator were chosen.[100] Nevertheless, at the bidding stage, prices have to reflect the suppliers predicted costs during the next Licence term. Bearing in mind the uncertainty of particular areas of cost for new bidder(s) which would only be finally determined by negotiations with the incumbent in the event of a transfer and after bids have been submitted, there is a clear advantage for the existing Operator under such conditions. The valuation of equipment transfers is problematic, and is such that bidding parity at the contract renewal interval between the original winner and rival successor firm(s) cannot be safely presumed.[101] Although there was a period of some 15 months between the (intended) announcement of the new Operator and the start of the new Licence,[102] this would be a time of uncertainty in the event of a new Operator securing the Licence. Camelot and the new Operator would negotiate the terms of the hand-over. But investment in the Lottery infrastructure at this time would be an area of concern. For a tenant (Camelot) will not make an improvement which would last beyond its lease (Licence),[103] unless it could secure full compensation. These uncertainties influenced the deliberations of the Commissioners, who were anxious not only to avoid controversy at a particularly sensitive and vulnerable time, but also to guarantee no disruption of service and consequent loss of monies to the Distribution Fund.[104] Their response to these concerns, and in the interests of creating a 'level playing field', was to require all applicants to install new lottery terminals.[105] For the incumbent this is expensive, and will involve Camelot, having secured the new Licence, replacing £100 million worth of equipment that is proven and in good working order.[106] This measure was certainly of considerable value in creating a fair and equal basis for competitive bids, in order to deliver the best possible outcome for the Good Causes.[107] Yet it remains the case that if Camelot's bid had been unsuccessful it would have been at liberty to retain the existing terminals and apply to the Gaming Board to become an external lottery manager, running both 'society' lotteries for a variety of charities and also lotteries on behalf of local authorities.[108] While the size of such lotteries is restricted, expenses of up to 35 per cent are permitted.[109] If Camelot, under this scenario, were able to generate a sufficient number of individual clients to whom the company would provide lottery services (it already has lottery interests abroad),[110] the business could have continued to be viable. The potential for Camelot to compete with a new National Lottery Licensee is a factor the Commissioners will have weighed in their deliberations. This prospect is likely to have strengthened the case for the incumbent.

One final aspect that should be borne in mind apropos the position of the incumbent, relates to the fact that Camelot is a single company made up of a consortium of shareholder/suppliers. This is one of the models for running the Lottery, referred to above, which the Commissioners considered appropriate for the new Licence. The Camelot model is best described as 'partial' vertical integration. That is to say some of the output of the upstream process of the shareholders/suppliers (including retail, marketing, security printing, computer technology, training and data communication skills) is sold to buyers other than Camelot, and some of the intermediate input for Camelot in the downstream process is purchased from suppliers other than the shareholders.[111] One of the potential benefits of vertically integrated firms is that they can make possible a closer synchronization of input and output flows, a closer control of quality and a better adjustment of capacity at the several stages of the production process than can be achieved by separate firms dealing with one another at arm's length.[112] Thus the upstream firm will be concerned with the net returns obtained downstream, since these contribute to the upstream firm's revenues and ultimately its profits.[113] Indeed the fact that Camelot's shareholders are also its chief suppliers was held out by the first Director General to be a particularly positive feature of the bid.

> One of the advantages to me of the Camelot bid was that we had five substantial corporations [Cadbury Schweppes 22.5 per cent, Racal 22.5 per cent, GTech 22.5 per cent, De La Rue 22.5 per cent and ICL 10 per cent] all of whom would have a trading relationship with Camelot and would want to support Camelot if times got tough.'[114]

While the traditional business explanation for vertical integration is that firms want to assure their control over the supply of inputs and their market for outputs, with the concomitant benefits of quality and cost control,[115] such arrangements pose a particular regulatory challenge. For vertical control arrangements are frequently characterized as a means by which the upstream firm can enhance and capture monopoly rents.[116] In the case of Camelot, much of its operating costs are for goods and services supplied by its owners. It may therefore be tempted to increase costs for services provided, which will depress its own profits while inflating those of the shareholder suppliers. In an effort to reduce this danger, the first Director General insisted as a condition of the Section 5 Licence that the Operator disclose in its annual accounts the amount of inter-company trading, to ensure complete transparency and visibility in relation to these transactions.[117] Camelot provides this information yearly in notes to the accounts under the heading 'Related party transactions'. Appendix III on pages 202–3 shows the cumulative benefit enjoyed by Camelot and the consortium members up to the financial year ending 31 March 2001.

There is clearly a need for regulatory vigilance in this area. The option of 'moving' profits upstream (in preference to dividends which are also politically sensitive) must have been tempting for Camelot and its share-holders during the time when media and public attention was particularly critical of the level of profits enjoyed by the Operator. The difficulties in this area and the potential for controversy are well illustrated by the fact that one of the bidders for the first Licence, *viz*. The Lottery (RT) Ltd, undertook to separate investors who would put up capital from service providers who would do the work, in order to make transparent the division between cost and profit.[118] Moreover the separation of suppliers from shareholders was a key feature of the bid from The People's Lottery, which argued that it had the capacity to be more efficient as it could go to the best suppliers in the world to secure the most appropriate arrange-ments and keenest prices.[119] This is without question an issue with which the Commissioners would have had to grapple in their deliberations on the terms and conditions of the new Licence, for it is important that in the design and execution of any bidding process the regulator is able to prevent, and be alert to the possibility that the 'original franchisee who is integrated backwards into equipment supply . . . can plainly rig the prices to the disadvantage of rival bidders at the contract renewal interval.'[120] It is worth remarking that the inherent and myriad problems of judging between an incumbent and rival bidder were to feature prominently in the award of the new Licence. Indeed the Commission's chairman alluded to these peculiar and innate difficulties during the bidding process.[121]

5.1.4 For Profit or Not-for-Profit?

As outlined at Table 4 (p. 78) the UK's National Lottery is arguably the most efficient in the world in terms of its fiscal contribution and its contribution to the Good Causes. This is a reflection both of the Operator's capabilities and of the scale economies that flow from being one of the world's largest lotteries. With after-tax profits typically being in the vicinity of 1 per cent of turnover, the idea of turning the Lottery into a not-for-profit entity, from an economic standpoint is likely to be a marginal exercise. Indeed it is possible to estimate that a decline in Lottery sales of less than 1 per cent would be more than sufficient to offset the benefits of the operator not retaining profits.[122] However, the fact that a not-for-profit option was considered for the new Licence term, was arguably driven less by considerations of economic efficiency than by a political and philosophical ambivalence with regard to the presence and size of the profit motive in what the Government had styled 'The People's Lottery'.

Political considerations aside, introducing a not-for-profit entity could have serious and adverse repercussions having regard to the funds raised for the Good Causes. Even if revenue raised by a not-for-profit entity were similar to that achieved by Camelot (itself a questionable prop-osition), there is no guarantee that running costs would not be higher.[123] By way of analogy it is perhaps worth pausing to consider 'If you had to choose between two retailers to promote your product would you place your business with the Co-op or with Tesco?'[124] However, in interviews carried out between 12 and 14 November 1999 NOP discovered that 51 per cent of lapsed players (some 6 million people) and 33 per cent of those who have never played the Lottery claimed they would be more likely to play if all profits went to good causes.[125] Those proponents of the existing arrangements argue that as the Lottery is working successfully (the over-arching criterion for success among advocates of the current model being the amount of money raised for the Distribution Fund) a miscalculation as to who runs the Lottery or how it is run could have a catastrophic impact on the cash flow to Good Causes; which are now working, as is the government, on the assumption that whoever runs the Lottery will do so at least as successfully as Camelot has in the past.[126]

The challenge for the Commissioners (one shared by many regulators) has been to put in place conditions that, while preventing the firm from exploiting its monopoly power, maintain incentives for the firm to pro-duce efficiently.[127] Designing a 'fair rate of return' which is reliable and not vulnerable to manipulation by the regulatee is not straightforward. A 'fair rate of return' criterion often employed by regulatory agencies maintains that after the firm subtracts its operating expenses from gross revenues, the remaining net revenue should be just sufficient to compen-sate the firm for its investment in plant and equipment.[128] Problems can arise if the rate of return allowed by the regulatory agency is greater than the cost of capital, but is less than the rate of return that would be enjoyed by the firm were it free to maximize profit without regulatory con-straint.[129] For under these conditions the firm will be tempted to over-invest in capital and substitute it for other factors of production and in so doing will operate at an output where costs are not minimized (the so-called Averch/Johnson effect).[130]

It is fair to posit that the optimum choice for the Regulator was to award the Licence to a commercial or for-profit operator. However, whatever the style of entity, in order to secure the new Licence the Operator was also required to undertake to make further 'secondary contributions' to the Distribution Fund from the profits generated. This concept is not new. During the bidding process for the first Licence, two applicants, The Enterprise Lottery Company Ltd and The Lottery (RT) Ltd offered contributions which were related to the profits they earned.[131] Arguably, 'a reasonable expectation of profit is the best way of maximising the Lottery's revenue.'[132] But this clearly begs the question of what is 'reasonable'? One measure might be the avoidance of monopolistic or supracompetitive profits. Under a case of perfect profit control where a firm's overall revenue requirements are equated to its cost of service and continuously revised upward or downward with any rise or fall in that cost, there would be no monopoly profits.[133] But neither would there be any incentive on the part of the monopolist to improve its efficiency, as lacking both the stick of competitive pressure or the carrot of supracompetitive profits, the managers of the firm would have no obvious reason to strive for a better performance.[134] To some extent this problem can be countered by the 'accident' of 'regulatory lag' where rates are periodically, not continuously, equated with costs.[135] Under such conditions the motivation or incentive for the firm to innovate is the temporary profits which the innovation permits between periodic regulatory reviews.[136]

During the initial Licence there has undoubtedly been evidence of regulatory lag in operation. Lessons learnt during the first half of the Licence find their expression in the 1998 Lottery Act. For example the Act, which *inter alia* extended to the Regulator the capacity to impose fines on the Operator, will have caused to a lesser or greater degree the latter to invest in measures designed to deliver more robust levels of player protection, especially having regard to the prevention of under-age sales. Another case in point is found in relation to the monopoly profits enjoyed by the Operator via interest earned on the Prize Target Shortfall, until these supranormal profits, themselves the by-product of Licence defects rather than Operator performance, were surrendered in the teeth of growing opposition from various members of the polity and media. The new Licence itself can also be seen in one way as a manifestation of regulatory lag. With the existing Operator having been successful in winning the right to run the Lottery for a further seven years, it will find the opportunities for profit more restricted than during the first term. The return on capital employed, which exceeded 20 per cent during the first Licence,[137] is also likely to be more modest.

Regulatory lag is not itself a complete answer to the incentive problem, for it is an inadvertent method of injecting a profit incentive. And while it permits supranormal profits, there is no express recognition that they are a legitimate and acceptable method of encouraging performance.[138] In this context, and in the context of the regulatory arrangements chosen for the new Licence it will be important that a clear distinction is made between profits or surpluses which can be identified as monopoly rents, perhaps as a consequence of Licence defects such as the profits generated as a result of the Prize Target Shortfall; and those 'legitimate' profits which are derived from the exploitation of, for example, a patented device or other innovative business process. This distinction is imperative and cannot be over-stressed, for as J. A. Schumpeter has demonstrated,[139] while competition (and by way of analogy regulation) tends to eliminate 'above-normal' profits in the long run, the motivation for a firm to innovate is the unusual and temporary profits which the innovation allows in the short to medium term.[140] This distinction, while of vital importance, is not the end of the problem. Even if rates of return are subject to regulatory review at agreed intervals, so as to provide a more consistent and predictable regulatory environment, there is a danger of a ratchet effect developing where the regulator infers from a high performance an ability to repeat a similar performance in the future and so becomes more demanding.[141] The operator who recognizes that high profits and greater efficiency will result in the regulator taxing the gains away will one day decide that efficiency is self-defeating – so why bother?[142] In the absence of a profit motive these technical considerations concerning Licence design would have been all but eliminated. But if the profit motive had been removed then there must be a serious question mark as to whether the motive of altruism would have been as effective in delivering a successful Lottery, and one capable of maximizing the return to the Good Causes.

During the course of the first Licence there have been important lessons learnt by both Operator and Regulator which in many instances have informed and have been introduced into the regulatory process. In terms of meeting the Lottery's *raison d'être*, i.e. improving the quality of life of the Nation, the Operator has played its part. While an ongoing debate has raged as to how the bounty should be most equitably apportioned between regions, categories and different social groups (a subject beyond the scope of this work), the funds raised have surpassed expectations. The placing of the Lottery in the private sector and the rôle of the profit motive have been important elements in this success. The first Licence term has seen some progress in the areas of propriety and corporate governance following painful experiences, and in the area of player protection with the introduction of new regulatory instruments. This period has also seen certain curbs placed on the Operator's capacity to extract supranormal profits through the surrendering of interest earned on the Prize Target Shortfall, and the extension to the Regulator of the power to fine. The notion of the Distribution Fund benefiting from 'secondary contributions' sounds seductive, yet the devil is likely to be found in the detail. It should be a central concern for the Regulator to avoid serious disincentives that might diminish the Operator's interest in pursuing future breakthroughs.[143] If this is not achieved it may be the case that 'secondary contributions' are more than outweighed by a loss in 'primary contributions', i.e. ticket sales.[144]

> The Lottery sits on every fault line in the British psyche – on what utilities should be public and what private; on what the State should pay for; . . . on how much the vulnerable should be protected or allowed to make wrong decisions; on how far can self-regulation work; on whether companies behave decently – and how we can guarantee that wealth-creation is a morally-based pursuit.[145]

The presence of the profit motive within the Lottery's operational arrangements lies at the heart of this debate. Tampering with these arrangements, however, is a fraught and potentially perilous process. With certain provisos that have been addressed in the course of this book the incentive of profit has served the Lottery's purpose well. It is instructive that in the year 2000, of the five most efficient lotteries in the world (in terms of percentage handed over to government and Good Causes) four of them incorporate a profit motive.[146] 'Given the cardinal importance of technological advance to economic welfare, and the fact that regulation includes no techniques for inducing a regulated firm to innovate at an optimal rate, this point argues strongly against profit controls.'[147] In relation to the next Licence period, those responsible for determining policy should be mindful that good regulation must not become obsessed with limiting profits, rather it should be a positive system allowing for the rôle of earnings to encourage and attract more capital.[148] Put another way, the goal of regulation should not be minimum profits to the regulated industry, but maximum service to the public at the lowest feasible cost.[149]

CHAPTER 6

THE OUTCOME

The National Lottery Commission was due to announce the name of the winning bidder by the end of June 2000. On 23 June, the Commission declared that the bidding period would be extended by a further month, as it believed that both bids could be substantially improved,[1] although it was unwilling to elaborate on the perceived weaknesses of either bid.[2] There was understandable concern at this delay, particularly among the consortium members of The People's Lottery, who feared the delay would jeopardize its hopes of replacing Camelot's terminals with its own, if it were to be successful.[3] On 23 August, and after five months of examination, involving the evaluation of 2 million words of evidence and 360 checks on the 100 companies involved in the two bids,[4] the Commission announced that neither of the bidders' plans met the statutory criteria for granting a licence.[5] However, the Commission added that it proposed to negotiate further with The People's Lottery only, and hoped to reach a satisfactory conclusion within a month.[6]

6.1 *The Rejection of Camelot*

Between the Commission's initial announcement that it had deferred its decision, and its subsequent statement that The People's Lottery's bid would be allowed to go forward for further consideration, there had been speculation in the press that the postponement of the Commission's decision was prompted by the revelation that there had been systems problems suffered by GTech, Camelot's main technology supplier.[7] In its announcement on 23 August, the Commission confirmed that during the evaluation process it had discovered that GTech had identified a software fault and corrected that fault secretly.[8] The fault had been in place between the launch of the Lottery and 27 July 1998 when it was rectified,[9] but it was only discovered in May 2000 when Mr David Armitage, a computer expert and former GTech employee, wrote to the Commission informing it of the cover-up.[10]

The decision to conceal the fault had been taken by the then Chairman and Chief Executive Officer, William O'Connor, and its then President and Chief Operating Officer, Steven Nowick.[11] The decision was taken against the advice of the head of GTech UK, Nigel Beaney, that both Camelot and Oflot should be told.[12] Neither the Operator nor the Regulator were notified. The GTech Board itself was not informed then or subsequently until the matter was raised by the Commission.[13] The fault itself involved a relatively small number of instances where two Draw Lottery tickets were printed for one transaction, which affected the payouts to winners below £50,000, but only by £2 to £3 per win.[14] Estimates suggest that the effect of these 'phantom' tickets is that between 50,000 and 78,000 winning tickets were underpaid by £59,000, and that between 35,000 and 38,000 were overpaid by a sum of £67,000.[15] Although it affected only 0.0007 per cent of transactions, the senior management determined to conceal the problem coming as it did just three months after the same management at GTech had provided assurances to the Director General, John Stoker, that (following the bribery scandal involving Snowden and Branson) the Company would observe the highest standards of corporate behaviour.[16]

Both GTech and Camelot took measures in response to the Commission's investigations. These included the resignation of the senior GTech executives involved in the decision not to notify Camelot or Oflot of the software problem.[17] Additionally GTech separated the posts of Chairman and Chief Executive, and created a new Compliance and Corporate Governance Committee made up of non-executives, which would provide an annual certificate of compliance to both Camelot and the National Lottery Commission, covering ethical and software issues.[18] Finally, the Company also agreed to have independent reviews undertaken of all its software development processes and process documentation, to make the findings available to Camelot and the Commission, to obtain certification against a number of international industry standards, and to have compliance with these standards independently audited and certified to Camelot and the Commission annually.[19] Camelot also agreed to extend the scope of its reviews of GTech's performance, including the introduction of more rigorous contract terms and the appointment of a quality assurance/IT specialist, to work full-time alongside GTech's quality assurance department.[20]

Notwithstanding the steps taken by Camelot and its principal supplier, the Commission's Chairwoman, Dame Helena Shovelton, made it clear that the Commission had lost confidence in Camelot's capacity to run the Lottery with 'all due propriety' for a further seven years.[21] Although both the Commission and Camelot had been deceived by GTech's blatant disregard for acceptable standards of corporate behaviour, it had become clear that Camelot could not demonstrate the capacity to manage GTech effectively.[22] It is a matter which defies credulity that GTech should have behaved in such a way so soon after the resignation of its chairman for attempted bribery and the forced sale of its shareholding in Camelot. The episodes only serve to underscore the gambling industry's historic and enduring association with misconduct and malfeasance. It is likely that if the matter had been properly disclosed at the time it was discovered by GTech, that it would have had only a marginal effect on the deliberations of the Commission and its Commissioners over the award of the next Licence. It is also a matter of supreme irony that the Company described as supplying Camelot with the 'blueprint' for the National Lottery should also come close to bringing about the Operator's downfall. In failing to put in place systems to ensure an acceptable level of performance by GTech, Camelot had undermined the propriety of the Lottery and had also failed to protect the interests of the participants. GTech's persistent failings led the Commission to conclude that it could not be certain that the measures offered by Camelot and GTech would be implemented in full, nor would it be in a position within the time-scale allowed to satisfy itself that the improvements in propriety and player protection were secure.[23]

In commenting on other aspects of the incumbent Operator's bid, the Commission recorded two further areas of concern. Firstly, a new corporate structure proposed by Camelot would have involved it, along with a sister company CISL, being structured within a new group, headed by a new holding company. The Commission was of the view that the structure carried with it the potential for the interests of the holding company and other group companies, to run counter to the overall interests of the National Lottery.[24] Secondly, the Commission was concerned that aspects of Camelot's game planning were unconvincing. In this context it should be noted (as outlined in Table 3, p. 71) from a peak in 1998, annual sales of Lottery tickets had declined in each of the subsequent two years. Furthermore, the Commission's deliberations on the award of the new Licence took place at a time when Lottery sales were lower still. During the first three months of the new financial year (1 April 2000–30 June 2000) Saturday Draw sales fell by nearly 7 per cent.[25] While accepting the credibility of the overall game strategy, the Commission was not convinced that the revenues projected by Camelot for a Euro Bloc game to be played across a number of countries with a combined prize fund, were achievable.[26] The Commission was also unconvinced that Camelot's plans to revive the Instants game which, as Table 3 demonstrates, has been in annual decline since the Lottery's first full operating year (£1523m for year ending 31 March 1996, to £561m for year ending 31 March 2000).[27] The Commission did not find plausible, Camelot's projection of a contribution of £15 billion to Good Causes over the course of the next Licence, which would have required an increase in sales of 43 per cent.[28] These concerns with regard to game plans and indeed corporate structure, it should be stated, were of considerably less importance in the Commission's decision to reject the Camelot bid for the new Licence, than the issues of propriety and player protection.[29] Yet up to the end of March 2001 no fine had been imposed on Camelot.[30]

6.2 The People's Lottery

In allowing The People's Lottery alone to go forward for further negotiations, it is entirely plausible to argue that the Commission's decision was based perhaps more on the continuing problems caused by GTech's relationship with Camelot, than on the inherent merits of the competing bid. In its deliberations the Commission highlighted two overriding reasons as to why it felt unable to award at once the new Licence to The People's Lottery, and thus why further, exclusive negotiations were necessary. Firstly, the Commission was concerned about the financial viability of the Company in lower revenue scenarios, in terms of both borrowing facilities available and their sufficiency, and in terms of profitability [sic] over the Licence period.[31] The adequacy of these arrangements the Commission averred would impact on the Company's ability to ensure funds were in place to guarantee prize security arrangements in the case of insolvency.[32] Secondly, during the improvement process (i.e. the period between the rejection of the Company's first bid, and the heavily qualified and conditional acceptance of its subsequent submission), The People's Lottery agreed to obtain an additional loan facility of £50 million.[33] The Commission wanted this facility not merely promised but unconditionally and irrevocably committed to ensure the Company's financial soundness in lower revenue scenarios.[34]

While being a central consideration for the Commission and its Commissioners, it would be unfair to claim that the problems having regard to integrity and player protection, which had hampered the incumbent Operator's bid, were the only reason for The People's Lottery being the preferred bidder. There is an argument to suggest that with Lottery sales declining since a peak of over £5.5 billion in 1997/98, giving Camelot control for a further seven years would not do enough to create fresh interest in the Lottery.[35] In Camelot's defence however, it should not be forgotten that long after the initial media excitement, 65 per cent of eligible players still participate at least monthly in the Lottery; and this is the second highest rate in the world after New Zealand.[36]

The People's Lottery proposed allocating 50p of each £1 to prizes, 30p to the Good Causes, 12p to Lottery duty, 5.2p to retailers and 2.8p for running costs.[37] However, the bid included some innovative game formats. These included the replacement of the current 6 from 49 numbers for the Draw game with a new 6 from 53 numbers format, designed to create at least eight double and two triple roll-overs a year.[38] As has been demonstrated in the course of this book roll-overs have a significant impact in increasing participation levels.[39] However, there is a danger in this strategy as players decide to wait for roll-over weeks and do not play in the meantime. In November 1999 the Florida State Lottery made a similar move to that proposed by The People's Lottery, and participation rates fell; the California State Lottery also experienced a sales decline in the 1980s from $31 million per annum to $15.7 million per annum in just 18 months when it altered its game matrix along the lines proposed by The People's Lottery.[40] The People's Lottery believed (which the Company claimed was supported by research) that while it would be likely that there would be a dip in player levels during non-roll-over weeks, this would be more than compensated for by sales during weeks when the jackpot did roll-over.[41]

In another innovation a 'Millionaires' game, which would run along-side the twice weekly Draw game, would allow players willing to spend an additional £1 to purchase an extra number.[42] The player would have a 1 in 3 million chance of becoming a millionaire if six of the seven numbers were drawn; and the game allowed the company to claim that it would create 2500 millionaires over the next Licence period.[43] This would have made players nearly five times more likely to become millionaires than the existing Draw game (odds 1 in 14 million). While welcoming these innovative game proposals, the Commission was concerned that the company's idea for inclusion of a regional lottery product in their on-line game portfolio, might not be viable within existing legislative con-straints.[44] The People's Lottery also included proposals to revive Instants Lottery sales with targeted products aimed at specific audiences such as football crowds and cricket crowds.[45] The Company aimed, with the aid of the Internet, to increase Instants sales to £1 billion a year.[46]

Like Camelot's bid, The People's Lottery is understood to have empha-sized a multi-channel approach to running the Lottery in order to increase sales,[47] including new interactive games to be played on the Internet, interactive television and WAP mobile telephone technology.[48] Also, as in the case of the incumbent's bid, the Commission assessed that the Com-pany's projections of an increase over current sales of 44 per cent to be unduly optimistic.[49] Finally, while having reservations concerning sales forecasts, the Commission was satisfied with the Company's technological solutions, which it considered credible and achievable to the required standards.[50] Technology suppliers to the Company included KPMG Con-sulting, Energis, Microsoft, Cisco Systems and AWI.[51] AWI provides services similar to those provided by GTech to Camelot and often com-petes with GTech to run state and national lotteries. During and before the bidding process AWI had succeeded in winning 7 of the last 14 licences awarded for running state lotteries in America.[52] Additional marketing and retail expertise was provided through the involvement, as suppliers, of J. Walter Thompson and Kellogg's .[53]

6.3 *Reaction and Events Following the 'Interim' Decision*

Whether or not the Commission's decision to defer the award of the new Licence not once, but twice, can be wholly justified is a moot point. However, the Commission's decision to find the bid from The People's Lottery unsatisfactory for a second time, yet to allow it, and it alone, to participate in further negotiations is less easy still to justify. The Commission's Chairwoman, Dame Helena Shovelton, defended the course of action, by explaining that the omission of Camelot from further negotiations was due to the belief that it would have taken the current Operator several months to meet the Commission's concerns (regarding the GTech cover-up) which was too long under the time-scale permitted.[54] Therefore, the Commission had determined that the flaws in the bid from The People's Lottery could be swiftly remedied, while those of Camelot could not.[55] The Commission's misgivings with regard to Camelot were clearly to do with the company's 'fit and proper' status. Yet, if the existing Operator was deemed unfit to run the Lottery under the new Licence, the corollary of this position is that Camelot was unfit to run the existing Licence. The implication of this line of thinking is that the Commission should have suspended the Lottery when the GTech deception came to light.[56] Indeed Dame Helena Shovelton confirmed that the Commission came very close to suspending Camelot's Licence,[57] which would have been an extreme and arguably heavy-handed measure.

Whether or not the course taken by the Commission was a prudent and measured response to its statutory remit or a demonstration of fainthearts and indecisiveness is debatable. However, it was irrefutably controversial. The environment of uncertainty was only added to by Dame Helena Shovelton's statements that Camelot was not entirely ruled out,[58] that if negotiations with The People's Lottery failed, negotiations with Camelot could be reopened,[59] that it might be possible for Camelot to re-enter the race if it could in some way remove the GTech connection,[60] and that if all talks failed the Commission might have to ask the government to find a way of running the Lottery.[61] To add to the confusion, Camelot successfully applied to the High Court to seek a judicial review of the Commission's decision, although the Company failed in its bid to halt its rival's talks with the Commission until after the review.[62] There was a feeling in some circles that Camelot had a strong case in terms of natural justice, and that it should have been allowed to continue negotiations with the Commission, alongside The People's Lottery.[63] This view gained currency when Camelot announced that it would buy GTech's UK operations by the end of September 2000, for over £100 million, including 24,000 lottery terminals, its computer system and specialized lottery software and the contracts of 70 staff.[64] By disassociating GTech from any future involvement in the management of the Lottery's software systems, and thereby removing an association that had become something of a 'moral hazard', Camelot addressed directly the Commission's overriding objection to allowing the company to participate in the ongoing negotiations for the new Licence.[65]

6.4 *Judicial Review*

Following a two-and-a-half-day High Court hearing, ending on 21 September, Mr Justice Richards found in Camelot's favour. Indeed the Judge's assessment of the Commission's behaviour was particularly damning. While accepting that the Commission had tried to be fair, the Judge accused it (in relation to the decision to allow The People's Lottery to participate exclusively in negotiations) of having demonstrated a 'marked lack of even-handedness'.[66] In omitting Camelot from the negotiating process, the Judge went so far as to accuse the Commission of behaviour 'so unfair as to amount to an abuse of power.'[67] Camelot argued in court that it had been misled by the Commission. The Company quoted a letter of 28 July 2000, in which the Commission declared that it had decided not to proceed with an enquiry re the GTech cover-up which could have resulted in the revocation of Camelot's Section 5 Licence.[68] The Company maintained that its action to remove GTech from any future involvement in the management of the Lottery would have been taken earlier if the Commission had made its position clearer.[69] Moreover, it was the judge's view that the Commission's decision had been based on the incorrect assumption that Camelot could do nothing to address its concerns over GTech.[70] The Commission had not anticipated Camelot's acquisition of GTech's operations.

The decision, although not entirely unexpected, brought the whole regulatory process centre stage and back into contention in a way which had not been seen since the time of the first Director General. The Commission had demonstrated a capacity for decisions of a maverick nature to match any of those taken during the personalized era of the Lottery's regulation. Indeed reviewing courts generally defer to the policy judgements of agency officials, provided they meet minimum standards of evidentiary support and rationale.[71] In this way the regulator as 'expert' may be said to be enshrined in historico-administrative legal precedent.

Successful judicial reviews of regulation are extremely rare. Courts tend to give regulators a large degree of latitude so that even if they disagree with what the regulator has done they are usually reluctant to interfere ... So courts have said they will interfere only if the regulator has acted with conspicuous unfairness and unreasonableness. Here they have applied that test and answered yes.[72]

The treatment of Camelot by the Commission was clearly an aberration and resurrects the issue addressed earlier of the proneness or susceptibility for decisions taken by commissions with so many competing views, to lack internal logic or consistency. The judge awarded Camelot more than £250,000 costs against the Commission,[73] and the Operator was given a further period, ending 24 October to put together a fresh bid.[74]

6.5 *Political Influence or Interference?*

The Commission's decision to exclude Camelot from the final bidding round had been found in the High Court to be tantamount to an abuse of power. Its error, it must be said, was not marginal: the decision the Commission took was inelegant, lacked intellectual rigour and was fundamentally unsound. A misjudgement of such proportions begs the question as to whether the Commission had been allowed to make its decision properly and independently, or whether it had been swayed by extra-mural influences which can be identified as political? In this connection it should be recalled that when in opposition the Labour Party championed the idea of the National Lottery being operated on a not-for-profit basis; this had been a key pledge in the Party's election manifesto. Indeed The People's Lottery had been the title of a White Paper presented by the New Labour government to Parliament in July 1997. It is also not unreasonable to remark on the close association of Sir Richard Branson and New Labour – both of whom had courted the other during Labour's time in opposition and once in power.[75]

Following the Commission's decision to allow The People's Lottery to participate in final negotiations, the Conservative Party Chairman, Michael Ancram, sought reassurances from the government's Minister for Culture, Media and Sport, Chris Smith, that he had played no part in influencing the decision.[76] Needless to say, the Secretary of State averred that the decision had been made 'entirely and solely' by the Commission.[77] This exchange can be reasonably dismissed as run-of-the-mill posturing or political point-scoring. Yet the Labour Party, both in opposition and in government, had been scathing on the subject of Camelot's level of profits and bonus payments. Having been awarded a seven-year Licence under the previous government, Camelot may have come to be seen as the

Conservative Party's Lottery Operator.[78] And having adopted a stance on the incumbent Operator which was both negative and at times highly voluble, it is not difficult to see how the rumour might emerge of members of the government having been heard muttering that they could not countenance the idea of Camelot winning a second contract.[79] While the Lottery's Commissioners are independent of government, having been selected by Ministers one might assume that their leanings and sympathies would not be entirely at odds with those who had appointed them. Perhaps, subconsciously, the Commissioners were reluctant to disappoint their principals.[80]

The mishandling of the selection process for the award of the Lottery's new Licence again raises the issue which has recurred throughout this book, of regulatory independence. The capacity for regulatory capture, although most often identified in respect of the relationship between regulator and regulatee, can also arise between regulators and other constituencies with a particular motive to alter the course of the regulatory process, to secure given outcomes. Arguably, the rôle of different groups trying to influence the course of regulation is a sign of democratic good health. In this way the politicization of regulation can be seen as a demonstration of a vigorous polity that is pluralistic and participatory. However, political involvement or influence in the narrow sense, i.e. by government, is more controversial, and can undermine the independence of regulators and so damage their credibility. With regard to the National Lottery *per se*, while capture might be too strong a term, there is certainly cause for concern that political influence, while not blatant or overt, may have been at work. In its deliberations to award the new Licence, the Regulator may have felt a silent weight of expectation to deliver an outcome that would meet with government approbation. Arguably, by making its preferences known, the government had undermined the principle of regulatory independence. Such implicit interference damages confidence in the regulatory process, will reduce the calibre of regulators and a priori the quality of the decisions made.[81] The foregoing also demonstrates that there is no guarantee that commissions are immune from the politics of regulation any more than are individual regulators.

6.6 *A Vulnerable Time*

The outcome of the judicial review threw the arrangements for the award of the new Licence into disarray. A decision which the Commission had been meant to deliver at the end of June, was now postponed until the end of November,[82] and was not eventually delivered until the middle of December. The implications of this delay would undoubtedly compromise the capacity of The People's Lottery to put into place its plans to guarantee an orderly and seemless take-up of the Lottery's operations by 1 October 2001. Even without the delay, the task for The People's Lottery would be an enormous one. Furthermore, questions had surfaced regarding the operational capabilities of The People's Lottery and of the ultimate source and integrity of the company's finances.

Firstly, to guarantee no disruption of service The People's Lottery would have to install some 35,000 terminals. A hand-over on such a scale has never been attempted anywhere in the world before;[83] indeed when Camelot launched the Lottery in 1994 there were fewer than 10,000 terminals in place and the network was augmented over time. While if Camelot were to be awarded the Licence it would also be required to replace the retail network, as the incumbent it enjoyed the not inconsiderable advantage of having run a network of similar size, with software and hardware systems that were proven and reliable. In addition, concerns were raised over the chosen suppliers of The People's Lottery, AWI, which had a patchy record with regard to commercial competency. The problems it encountered with regard to the Arizona State Lottery have already been referred to;[84] however, the Company also had damages of $600,000 laid against it in 1996, after the system it installed for the Minnesota State Lottery failed and took two years to rectify.[85] In addition AWI had to pay $1 million to the Maryland State Government because of delays caused by faulty software, and the Company was (at the end of August 2000) four months behind schedule on a contract involving the conversion of lottery terminals in Florida.[86] Additionally, The People's Lottery agreed to have the UK Lottery's terminals made and supplied by a Swiss company, Wincor Nixdorf – better known for making cash dispensers for banks.[87] Wincor Nixdorf's ability to mass-produce lottery terminals had yet to be seriously tested as its biggest order at this time had been for 1500 terminals for the Shanghai Lottery.[88] In contemplating a change in the management of the lottery, Dianne Thompson, Chief Executive designate of Camelot, inveighed

> There have been changes of operators but not systems; there have been changes of systems and computer software but not operators. Nowhere else in the world has there been a change of this magnitude, if that is what happens here in the UK.[89]

Secondly, while The People's Lottery had agreed borrowing facilities of £170 million, backed by the City bank J. P. Morgan and Lloyds TSB, the company still had to satisfy the Commission that a further £50 million was in place.[90] Concern was quite rightly raised by some commentators over Sir Richard Branson's complex web of off-shore trusts, where much of his wealth and the beneficial ownership of his far-reaching business empire is based.[91] The lack of transparency was without doubt a material issue, as absolute transparency in all aspects of the Lottery's workings is vital to help preserve the operation's propriety. Indeed this had been one of the areas of disputation between the PAC and the first Director General. The Byzantine nature of Sir Richard Branson's finances inevitably posed questions that go to the very heart of the bid from The People's Lottery and that are concerned with integrity and trust. The waters were further muddied by the publication, on 21 September, of a biography entitled *Branson* written by the investigative journalist Tom Bower, which raised further issues regarding the tycoon's business practices and the state of health of his companies' finances.[92] Most damaging of these allegations related to 1988 when Mr Branson (as he then was) attempted to return his company to the private sector and offered investors cash for their shares, valuing the Company at £248 million, at a time when he had already agreed to sell a stake in the Company, when once again privately owned, to the Japanese media company Pony Canon, which valued the group at £377 million.[93] The implication of this allegation, if true, is that Branson may have held back material information, possibly breaking the City's take-over panel code.[94] Whether or not the allegations are true, these are issues which one would expect the Commission to include in its enquiries with regard to the 'fit and proper' status of those associated with The People's Lottery.

All the above considerations served to a lesser or greater extent to surround the Lottery with an atmosphere of instability and uncertainty. The Commission's deliberations and its mishandling of the bidding process brought the Lottery's regulation into disrepute, while weakening its own credibility. The ramifications of the judicial review were that the Commission should allow Camelot to run the Lottery on an interim basis beyond 30 September, to allow the new Licensee to have a notice period of at least a year to install the new equipment.[95] However, Camelot was under no legal compunction to agree to have its Licence extended. One would rightly have to question how willing the Company would be to agree to such a temporary expedient (especially if it had not secured the new Licence). Although Camelot had agreed to cooperate in the hand-over of operations in the event of it not securing the new Licence, the Company's willingness to cooperate beyond the existing Licence (if it had not been the successful bidder) would be likely to be a function of the period of time over which the interim licence would be expected to run. The Company would in all probability be less likely to extend property leases, retain staff and extend contracts for a few months than it would for a more meaningful period of perhaps up to a year.[96]

The uncertainty was only added to at this time by speculation (including the musings of Home Secretary Jack Straw)[97] that there should either be voluntary resignations of all or some of the Commissioners, or that the

Secretary of State should intervene to alter the Commission's member-ship.[98] In rapid succession, the Commission's Chairwoman resigned to be replaced temporarily by Harriet Spicer (one of the existing Com-missioners),[99] and the Commission sacked the Treasury solicitor for hav-ing provided it with unsound advice on the decision to allow The People's Lottery to participate in exclusive negotiations.[100] In the Treasury solici-tor's place, the Commission appointed the City law firm Freshfields.[101] This step is noteworthy, as it is very unusual for a quango to dismiss its own government advisers and replace them with a private sector firm.[102] The Commission conceded that it had been at fault in the mistaken assumption that Camelot could not address expeditiously its concerns. In the Treasury solicitor's defence, it was on the basis of information pro-vided to him by the Commission that he gave his opinion. If the Commis-sion's assumption had been correct it would have been inappropriate and arguably open to challenge for both bids to have been allowed to proceed. The Commission accepted that there had been a consequential distortion of process emanating from the initial error.[103] Additionally and under pressure from Camelot the Commission issued a formal apology to the Operator declaring that it was 'sincerely sorry' for having illegally barred Camelot from further talks.[104] Finally, on 12 October, Lord Burns was appointed to the Commission, as Chairman.[105] He conceded that the Commission had made a mistake, and he also confirmed that the four other Commissioners had offered their resignations in response to the débâcle: the offers were not accepted.[106]

The successful judicial challenge by Camelot (and its insistence on a formal apology) without doubt served to humiliate the Commission and to add a fresh layer of ice to an already frosty relationship.[107] As a consequence, Camelot must have been concerned as to whether it could expect to receive full and impartial consideration from the Commission. It follows from this that if Camelot were again to be rejected it would have been likely to return to the courts, arguing that under such circumstances, the company could never have received a fair hearing.[108] If on the other hand, as transpired, the Commission accepted the revamped Camelot bid, there was a real danger that The People's Lottery could object on the grounds that it had ultimately been rejected only to save the Commission's face in the wake of the High Court's condemnation of its incompetence.[109] Either way the Commission's and more especially the Commissioner's credibility had been severely compromised. Under these circumstances Lord Burns may well have been ill advised in not accepting the offer of the Commissioner's resignations.

6.7 The Final Result

At 4 p.m. on 19 December the National Lottery Commission announced on its website and by fax to the bidders that the new Licence had been awarded to Camelot. By announcing the winner on its website, the Commissioners having already lost in court once, were in all likelihood mindful of the risks of losing further time by giving answers to press questions that could be used in evidence against them, should The People's Lottery seek a judicial review.[110] The reasons given by the Commission for its choice focused principally on the uncertainty relating to achievable sales being greater in the case of The People's Lottery when compared with Camelot, and also the greater risks in its bid having regard to costs and financial soundness.[111] The Commission was especially concerned that the 6 from 53 number format chosen by The People's Lottery for the main Draw game could lead players to defer playing the twice weekly game during weeks when there was no roll-over.[112] In other words, the Commission doubted whether the format would raise new sales rather than merely displace or defer existing sales. The Commission was also sceptical with regard to plans to introduce a large number of new games at one time, and had reservations with regard to the practicalities of the company's plans for a regional game.[113]

Most importantly, the Commission's decision related not just to the likely returns to the Good Causes included in the two bids, but also to the financial soundness of the bidders themselves. The potential bankruptcy of a licensee, leading to the cessation of the service, could be costly to the franchisor/licensor, i.e. the National Lottery Commission (and government, and ultimately the taxpayer) in terms of obtaining a replacement licensee and bridging any potential gaps in service.[114] Furthermore, any interruption in service or other disruption might be very damaging for the commercial prospects of a future franchisee/licensee.[115] While the Commission considered the annual sales projections of £7.3 billion and £7.4 billion for Camelot and The People's Lottery respectively, to be excessive, it was concerned with the financial soundness of The People's Lottery in lower revenue scenarios, and in particular when not far below the figure of £5 billion annual sales which the Commission considered (based on recent evidence) to be realistic.[116] The People's Lottery projected a contribution to Good Causes some £160 million higher than Camelot at the principal forecasts, and some £110 million more at £5 billion sales.[117] However, if sales fell only slightly below £5 billion per annum, the Commission concluded that The People's Lottery might incur losses which would not be sustainable within its proposed financial structure.[118] The Regulator also determined the projected running costs of The People's Lottery of 2.8 per cent of sales, compared with Camelot's projection of 4.2

per cent to be overly optimistic.[119] Ultimately it was perhaps the Commission's concern that the risks in the bid, particularly in the early stages were too great, and that the Company had not sufficiently recognized the resources required for the management tasks involved in start-up as well as subsequent operations.[120] This may be seen at least to some degree as a function of the company's structure as a not-for-profit entity. For without the cushion of equity risk-takers, the Company had been forced to seek extra funds to insure itself against insolvency, thereby incurring additional debt servicing costs.[121] Furthermore, because each year The People's Lottery proposed to hand over any surplus to the Distribution Fund, it would not be building a reserve to cushion it in the event of adverse trading conditions in future years.[122] These points go to the very heart of the for-profit/not-for-profit debate.

Notwithstanding the foregoing reservations *vis-à-vis* The People's Lottery bid, the decision to reject the application was not unanimous – the Commissioners voted in favour of Camelot by four to one.[123] Indeed one of the Commissioners, Hilary Blume (having voted in favour of TPL), resigned, citing the need to relaunch the Lottery to arrest declining sales, the use by Camelot of outdated technology which presented a risk later in the Licence period (a point conceded by the Commission),[124] and the overstatement of concerns having regard to the financial soundness of The People's Lottery, which she believed would be mitigated by the ancillary earnings derived from the Company's more sophisticated terminal network.[125] Ms Blume felt that the Commissioners had played it too safe;[126] and she was not alone in this view: 'For the NLC, unimaginative caution seems to have been the watchword in sticking with Camelot.'[127]

While this position certainly holds currency, the judgement is perhaps a harsh one. Clearly there were risks in The People's Lottery bid which when taken together were greater in comparison with the incumbent's bid. The Commission acknowledged that the IT systems proposed by The People's Lottery 'had considerable potential to benefit the National Lottery'.[128] Yet the reservations concerning the untried nature of its technological solutions especially having regard to scale, and referred to earlier,[129] cannot be overlooked. To have relied on notional, unspecified and untried ancillary income generated by the terminal network to compensate for financial shortcomings in its overall bid would have been imprudent. The precise nature of this income is not disclosed as the bids are not in the public domain.[130] The Commissioner's decision not to award the Licence to The People's Lottery was in the final analysis a determination based on an assessment of a combination of risks. Changing operator and Lottery systems on a scale lacking any clear precedent, together with concerns over the financial standing of The People's Lottery led the Commissioners to conclude that the overall risk was just too great.[131]

The Commissioner's decision had taken nearly six months longer than the bidding timetable had allowed. The implications of this delay were for the commencement of the new Licence period, which had been due to start on 1 October 2001, to be deferred to (at least) January 2002.[132] However, the uncertainty was to last into 2001 as The People's Lottery deferred until the new year its decision as to whether to seek a judicial review of the National Lottery Commission's decision.[133] The effect of this was in turn to delay Camelot's willingness to prepare in earnest for the new Licence, and in particular to commit itself to place orders for the new lottery terminals.[134] Matters were finally settled on 10 January 2001 when Sir Richard Branson declared that The People's Lottery would not be seeking a judicial review.[135] Sir Richard suggested that he would not be appealing against the Commission's decision as a further delay of three or four months could lead to a suspension of the Lottery and a loss of funds for Good Causes – as Camelot had not signed an interim licence.[136] However, this would have been unlikely as the Commission and Camelot had already agreed in principle to an initial four-month interim licence.[137]

CHAPTER 7

COMMENT

The bidding process re-enacted and brought into sharp relief many of the regulatory issues addressed in the course of this work. Uncertain and untried regulatory apparatus, the rôle of rules versus discretion, conflicts of interest, politicization and regulatory independence/capture were all to a lesser or greater extent brought to the fore. The National Lottery etc. Act 1993 gave little direction with regard to the management of the bidding process, and the 1998 Act did not improve matters. Indeed in resigning her post as Chairwoman of the National Lottery Commission, Dame Helena Shovelton opined to the Minister, Chris Smith, that the law on how the Commission should select an operator was too vague, for the Commission is not strictly required to even stage an open competition, nor is it prevented from only allowing one applicant to bid.[1] It was this lack of clear direction and unequivocal guidelines that led the Treasury solicitor to believe (incorrectly as events turned out) that the Commission was legally competent to hold exclusive talks with The People's Lottery, before awarding the Licence.[2]

> Contestants parade their attributes before a panel of well meaning, intelligent people, and these people really have no basis on which to make comparisons, they have no specific methodology by which to make choices between the alternatives they are offered, so they make choices on the basis of other criteria which they can understand.[3]

This tension between the need for objective standards and the importance of subjective judgements is an ongoing and long-standing problem that exercises most, if not all regulatory schemes. In respect of the National Lottery *per se*, the need for a clearer scheme of delegation and regulation especially with regard to the bidding process is something that the Minister for Culture Media and Sport accepted should be in place in the future.[4] With regard to the selection of the new Licensee, the absence of clear rules forced the regulatory agency to operate on a discretionary basis in areas which proved contentious, and where it was least appropriate. Additionally, and taking up a theme explored earlier, the Culture, Media and Sport Committee were of the opinion that 'the Commission's functions of regulation and selection may not necessarily be best performed by the same people'.[5]

As well as the need to review the legislation, there are two other areas of note that were highlighted during the bidding process. Firstly, the issue of 'incumbent advantage' was undoubtedly raised and is likely to be at the forefront of the government's thinking in any review of the legislation which may take place in the future.[6] The classic disadvantage of long-term contracts like that for the National Lottery is that incumbents become difficult to remove, new entrants having to make a particularly powerful case are discouraged and licensing turns into little more than a scheme of regulation.[7] A fortiori when the initial-entry investment is substantial and not readily saleable[8] as also applies in the case of the National Lottery. The foregoing is confirmed by the fact of there being only two bidders for the new Licence. However, this is also a function of the esoteric nature of the industry concerned, as there are only two companies worldwide who can provide the requisite software for computer systems, viz. GTech and AWI.[9] It has also been estimated that the failed bid of The People's Lottery cost between £25 million[10] and £40 million – £3 million of which is believed to have come from Sir Richard Branson's personal fortune.[11] The Culture, Media and Sport Committee in reporting on the Lottery's operation recommended that legislative action is taken if the project is not to become a perpetual private monopoly for the Licensee.[12]

One way around this problem of prohibitive investment costs, and referred to at the beginning of this book, would be to award a National Lottery operating franchise (or franchises), with the state or government agency retaining ownership of the capital assets (i.e. terminal network).[13] Under such an arrangement, responsibility for maintenance and investment in infrastructure would remain with the franchisor or some other appointed government body.[14] By disassociating the franchisee(s) from the investment risk of sunk costs of plant and equipment, entry and exit costs can in turn be kept to a minimum. Furthermore, by divorcing ownership from control, franchise or licensing auctions could thus be held without large entry costs (and perhaps more frequently than once every seven years), thereby encouraging a higher number of bids.[15] This arrangement has been tried (although not without its own problems) in the rail industry, with the separation of ownership of the rail network by Railtrack from the individual operating companies. A scheme with comparable goals with regard to water delivery was also explored by a number of the large UK utilities during 2000 and 2001, although as yet the schemes have not been approved or adopted.

A National Lottery operating franchise or licence or indeed licences may, by removing prohibitive entry costs, encourage a greater level of competition at the bidding stage and thereby help eliminate incumbent advantage. However, operating franchises create their own problems. Who and what sort of body should the franchisor or licensor be? Should it be a state agency and/or an intermediary body situated between the regulator and licensee – with the regulator acting as arbiter? The relationship between the 'natural monopoly' entity owning the equipment and the entity or entities running Lottery operations is certainly likely to be one which has the capacity to be as adversarial as it is cooperative. Such a relationship raises fundamental questions regarding monitoring and control. If a licensee owns the assets then it has an incentive to look after them.[16] If not, then it has no built-in incentive not to run down the rented assets without proper maintenance.[17] Clearly there is ample room for conflict between the body owning the equipment and the operating body or bodies. Furthermore, the licensor, i.e. the plant-owning entity has its own internal conflicts as principal of the operating company or companies, and as agent of the government. The conflict is whether to invest in the infrastructure with a view to improving service to the public, or to resist spending and endeavour to obtain an improved performance from the operator(s).[18] Such a system provides both franchisor/licensor and the operating company, with opportunities to game the system. Opportunism on the part of the franchisor/licensor could lead to franchisees/licensees reducing their bids.[19] Alternatively the operator (or operators) with little incentive to care for the assets, may become a free rider, and may be tempted to claim that the facilities are inadequate to provide the quality of service required.[20]

Switching to a new scheme of regulation to encourage greater efficiencies and/or a greater number of bids clearly carries its own risks. Moreover, while only two bidders emerged to compete for the new Licence is there any evidence to suggest that the result was less than optimal? Already the most efficient lottery in the world in terms of contribution (to Good Causes and the Treasury), any improvement at all in that area would arguably represent a successful outcome of the bidding process. In this way The People's Lottery bid may be said to have done much good. For

> Camelot will render more to charity [the Good Causes] than it would have done without [the] rival bid; it has been forced to justify every aspect of management and shed its worst aspects. The Lottery may look more than ever like a natural monopoly. But Sir Richard [Branson] has aerated it with the breath of competition.'[21]

Certainly controls will be tighter (including internal controls)[22] and the profit or 'rent' Camelot can expect to extract from the Licence over the next seven years will be lower and harder won than during the first period. Indeed, under the heading of 'secondary contributions' Camelot is committed to paying over to the Good Causes half of all profits in excess of those included in its principal forecasts.[23] However in terms of the contribution to Good Causes it is the volume of sales generated which will be the arbiter of the Lottery's success. Although not conceded by the Commission,[24] this is an area in which The People's Lottery's bid may have carried some benefits, as Camelot has struggled to maintain sales since its peak performance in the year to March 1998.[25] Both The People's Lottery and Camelot pledged in the region of £15 billion to the Good Causes over the next Licence – a figure over £4 billion higher than is likely to be achieved during the first licensing period. The Commission did not find this aspect of either bid to be plausible. With ongoing liberalizing and derestricting measures being introduced in to the gambling industry,[26] the target of £15 billion would indeed appear to be very challenging. If the Government were to adopt futher measures to free up the industry, as recommended by the Budd Report, including side-betting on the National Lottery[27] then the target of £15 billion would be even less feasible. There is clear evidence of deliberate 'overbidding' here, as the winner knows it cannot be held to account afterwards. For the amount pledged to Good Causes is not a commitment, it is a target and as such the Operator is not contractually bound in any way to the figure included in its bid. This tendency to overbid will also be likely to apply where a highly competitive pre-contract situation is turned into one of limited, if any, competition thereafter.[28] Indeed Lord Burns has alluded to the need to find a way of injecting more competition into the Lottery not just during the bidding phase to award the licence, but during the Licence period itself.[29] This would almost certainly involve the introduction of new legislation. While addressing this problem for the next Licence (from 2009) would not necessarily eliminate 'incumbent advantage' it would result in more measured and deliverable pledges from bidders as well as bids which are more easily compared. However, finding a mechanism or formula to hold a successful bidder to account *ex post* is a challenging task. An auction process (similar to that used in 2000 to award frequencies to mobile telephone operators) where the operator(s) guarantees a return to Good Causes might be one option.[30] Under such a system, however, Operators would probably require a greater share of revenue to compensate them for carrying the risk of sales shortfalls.[31] But an auction mechanism carries the potential to offer more certain, if lower, returns than the current system.[32] It remains to be seen whether a fair and practicable method can be found for introducing greater levels of competition during the Licence term. One option the government is likely to explore in anticipation of the expiry of the second Licence term,[33] is to consider placing the Lottery in the state sector as obtains in most US lotteries,[34] and to hire a variety of contractors to provide different services including marketing, advertising, game design, as well as the design and delivery of both hardware (terminal network) and software solutions. Such contracts could be reviewed on a more frequent basis than once every seven years. Another, and perhaps more likely possibility, as outlined above, would be to place the assets and terminal infrastructure in the public sector, or some other model such as a not-for-profit company, with the private sector competing on a more ongoing basis to provide the outsourced work – including game design and delivery.[35]

The final area for comment relates to politics and accountability. Indeed the politicization of regulation has been a recurrent theme throughout this book. All institutions are imperfect, yet a particular and inherent weakness of regulation is its inescapable involvement with the political process.[36] While it is generally accepted as being desirable for the regulator to be as far as possible disinterested, and above the political fray, if there is a divergence of objectives between principal and agent, this divergence will remain whatever structures or mechanisms of regulation are put in place.[37] Without doubt there was dissonance between the Commission's statutory mandate to deliver its triumverate of objectives (player protection, propriety, maximize the proceeds to the Good Causes) and the government's election pledge of finding a not-for-profit entity as the preferred solution for the Lottery's operation. This divergence of interest served to politicize the bidding process and to some extent compromise or at least bring into question the National Lottery Comission's independence. This influence, whether advertent or inadvertent and while difficult to quantify, should not be overlooked.

In an ideal world the political process should generate precise, clear-cut objectives to allow the managerial accountability of the regulator to be a neutral exercise in the application of value-free techniques.[38] However, in many cases the institutional and organizational links between political and managerial accountability are ineffective, do not properly mesh and become blurred – leading to objectives and criteria being generated at all levels in the hierarchy.[39] This can and often does lead to conflicts of interest and does not make for good regulation. The problem for the regulator is arguably made more difficult still if this tendency is implicit, rather than enshrined overtly in, by way of example, a flawed ministerial directive or new legislation, which is in some way equivocal. Here at least the regulator can point to the defect in defence of its position. While always susceptible to criticism for mishandling its statutory brief, the regulator is also vulnerable (perhaps more so) to criticism if it allows some unlisted criterion to have an evident influence upon its conclusions.[40] Indeed to give up on a course of conduct that one thinks is right in favour of another course simply because the latter reflects the will of those to whom one is accountable is to act irresponsibly.[41] It is not an uncommon problem for professionals in bureaucracies to be concerned that they will be obliged to act against their consciences (or better judgement) in order to deliver the bureaucratic (or ideological) imperatives of their hierarchal superiors.[42]

It is not possible to assess, with any precision, the degree to which the flaws in the process to award the second National Lottery main Licence were the result of incompetence, vague and imprecise statutory criteria, political interference or a sympathy among the Commissioners (themselves political appointees) with the Government's stated policy preference. The Culture, Media, and Sport Committee investigating the Lottery's regulation concluded that prior to the appointment of Lord Burns, the Commission lacked the requisite skills or expertise; and that this shortcoming which was ultimately a failing of the Secretary of State, proved instrumental in the problems that arose during the selection process.[43] After the finalization of the bidding process, however, one must question the willingness of the Commission's newly appointed chairman to raise doubts very publicly about several aspects of the Lottery's regulatory regime. At one level this openness is refreshing, at another, it raises the hoary issue of whether by criticizing in public the Lottery's regulation, the Regulator encroaches on the domain of the politician, and thereby undermines his/its own political independence. Clearly Lord Burns does not regard himself or his rôle *qua* Chairman of the Lottery Commission as being that of merely a 'Creature of Statute'. Admitting to a lack of confidence in the Lottery's regulatory architecture may prepare the way for change, but it can also serve to undermine and destabilize and further discredit the existing regime at a particularly vulnerable time (i.e. following the flawed bidding process). There is a powerful argument which says that any misgivings the Chairman of the Commission may have are best discussed with his fellow Commissioners and Ministers in private. Overall, however, and most especially during the bidding process, the Commission's conduct whatever its reasons or motives demonstrates that just as the consumer needs protection from the abuse of monopoly power, so too does industry, from the abuses of the regulator, in its capacity as a monopolist in the supply of regulation.[44] In the case of the National Lottery this protection was provided by the Courts. More isolated from political control or interference than any agency, it was the judiciary that was to play a pivotal rôle in ensuring that the bidding process for all its procedural faults was at least, in the end, fair and even-handed.

Privatization and the creation of regulatory agencies has been part of a wider process of institutional reform in the UK which has raised important questions about the effectiveness of constitutional structures for delivering the accountability of public agencies.[45] Criticism though should perhaps be more appropriately addressed to the politicians who devised the framework, rather than the regulators who struggle to operate within it.[46] For while responsibility comes from within an agency, accountability comes from without; and should be placed on the shoulders of the principal.[47] With regard to the National Lottery *per se*, the Regulator, during the era of both the Director Generals and the Commission suffered not only from a legislative framework that was incomplete but also, with the change in government, from an unstable policy framework. In modern complex societies it remains a central question as to whether the linkages are in place between action and explanation.[48] This impinges critically on the issue of ultimate accountability. In the case of the National Lottery these linkages have not been clearly established. It is to be welcomed that the Culture, Media and Sport Committee has recommended that unless in the case of any particular issue, the interests of public disclosure are outweighed by the need for commercial confidentiality, the National Lottery Commission should hold its formal meetings in public.[49] In reviewing the workings of the political economy and the rôle of regulation in serving the public interest the experience of the Lottery has posed difficult and uncomfortable questions having regard to the adequacy of the structures of our democracy. These questions are concerned most pertinently with the need for greater openness, accountability and transparency in the public life of the nation and its institutions.

NOTES

Chapter 1

1. Peter M. Jackson and Catherine M. Price 'Privatisation and regulation: a review of the issues', in Peter M. Jackson and Catherine M. Price (eds), *Privatisation and Regulation: A Review of the Issues* (Longman, Harlow, 1994), p. 1.
2. Cosmo Graham, *Is There a Crisis in Regulatory Accountability? Discussion Paper 13* (Centre for the Study of Regulated Industries, London, 1995), p. 50.
3. *Idem.*
4. *Idem.*
5. James McCormick and Elizabeth Kendall, *A Flutter on the Future? Why the National Lottery Needs Citizens' Juries* (Institute for Public Policy Research, London, November 1995), p. 1. The Lottery is more properly described as a near-monopoly. The reason for this is explained fully on pages 18, 69 and 72.
6. Home Office, *A National Lottery Raising Money for Good Causes CM 1861* (HMSO, London, March 1992), p. 2, para. 9. Although the sale of foreign lottery products in the UK is illegal, 2.6 million illegal foreign lottery direct-mail offers were seized by Customs and Excise in the first five months of 1990 alone. '2.6 million lottery offers seized', *Daily Telegraph* (09/06/90).
7. Home Office, *A National Lottery*, p. 2, para. 10.
8. Jackson and Price, 'Privatisation and regulation', p. 4.
9. This has not meant state lotteries are immune from corruption and misconduct. In America, for example, allegations of malfeasance of varying degrees of seriousness have been associated with the lotteries of New York, New Jersey, the District of Columbia and Pennsylvania. See Vicki Abt, James F. Smith and Eugene Martin Christiansen, *The Business of Risk: Commercial Gambling in Mainstream America* (University of Kansas Press, Lawrence, 1985), p. 212, and Charles T. Clotfelter and Philip J. Cook, *Selling Hope: State Lotteries in America* (Harvard University Press, Cambridge, MA, 1989), pp. 170–1.
10. *La Fleur's 1999 World Lottery Almanac* (TLF Publications Inc., Boyds, MD, 7th edn, 1999), p. 8.
11. *Ibid.*, p. 9.
12. Graeme Evans and Judy White, *The Economic and Social Impact of the National Lottery* (University of North London Press, Centre for Leisure and Tourism Studies, London, 1996), p. 6. Some American states club together in order to generate greater sales and greater jackpots, which in turn helps to increase sales further. See Andrew Douglas, *British Charitable Gambling 1956–1994* (The Athlone Press, London, 1995), p. 123, and *1999 Almanac*, p. 6.

13. Commission of the European Communities, *Gambling in the Single Market: A Study of the Current Legal and Market Situation vol. I* (Office for Official Publications of the European Communities, Luxembourg, 1991), p. 47 sect. 3.2.3, and *1999 Almanac*, p. 9.

14. Commission of European Communities, *Gambling in the Single Market*, p. 47, sect. 3.2.3.

15. National Gambling Impact Study Commission, *Final Report* (National Gambling Impact Study Commission, Washington, DC, June 1999) pp. 1–4.

16. Clotfelter and Cook, *Selling Hope*, p. 160.

17. David Miers, 'Regulation and the public interest: commercial gambling and the National Lottery' *Modern Law Review*, vol. 59, no. 4 (July 1996) p. 492.

18. *La Fleur's 1996 World Lottery Almanac* (TLF Publications Inc., Boyds, MD, 1996), p. 79.

19. *1999 Almanac*, pp. 91 and 95.

20. *Ibid.*, p. 9.

21. Melissa Simard (Public Relations Account Co-ordinator to Connecticut Lottery), telephone interview (27/04/98).

22. *1996 Almanac*, p. 151, and *1999 Almanac*, p. 167.

23. National Gambling Impact Study Commission, *Final Report*, pp. 3–4.

24. *Idem.*

25. John Kay and John Vickers, 'Regulatory reform: an appraisal', in Giandomenico Majone (ed.), *Deregulation or Re-regulation? Regulatory Reform in Europe and the United States* (Pinter, London, 1990) p. 224.

26. See pages 18, 69 and 72.

27. Kay and Vickers, 'Regulatory reform', p. 225.

28. Clair Wilcox, *Public Policies Toward Business* (Richard D. Irwin Inc., Homewood, IL, 1966), p. 476.

29. *Idem.*

30. Alfred E. Kahn, *The Economics of Regulation: Principles and Institutions*, vol. 2 (John Wiley, New York, 1970), p. 178.

31. Catherine Price, 'Economic regulation of privatised monopolies', in Jackson and Price (eds), *Privatisation and Regulation*, p. 78.

32. *Idem.*

33. See S. B. Caudill, S. K. Johnson and F. G. Mixon, 'Economies of scale in state lotteries: an update and statistical test', *Applied Economics Letters*, vol. 2, no. 4 (1995), pp. 115–17.

34. National Lottery etc. Act 1993, Part I, Section 4 (2).

35. Larry de Boer, 'Jackpot size and Lotto sales: evidence from Ohio 1986–1987', *Journal of Gambling Studies*, vol. 6, no. 4 (winter 1990), pp. 345–54.

36. Clotfelter and Cook, *Selling Hope*, p. 247.

37. Anthony I. Ogus, *Regulation: Legal Form and Economic Theory* (Clarendon Press, Oxford, 1994), p. 319.

38. *Idem.*

39. Cento Veljanovski, *The Future of Industry Regulation in the U.K.: A Report of Independent Inquiry* (European Policy Forum for British and European Market Studies, London, January 1993), p. 60.

40. David Souter, 'A stakeholder approach to regulation', in Dan Corry, David Souter and Michael Waterson, *Regulating Our Utilities* (Institute for Public Policy Research, London, 1991), p. 12.

41. Eamonn Butler, 'But who will regulate the regulators?', in Adam Smith Institute, *But Who Will Regulate the Regulators?* (Adam Smith Institute, London, 1993), p. 3.

42. Veljanovski, *Industry Regulation in the U.K.*, p. 60.

43. Souter, 'Stakeholder approach', p. 80.

44. *Ibid.*, p. 12.

45. *Ibid.*, p. 80.

46. *Ibid.*, p. 67.

47. National Lottery Act 1998, Part I, Section 1 and Part II, Schedule 2 (l).

48. Office of the National Lottery (Oflot) *The Director General of the National Lottery: Background Note* (Oflot, London, n.d.).

49. James Keulemans (Oflot Public Affairs representative), telephone interview (05/03/99).

50. Oflot, *Director General of the Lottery: Background Note.*

51. Carol Midgely, 'How life turned too exciting for dull accountant', *The Times* (02/04/98).

52. Chris Blackhurst, 'Man who has pride in being boring', *Independent* (13/12/95).

53. Philip Webster and Joanne Bale, 'Peter Davis sacked as Lottery chief', *The Times* (04/02/98).

54. Michael E. Levine and Jennifer L. Forrence, 'Regulatory capture, public interest and the public agenda: toward a synthesis', *Journal of Law, Economics and Organisation* (special issue) (1990), p. 168.

55. *Idem.*

56. Ben W. Lewis, 'Emphasis and misemphasis in regulatory policy', in William G. Shephard and Thomas G. Gies (eds), *Utility Regulation: New Directions in Theory and Practice* (Random House, New York, 1996), p. 245.

57. Marver H. Bernstein, 'The regulatory process: a framework for analysis', *Law and Contemporary Problems*, vol 6 (1961), pp. 329 and 332.

58. Eugene Bardach and Robert A. Kagan, 'Conclusion: responsibility and accountability', in Eugene Bardach and Robert A. Kagan (eds), *Social Regulation: Strategies for Reform* (Institute for Contemporary Studies, San Francisco, 1982), p. 356.

59. Charles F. Phillips Jr, *The Economics of Regulation: Theory and Practice in the Transportation and Public Utility Industries* (Richard D. Irwin, Homewood, IL, 1969), p. 710.

60. Graham, *Is There a Crisis?*, p. 49.

61. Ogus, *Regulation*, p. 111.

62. *Idem.*

63. Alan Peacock and Ian Orton, 'The bargaining process as a means of implementing and enforcing regulations in the United Kingdom', in Alan Peacock (ed.), *The Regulation Game* (Blackwell, Oxford, 1984), p. 96.

64. National Lottery etc. Act 1993, *passim.*

65. Ogus, *Regulation*, p. 105.

66. Peter Davis (Director General of the National Lottery), *Minutes of Evidence Taken Before the Committee of Public Accounts* (13/11/96). *Payments to the National Lottery Distribution Fund. Twentieth Report. H.C. 99, Session 1996–97* (The Stationery Office, London, 17/03/97), p. 10, para. 94.

67. National Lottery etc. Act 1993, Part I, Sections 5–7.

68. *Ibid.*, Section 8.
69. *Ibid.*, Section 9.
70. *Ibid.*, Section 11.
71. Ogus, *Regulation*, p. 112.
72. *Idem.*
73. *Ibid.*, pp. 105–6.
74. Eugene Bardach and Robert A. Kagan, *Going by the Book: The Problem of Regulatory Unreasonableness* (Temple University Press, Philadelphia, 1982), pp. 152–3.
75. Graham K. Wilson, 'Social regulation and explanations of regulatory failure', *Political Studies*, vol. 32 (1984), p. 218.
76. Bardach and Kagan, *Going by the Book*, p. 134.
77. Bruce M. Owen and Ronald Braeutigam, *The Regulation Game* (Billinger, Cambridge, MA, 1978), pp. 16–17, and Robert H. Miles and Arvind Bhambri, *The Regulatory Executives* (Sage, Thousand Oaks, CA, 1983), pp. 9–10.
78. Bardach and Kagan, *Going by the Book*, p. 153.
79. Robert Sheldon (Chairman) *Minutes of Evidence, Twentieth Report*, p. 4, para. 34.
80. Alan Williams, *Minutes of Evidence, Twentieth Report*, p. 8, para. 82.
81. 'The National Lottery – an easy going lot', *The Economist*, vol. 340, no. 7981, (31/08/96), p. 29.
82. Williams, *Minutes of Evidence*, p. 9, para. 85.
83. 'The jury's verdict damned the lottery regulator too', *Independent* (03/02/98).
84. Roger Lowe, Keith Harper and Celia Watson, 'Labour hits the profiteers for six', *Guardian* (07/06/97).
85. *Idem.*
86. Roger G. Noll, 'Government regulatory behaviour: a multi-disciplinary survey and synthesis', in Roger G. Noll (ed.), *Regulatory Policy and the Social Sciences* (University of California Press, Los Angeles and Berkeley, 1985), p. 41.
87. Phillips Jr, *Economics of Regulation*, p. 692.
88. David Currie, 'Regulating utilities – the Labour view', in M. E. Beesley (ed.), *Regulating Utilities: Broadening the Debate Readings 46* (Institute of Economic Affairs, London, 1997), p. 21.
89. Progress in the Next Steps initiative, *The Government's Reply to the Eighth Report from the Treasury and Civil Service Committee, CM 1263, Session 1989–90* (HMSO, London, October 1990), cited by Philip Giddings, 'The Treasury Committee and the Next Steps agencies', in Philip Giddings (ed.), *Parliamentary Accountability* (Macmillan, London, 1995), p. 65.
90. *Idem.*
91. Phillips Jr, *Economics of Regulation*, p. 693.
92. Noll, 'Government regulatory behaviour', p. 41.
93. Marver H. Bernstein, *Regulating Business by Independent Commission* (Princeton University Press, Princeton, NJ, 1995), p. 149.
94. Bardach and Kagan, *Going by the Book*, p. 320.
95. Miles and Bhambri, *Regulatory Executives*, p. 17.
96. Ogus, *Regulation*, p. 90.
97. Jean-Jacques Laffont and Jean Tirole, *A Theory of Incentives in Procurement and Regulation* (MIT Press, Cambridge, MA, and London, 1993), p. 475.

98. *Idem.*

99. Barry M. Mitnick, *The Political Economy of Regulation* (Columbia University Press, New York, 1980), p. 242.

100. E. Pendleton Herring, *Public Administration and the Public Interest* (McGraw-Hill, New York and London, 1936), p. 68.

101. An Advisory Group Report, *The National Lottery Initiatives and Recommendations* (Labour Party, London, 1996), *passim*, and *Labour Party Manifesto* (April 1997), p. 31.

102. C. D. Foster, *Privatization, Public Ownership and the Regulation of Natural Monopoly* (Blackwell, Oxford and Cambridge, MA, 1992), p. 414.

103. Noll, 'Government regulatory behaviour', p. 41.

104. Graham, *Is There a Crisis?*, p. 7.

105. Foster, *Privatization.*

106. *Idem.*

Chapter 2

1. National Lottery etc. Act 1993, Part I, Section 4.

2. *Ibid.*, Sections 5–10.

3. *Ibid.*, Section 11.

4. *Ibid.*, Section 12.

5. *Ibid.*, Part II, Sections 22–3.

6. Report of the Comptroller and Auditor General, *Evaluating the Applications to Run the National Lottery H.C. 569 Session 1994–95* (National Audit Office, HMSO, London, 07/07/95), p. 1, para. 3.

7. C. D. Foster, *Privatization, Public Ownership and the Regulation of Natural Monopoly* (Blackwell, Oxford and Cambridge, MA, 1992), p. 186.

8. Director General of the National Lottery, *Annual Report 1994/95* (HMSO, London, 16/10/95), p. 5.

9. National Lottery etc. Act 1993, Part I, Section 4.

10. Charles F. Phillips Jr, *The Economics of Regulation, Theory and Practice in the Transportation and Public Utilities Industries* (Richard D. Irwin, Homewood, IL, 1969), p. 710.

11. Consumers' Association 'The National Lottery – who wins who loses?', *Which?* (Consumers' Association, January 1997), p. 7.

12. David Miers, 'Regulation and the public interest: commercial gambling and the National Lottery', *Modern Law Review*, vol. 59, no. 4 (July 1996), p. 516.

13. Luke FitzHerbert and Lucy Rhoades (eds), *The National Lottery Yearbook 1997 Edition* (Directory of Social Change, London, 1997), p. 22.

14. Michael E. Levine and Jennifer L. Forrence, 'Regulatory capture, public interest and the public agenda: toward a synthesis', *Journal of Law, Economics and Organisation* (special issue) (1990), p. 168.

15. Consumers' Association, 'National Lottery', p. 8, and Fitzherbert and Rhoades, *National Lottery Yearbook*, p. 22.

16. See Director General of the National Lottery, *Annual Report 1995/96* (Oflot, London, 17/07/96), p. 9.

17. Consumers' Association, 'National Lottery', p. 8, and FitzHerbert and Rhoades, *National Lottery Yearbook*, p. 22.
18. Cento G. Veljanovski, 'The economics of regulatory enforcement', in Keith Hawkins and John M. Thomas (eds), *Enforcing Regulation* (Kluwer-Nijhoff, Boston, 1984), p. 174.
19. Anthony I. Ogus, *Regulation: Legal Form and Economic Theory* (Clarendon Press, Oxford, 1994), p. 90.
20. Rupert Brooke (Secretary of State for National Heritage), *Minutes of Evidence National Lottery etc., Bill 389-i, Session 1992–93* (HMSO, London, 13/01/93), p. 2, para. 1, and National Lottery etc. Act 1993, Part I, Section 22.
21. Ogus, *Regulation*, p. 92.
22. Director General of the National Lottery *Annual Report 1996/97* (The Stationery Office, London, 26/06/97), p. 15.
23. Foster, *Privatization*, p. 186.
24. *Idem*.
25. Graham, *Is There a Crisis?*, p. 8.
26. Cento Veljanovski, *The Future of Industry Regulation in the U.K.: A Report of Independent Inquiry* (European Policy Forum for British and European Market Studies, London, January 1993), p. 60.
27. Irwin M. Stelzer, 'Lessons for the UK regulation from recent US experience', in M. E. Beesley (ed.), *Regulating Utilities: A Time for Change? Readings 44* (Institute of Economic Affairs, London, 1996), p. 196.
28. Marver H. Bernstein, *Regulating Business by Independent Commission* (Princeton University Press, Princeton, NJ, 1995), p. 149.
29. E. Pendleton Herring, *Public Administration and the Public Interest* (McGraw-Hill, New York and London, 1936), p. 116.
30. *Idem*.
31. Director General of the Lottery, *Annual Report 1995/96*, p. 9.
32. An Advisory Group Report, *The National Lottery Initiatives and Recommendations* (Labour Party, London, 1996), p. 6.
33. John Kay and John Vickers, 'Regulatory reform: an appraisal', in Giandomenico Majone (ed.), *Deregulation or Re-regulation? Regulatory Reform in Europe and the United States* (Pinter, London, 1990), p. 233.
34. Peter M. Jackson and Catherine M. Price, 'Privatisation and regulation: a review of the issues', in Peter M. Jackson and Catherine M. Price (eds), *Privatisation and Regulation: A Review of the Issues* (Longman, Harlow, 1994), p. 12.
35. National Heritage Committee, *Minutes of Evidence. The National Lottery H.C. 240–I Session 1995–96* (HMSO, London, 20/02/96), p. 2, para. 9.
36. James McCormick and Elizabeth Kendall, *A Flutter on the Future? Why the National Lottery Needs Citizens' Juries* (Institute for Public Policy Research, London, November 1995), p. 5.
37. Camelot, *Annual Report and Accounts 1999* (Camelot Group plc, Watford, 1999), p. 2.
38. Comptroller and Auditor General, *Evaluating the Applications*, p. 6, fig. 2, p. 4, para. 1.6.
39. *Ibid.*, p. 9, paras 2.1–2.2.
40. Kay and Vickers, 'Regulatory reform', p. 233.
41. National Lottery etc. Act 1993, Part I, Section 5 (4).

42. Director General of the Lottery, *Annual Report 1994/95*, p. 18, para. 2.26.
43. *Ibid.*, p. 18, para. 2.27.
44. Comptroller and Auditor General, *Evaluating the Applications*, p. 1, para. 3.
45. It is arguable that any heading dealing with 'player protection' automatically addresses the issue of 'propriety'. If the players are not adequately protected the propriety of the Lottery is inevitably brought into question.
46. Comptroller and Auditor General, *Evaluating the Applications*, p. 35, para. 4.5.
47. Peter Davis (Director General of the National Lottery), *Minutes of Evidence Taken Before the Committee of Public Accounts on 13/11/96 Payments to the National Lottery Distribution Fund Twentieth Report H.C. 99 Session 1996–97* (The Stationery Office, London, 17/03/97), p. 5, para. 39.
48. Peter Davis (Director General of the National Lottery), *Minutes of Evidence Evaluating the Applications to Run the National Lottery and the Director General's Travel and Hospitality Arrangements Taken Before the Committee of Public Accounts on 11/12/95. Forty-First Report* (HMSO, London, 15/07/96), p. 16, para. 166. The Director General somewhat contradicted himself on this point elsewhere in the minutes. Davis, *ibid.*, p. 26, para. 293, and p. 27, para. 307.
49. Director General of the Lottery, *Annual Report 1994/95*, p. 14, para. 2.4.
50. Comptroller and Auditor General, *Evaluating the Applications*, p. 27, para. 3.18.
51. *Idem.*
52. Director General of the Lottery, *Annual Report 1994/95*, p. 14, para. 2.5.
53. Davis, *Minutes of Evidence Forty-First Report*, p. 2, para. 12.
54. Director General of the Lottery, *Annual Report 1994/95*, p. 15, para. 2.5.
55. *Idem.*
56. Comptroller and Auditor General, *Evaluating the Applications*, pp. 50–1, app. I.
57. *Ibid.*, p. 51.
58. Andrew Alderson, 'Will this man's numbers finally come up?', *Sunday Telegraph* (20/02/00).
59. Director General of the Lottery, *Annual Report 1995/96*, p. 39.
60. National Lottery etc. Act 1993, Schedule 2–1 (4).
61. 'Unsackable should not mean unaccountable', *Independent* (21/12/95).
62. *Licence to Run the National Lottery under Section 5 of the National Lottery etc. Act 1993* (Oflot, London, July 1994).
63. National Lottery etc. Act 1993, Part II, Section 21 (1).
64. *Ibid.*, Sections 22 and 23.
65. *National Lottery Act 1998*, Part I, Section 7. See also page 64.

Chapter 3

1. Report of the Comptroller and Auditor General, *Payments to the National Lottery Distribution Fund H.C. 678 Session 1995–96* (National Audit Office, HMSO, London, 23/07/96), p. 5, para. 13.
2. Director General of the National Lottery, *Annual Report 1993/94* (HMSO, London, 01/11/94), p. 20, app. A.
3. Director General of the National Lottery, *Annual Report 1996/97* (The Stationery Office, London, 26/06/97), p. 12.
4. *Ibid.*, pp. 12–13.
5. *Ibid.*, p. 13. In the following 12 months 37 individuals and 6 companies were

vetted for the first time, and re-vetting was carried out on 141 individuals and 2 companies. Director General of the National Lottery, *Annual Report 1997/98* (Stationery Office, London, 09/07/98), p. 5.

6. *Licence to Run the Lottery under Section 5 of the National Lottery etc. Act 1993* (Oflot, London, July 1994), condition 17.

7. Director General of the National Lottery, *Annual Report 1994/95* (HMSO, London, 16/10/95), p. 11.

8. Director General of the National Lottery, *Annual Report 1995/96* (Oflot, London, 17/07/96), p. 29.

9. *Idem* and Director General of the Lottery, *Annual Report 1994/95*, p. 21.

10. Camelot, *Annual Report and Accounts 1999* (Camelot Group plc, Watford, 1999), p. 18.

11. Director General of the Lottery, *Annual Report 1994/95*, p. 22.

12. *Idem.*

13. *Idem.*

14. National Lottery Commission, *Annual Report 1998/99* (The Stationery Office, London, 20/07/99), p. 6.

15. Director General of the Lottery, *Annual Report 1995/96*, p. 25, and *Annual Report 1996/97*, p. 12.

16. *Idem* and the Director General of the Lottery, *Annual Report 1994/95*, p. 17.

17. David Miers, 'Regulation and the public interest: commercial gambling and the National Lottery, Modern Law Review, vol. 59, no. 4 (July 1996), p. 512; see also National Lottery etc. Act 1993, Part I, Sections 6 and 7.

18. Committee of Public Accounts, *Payments to the National Lottery Distribution Fund, Twentieth Report* (The Stationery Office, London, 17/03/97), p. x, para. 10. This criticism would seem to carry some weight as in April 2000 it was discovered that between November 1994 and July 1998, due to computer error, certain payments (below £50,000) on the Draw game made to winners were lower than they should have been. Sophie Goodchild, 'Lottery glitch leaves winners out of pocket', *Independent on Sunday* (21/05/00).

19. Committee of Public Accounts, *Payments to the Distribution Fund, Twentieth Report*, p. x, para. 11.

20. *Ibid.*, p. ix, para. 7.

21. Director General of the Lottery, *Annual Report 1994/95*, p. 12, para. 1.14.

22. Camelot, *Annual Report and Accounts 1997* (Camelot Group plc, Watford, 1997), p. 16.

23. Director General of the Lottery, *Annual Report 1995/96*, p. 19.

24. *Idem.*

25. In the year to 31 March 1996, for example, there were 4700 security 'incidents' including 1400 relating to the theft of Instants tickets. Peter Davis (Director General of the National Lottery), *Minutes of Evidence Taken Before the Committee of Public Accounts on 13/11/96. Twentieth Report, H.C. 99, Session 1996–97* (The Stationery Office, London, 17/03/97), p. 11, para. 96.

26. *Directions to the Director General of the National Lottery under Section 11 of the National Lottery etc. Act 1993*, Section 2 (1) (b), cited in Director General of the Lottery, *Annual Report 1994/95*, p. 34, app. C.

27. Benedict Brogan, 'Lottery bosses told to beware crooked traders', *Daily Mail* (30/08/96).

28. *Idem.*

29. *Idem.*
30. Nick Pryer, 'Big Lottery fiddle probe', *Evening Standard* (25/04/95).
31. *Idem.*
32. Peter Davis (Director General of the National Lottery), *Minutes of Evidence Evaluating the Applications to Run the National Lottery and the Director General's Travel and Hospitality Arrangements Taken Before the Committee of Public Accounts on 11/12/95. Forty-First Report* (HMSO, London, 15/07/96), p. 22, para. 246. Camelot was unwilling to provide more recent information on retailer contract termination. Gail Farley (Camelot Lottery Line Team Manager, Player Services Division), correspondence from (ref GF/SRI/99/02/813436, 03/08/99). By November 2000, a total of 132 terminals had been withdrawn. Memorandum submitted by Camelot Group plc to Culture, Media and Sport Committee, *Minutes of Evidence. The Operation of the National Lottery First Report, Vol. II, H.C. 958–i, Session 1999–2000* (The Stationery Office, London, 09/11/00), p. 6, para. 6.1.
33. Director General of the Lottery, *Annual Report 1997/98*, p. 6.
34. Paul Farrelly, 'Camelot accused', *Independent on Sunday* (21/01/96).
35. Luke FitzHerbert, Faisel Rahman and Stan Harvey (eds), *The National Lottery Yearbook 1999 Edition* (Directory of Social Change, London, 1999), p. 14.
36. *Idem.*
37. Davis, *Minutes of Evidence. Forty-First Report*, p. 15, para. 148.
38. Mark Slattery (Head of Public Affairs to National Lottery Commission), telephone interview (08/07/99).
39. NLC, *Annual Report 1998/99*, p. 12.
40. Director General of the Lottery, *Annual Report 1993/94*, p. 20, app. A.
41. *The National Lottery Regulations 1994 (No 189)*, Conditions 4 (1) and 7, and Camelot, *The Advertising Code of Practice* (Camelot Group plc, Watford, 2nd edition, November 1995), p. 3.
42. Steve Boggan, 'Victory of the Lottery fat-cats', *Independent* (07/06/97).
43. Camelot, *Annual Report 1997*, p. 35. The figures provided by Camelot for the amounts passed to the Distribution Fund are different from those included in Oflot's reports due to different accounting practices. See note at Table 3, page 71 in this volume.
44. Raymond Snoddy, 'Lottery chief summoned to talks', *Financial Times* (29/05/97).
45. Polly Toynbee, 'The man from the ministry of culture', *Independent* (03/06/97).
46. Carol Midgley, 'Lottery chiefs ordered to give up bonus', *The Times* (03/06/97).
47. Toynbee, 'The man from the ministry'.
48. Snoddy, 'Lottery chief summoned'.
49. Toynbee, 'The man from the ministry'.
50. Jon Ashworth, 'Compromise likely on Camelot pay', *The Times* (06/06/97).
51. Boggan, 'Lottery fat cats'.
52. Director General of the Lottery, *Annual Report 1996/97*, introductory remarks. The Prize Target Shortfall is how much less in percentage terms the actual prizes won in any year amount to when compared with the target specified in the Licence. In practice there will almost always be a difference between the two as each individual game has its own prize structure and payout

percentages. Camelot must pay the difference on any shortfall to the Distribution Fund on or before 28 July in the following financial year. The prize shortfall has been greater than anticipated due to the success of the on-line game relative to the Instants scratch-card games, which have a higher percentage payout (55 per cent *vis-à-vis* 45 per cent for the on-line game). The shortfall amounted to £135 million in the year to 31 March 1996. Camelot benefited from the interest earned on this money in the year – some £6 million. Committee of Public Accounts, *Payments to the Distribution Fund Twentieth Report*, pp. xiv–xv, paras 34–6.

53. Boggan, 'Lottery fat cats'.
54. *The Shorter Oxford English Dictionary (on Historical Principles)*, Vol. II (Clarendon Press, Oxford, 3rd ed, 1978), p. 1689.
55. Boggan, 'Lottery fat cats'.
56. 'English soundbites', *Independent on Sunday* (08/06/97).
57. Paul Vallely, 'It's a lottery but Camelot has earned its dosh', *Independent* (30/05/97).
58. *Idem.*
59. David Souter, 'A stakeholder approach to regulation', in Dan Corry, David Souter and Michael Waterson, *Regulating Our Utilities* (Institute for Public Policy Research, London, 1991), p. 81.
60. 'Smith in Camelot', *The Times* (07/06/97).
61. Jean-Jacques Laffont and Jean Tirole, *A Theory of Incentives in Procurement and Regulation* (MIT Press, Cambridge, MA, and London, 1993), p. 638.
62. John Kay and John Vickers, 'Regulatory reform: an appraisal', in Giandomenico Majone (ed.), *Deregulation or Re-regulation? Regulatory Reform in Europe and the United States* (Pinter, London, 1990), p. 234.
63. Laffont and Tirole, *A Theory of Incentive*, p. 234.
64. Anthony I. Ogus, *Regulation: Legal Form and Economic Theory* (Clarendon Press, Oxford, 1994), p. 106.
65. Report of the Comptroller and Auditor General, *Evaluating the Applications to Run the National Lottery, H.C. 569, Session 1994–95* (National Audit Office, HMSO, London, 07/07/95), p. 11, para. 2.5.
66. *Idem.*
67. Davis, *Minutes of Evidence. Forty-First Report*, p. 5, para. 38.
68. *Ibid.*, pp. 5–6, para. 38.
69. John Mason and Richard Tomkins, 'Serious blow for world's biggest Lottery operator', *Financial Times* (03/02/98).
70. Committee of Public Accounts, *Evaluating the Applications to Run the National Lottery and the Director General's Travel and Hospitality Arrangements. Forty-First Report* (HMSO, London, 15/07/96), p. xvi, para. 48.
71. Committee of Public Accounts, *Appendices to the Minutes of Evidence. Forty-First Report* (HMSO, London, 15/07/96), p. 41, app. 3. A senior employee of GTech at this time, Mr J. David Smith, although not involved in the UK National Lottery bid, was subsequently jailed for five and a half years for accepting inducements from lobbyists involved in winning lottery contracts (in Kentucky and New Jersey). Mr Smith's employment ceased before the allegations were discovered by GTech. See Peter Foster, 'How Camelot lost the biggest prize', *Daily Telegraph* (24/08/00), and Committee of Public

Accounts, *Appendices to Minutes of Evidence. Forty-First Report*, pp. 41 and 64, annex 3.

72. Committee of Public Accounts, *Forty-First Report*, p. 48, para. 50.

73. *Ibid.*, p. vii, para xvii.

74. *Ibid.*, p. vii, para xviii.

75. Virginia Bottomley (Secretary of State for National Heritage), 'Letter to Peter Davis (Director General of the National Lottery) (19/12/95)', cited in Committee of Public Accounts, *Appendices to Minutes of Evidence. Forty-First Report*, p. 61, app. 4.

76. 'Unsackable should not mean unaccountable', *Independent* (21/12/95).

77. Committee of Public Accounts, *Forty-First Report*, p. xviii, para. 64.

78. *Ibid.*, p. viii, para xx, and p. xviii, para. 63, and Committee of Public Accounts, *Appendices to Minutes of Evidence. Forty-First Report*, p. 37, app. I, annex C.

79. Committee of Public Accounts, *Minutes of Evidence to Forty-First Report* (HMSO, London, 15/07/96), p. 28, para. 321.

80. Gaming Board for Great Britain, *Annual Report 1994/95* (HMSO, London, 11/07/95), p. 7, para. 2.2.

81. Robert Miller, 'Lottery tickets seized in £100m scam inquiry', *The Times* (27/09/95).

82. Jon Ashworth and Oliver August, 'Cutting American lifeline would spell the end of Camelot's reign', *The Times* (04/02/98).

83. George Kuempel and Tom Steinert-Threlkeld, 'Lottery firms tactics gall rivals; GTech notes clean record, seeks new challenges', *Dallas Morning News* (17/04/94).

84. Neil Tweedie, 'There's always a bottom line, what can I do for you personally? Everyone needs something', *Daily Telegraph* (03/02/98).

85. Kamal Ahmed, 'Bribes verdict ignites Lottery crisis', *Guardian* (03/02/98), and Cyril Dixon, 'Lottery supremo offered Branson bribe over lunch', *Daily Mail* (14/01/98).

86. Ahmed, 'Bribes verdict'.

87. Tweedie, 'There's always a bottom line'.

88. Anne Rafferty QC, *Enquiry into National Lottery Application Allegations* (Temple, London, 31/05/96), p. 6.

89. *Ibid.*, p. 1.

90. 'The jury's verdict damned the lottery regulator too', *Independent* (03/02/98).

91. Ahmed, 'Bribes verdict'.

92. John Stoker (Acting Director General to the National Lottery), Note re GTech, appended to news release (Oflot, 09/04/98). Mr Snowden retained a shareholding of just under 1 per cent in GTech. Philip Webster and Joanna Bale, 'Peter Davis sacked as Lottery chief', *The Times* (04/02/98).

93. Webster and Bale, 'Peter Davis sacked'.

94. Joanna Bale and Andrew Pierce, 'Davis did not deserve humiliation, says wife', *The Times* (05/02/98).

95. Webster and Bale, 'Peter Davis sacked'.

96. *Idem.*

97. Nicholas Bannister, 'Watchdogs held at bay', *Guardian* (05/02/98).

98. Webster and Bale, 'Peter Davis sacked'.

99. National Lottery etc. Act 1993, Schedule 2 (1) (4).

100. Philip Johnston, 'Why Lottery watchdog failed to bite', *Daily Telegraph* (04/02/98).
101. Committee of Public Accounts, *Forty-first Report*, p. xii, para. 25.
102. *Idem.*
103. Patricia A. McQueen and John Frank-Keyes, 'GTech buyout boosts Camelot', *International Gaming and Wagering Business*, vol. 19, no. 5 (May 1998), p. 63. John Stoker succeeded Peter Davis on 9 February 1998. Director General of the Lottery, *Annual Report 1997/98*, p. 17, app. G.
104. Carol Midgley and Jon Ashworth, 'GTech to sell Lottery stake in £51m deal', *The Times* (02/04/98).
105. Kamal Ahmed, 'Lottery operator Camelot dumps UK shareholder', *Guardian* (02/04/98).
106. Stoker, Note re GTech, p. 1.
107. Jason Burt, 'Camelot told: we may halt Lottery', *Daily Mail* (07/03/98).
108. Robert A. Kagan, *Regulatory Justice* (Russell Sage Foundation, New York, 1978), p. 10.
109. Carol Midgley, 'Changes drive punters away', *The Times* (04/02/98).
110. Jon Ashworth and Oliver August, 'Cutting American lifeline'.
111. *Idem.*
112. Stoker, Note re GTech, pp. 2–3.
113. *Ibid.*, p. 3.
114. *Idem.*
115. *Idem.*
116. *Labour Party Manifesto* (April 1997), p. 31.
117. Chris Smith (Secretary of State for Culture, Media and Sport), *The People's Lottery* (Cm. 3709, July 1997), p. 28.
118. 'The winners: £1.5m a week for Camelot', *Independent* (03/06/98), and Midgley, 'Lottery chiefs ordered to give up bonus'.
119. Miers, 'Regulation and the public interest', p. 492.
120. *Idem.* Notwithstanding the fact that the majority of lotteries in America are run by state agencies, they have been dogged by controversy over aggressive marketing and advertising techniques, such as the alleged targeting of vulnerable populations including possible pathological gamblers and economically disadvantaged groups. See National Gambling Impact Study Commission, *Final Report* (National Gambling Impact Study Commission, Washington, DC, June 1999), p. 3–4, and Charles T. Clotfelter and Philip J. Cook, *Selling Hope: State Lotteries in America* (Harvard University Press, Cambridge, MA, 1989), pp. 186–212.
121. Joseph M. Kelly, 'British Gaming Act of 1968', *New York Law School Journal of International and Competition Law*, vol. 8 (1986), p. 55, n. 163.
122. Gaming Board for Great Britain, *Annual Report 1996/97* (The Stationery Office, London, 10/07/97), p. 13, para. 2.5.
123. Gaming Act 1968, Part II, Section 10.
124. Gaming Board for Great Britain, *Annual Report 1993/94* (HMSO, London, 11/07/94), p. 2, para. 8.
125. Peter Dean (Chairman), *Report of the Gaming Board for Great Britain* (The Stationery Office, London, 14/07/99), p. v.
126. Gaming Board for Great Britain, *Annual Report 1995/96* (HMSO, London, 11/07/96), p. 7, para. 1.30.

127. David Miers, 'Objectives and systems in the regulation of commercial gambling', in Jan McMillen (ed.), *Gambling Cultures: Studies in History and Interpretation* (Routledge, London, 1996), p. 306.

128. Gaming Board, *Annual Report 1995/96*, p. 7, para. 1.30.

129. Director General of the Lottery, *Annual Report 1994/95*, p. 12, para. 1.13.

130. Marianne Macdonald, 'Camelot plays £40m hand to launch Lottery', *Independent* (04/11/94).

131. For an exposition of the semantics of 'gaming' and 'gambling' see Andrew Douglas, *British Charitable Gambling 1956–1994* (The Athlone Press, London, 1995), pp. 3–6.

132. Miers, 'Regulation and the public interest', p. 492.

133. Director General of the Lottery, *Annual Report 1994/95*, p. 11, para. 1.12.

134. *Licence to Run the National Lottery under Section 5*, pp. 32–7, conditions 11–13.

135. *Ibid.*, p. 28, condition 9 (1).

136. *Ibid.*, p. 28, condition 9 (2).

137. *Ibid.*, pp. 28–29, condition 9 (2) (f).

138. Alan J. Karcher, *Lotteries* (Transaction Publishers, New Brunswick, NJ, 1989), pp. 77–9.

139. Camelot, *Advertising Code of Practice* (Camelot Group plc, Watford, January 1998), p. 5, sect. 2.2, and pp. 5–6, sect. 2.3.

140. Director General of the Lottery, *Annual Report 1994/95*, p. 24, para. 4.5.

141. *Ibid.*, p. 25, para. 4.6.

142. Director General of the Lottery, *Annual Report 1995/96*, p. 16, and *Annual Report 1996/97*, p. 10.

143. *Idem.*

144. The Operator also provides a Lottery telephone line (which dealt with two million calls in the financial year 1996/97). The performance and customer satisfaction levels achieved in this area were monitored closely by Oflot. Director General of the Lottery, *Annual Report 1996/97*, p. 10.

145. Director General of the Lottery, *Annual Report 1995/96*, p. 17. As well as providing information, the Operator also has a responsibility to provide confidentiality to winners. During the early stages of the Lottery's life the arrangements made by Camelot with regard to protecting the confidentiality and privacy of winners were found to be less than adequate. This problem has since been rectified. *Ibid.*, p. 16.

146. *Directions to the Director General*, Section 2 (1) (a).

147. *Ibid.*, Section 2 (1) (b).

148. *Ibid.*, Sections 4 and 2 (2). If a jackpot is not won in a particular Lottery it can be 'rolled-over' to the next three draws, *ibid.*, Section 4(1). As well as forbidding the association of the National Lottery with other betting or gaming products, the Licence also underpins the Secretary of State's Directions by forbidding the sale of Lottery tickets by telephone. *Licence to Run the National Lottery under Section 5*, p. 35, condition 12 (8).

149. Miers, 'Regulation and the public interest', p. 511.

150. James M. Stearns and Shaheena Borna, 'The ethics of lottery advertising: issues and evidence', *Journal of Business Ethics*, vol. 14, no. 1 (1995), p. 46.

151. Stephen Breyer, *Regulation and Its Reform* (Harvard University Press, Cambridge, MA, 1982), p. 33.

152. Stephen Breyer, 'Analyzing regulatory failure: mismatches, less restrictive

alternatives and reform', *Harvard Law Review*, vol. 92, no. 3 (January 1979), p. 559.

153. Judith A. Osborne, 'Licensing without law: legalized gambling in British Columbia', *Canadian Public Administration – Administration Publique du Canada*, vol. 35, no. 1 (1992), p. 60.

154. Ogus, *Regulation*, pp. 191–2.

155. David Miers, 'The national regulation of gambling and the completion of the internal market in the European Community', in William R. Eadington and Judy A. Cornelius (eds), *Gambling and Public Policy* (University of Nevada, Reno, 1991), p. 420.

156. T. H. Jackson, 'The fresh start policy in bankruptcy law', *Harvard Law Review*, vol. 98 (1983), p. 1393 and pp. 1408–14, and P. Asch, *Consumer Safety Regulation* (Oxford University Press, Oxford, 1988), pp. 74–9.

157. Players can also underestimate their chances of winning. See Clotfelter and Cook, *Selling Hope*, p. 76.

158. M. Griffiths, *Adolescent Gambling* (Routledge, London, 1995), pp. 21–6. Other irrational thinking patterns include chasing losses (cognitive entrapment or sunk-cost bias), a belief in 'hot and cold' numbers, unrealistic optimism, a belief in personal luck, superstitious thinking, the erroneous perception of near-misses, and a susceptibility to prize size and roll-over effects. Paul Rogers, 'The cognitive psychology of lottery gambling: a theoretical review', *Journal of Gambling Studies*, vol. 14, no. 2 (summer 1998), pp. 119–29. See also Elliot Coups, Geoffrey Haddock and Paul Webley, 'Correlates and predictors of lottery play in the United Kingdom', *Journal of Gambling Studies*, vol. 14, no. 3 (Fall 1998), pp. 290–302.

159. R. K. Kinsey, *The Rôle of Lotteries in Public Finance* (PhD thesis, Columbia University, Canada, 1959), p. 142. Prospect theory assumes the values placed on wins and losses by lottery players are not directly related to the probability of such events occurring. See Rogers, 'The cognitive psychlogy', pp. 127–9.

160. The concept of 'bounded rationality' was developed by H. A. Simon, *Administrative Behavior* (Free Press, New York, 1975).

161. Edward J. McCaffery, 'Why people play lotteries and why it matters', *Wisconsin Law Review* (1994), p. 82.

162. *Ibid.*, pp. 121–2.

163. Raj Persaud (consultant psychiatrist), 'Letter', *British Medical Journal*, vol. 311 (04/11/95), p. 1225.

164. Oflot, *Social Research Programme 01/03/97–01/09/97* (Oflot, London, 1997), p. 11.

165. McCaffery, 'Why people play', p. 122.

166. Ogus, *Regulation*, p. 227.

167. Stephen Breyer, 'Regulation and deregulation in the United States: airlines, telecommunications and antitrust', in Majone, *Deregulation or Re-regulation*, p. 10.

168. *The 1998 La Fleur's World Lottery Almanac* (TLF Publications Inc., Boyds, MD, 6th edn, 1988), pp. 65, 89 and 109; 'Compulsive gambling? Lotteries are not a problem', *Public Gaming International*, vol. 19, no. 5 (May 1991), p. 38; Kathleen Ward, 'Lotteries address responsible play', *Public Gaming International*, vol. 26, no. 8 (September 1998), p. 32; 'Lottery jurisdiction response to problem gambling', *Public Gaming International*, vol. 26, no. 9 (October 1998), p. 21.

169. Camelot, *Camelot and Social Responsibility Social Report 1999* (Camelot Group

plc, Watford, 2000), p. 22, para. 10.4.4. GamCare (The National Association for Gambling Care, Educational Resources and Training) was established in 1997 to improve understanding of the social impact of gambling, promote a responsible approach to gambling and to address the needs of those adversely affected by gambling dependency. Luke FitzHerbert and Mark Paterson (eds), *The National Lottery Yearbook 1998 Edition* (Directory of Social Change, London, 1998), p. 19.

170. 'Lottery jurisdiction response to problem gambling', pp. 19–21.
171. Vicki Abt and Martin C. McGurrin, 'Commercial gambling and values in American society: the social construction of risk', *Journal of Gambling Studies*, vol. 8, no. 4 (winter 1992), p. 416.
172. Breyer, *Regulation and Its reform*, p. 26.
173. *Idem.*
174. Richard McGowan, 'The ethics of gambling research: an agenda for mature analysis', *Journal of Gambling Studies*, vol. 13, no. 4 (winter 1997), p. 287, and Bernard P. Horn, 'The courage to be counted', *Journal of Gambling Studies*, vol. 13, no. 4 (winter 1997), p. 305.
175. Horn, 'The courage to be counted, p. 305.
176. Director General of the Lottery, *Annual Report 1994/95*, p. 15, para. 2.11, *Annual Report 1995/96*, p. 18, *Annual Report 1996/97*, p. 9, *Annual Report 1997/98*, p. 2, and NLC, *Annual Report 1998/99*, p. 8. Although the last report was issued by the Lottery Commission it related to the period of the Oflot regime.
177. Luke FitzHerbert, Celia Guissani and Howard Hurd (eds), *The National Lottery Yearbook 1996 Edition* (Directory of Social Change, London, 1996), p. 292, Luke FitzHerbert and Lucy Rhoades (eds), *The National Lottery Yearbook 1997 Edition* (Directory of Social Change, London, 1997), p. 23, and FitzHerbert and Paterson (eds), *Lottery Yearbook 1998*, p. 18.
178. Dr Mark Griffiths (Psychology Division, Nottingham Trent University), 'The National Lottery and Instant scratch cards: some comments on research', in FitzHerbert and Rhoades, *Lottery Yearbook 1997*, p. 25, and FitzHerbert and Paterson, *Lottery Yearbook 1998*, p. 18.
179. Oflot, *Social Research Programme 31/01/95–31/01/96* (Oflot, London, 1996), sect. D5.
180. In June 1999 a new format for the main Draw game was launched, 'Thunderball', which pays out £5 for matching just one number with the prescribed 'Thunderball' number. Camelot, 'Thunderball', advertisement in *Independent* (07/06/99).
181. The new 'Thunderball' game presents players with odds of 1 in 33 of winning £5. "Thunderball' advertisement' in *Independent* 07/06/99).
182. Oflot, *Research Programme 31/01/95–31/01/96*, sect. B2.
183. John Deans and Jason Burt, 'Bottomley tells churchmen to count their good fortune', *Daily Mail* (05/01/96), and the Lord Bishop of Leicester, *National Lottery Bill House of Lords*, vol. 584, no. 82 (Hansard, 18/12/97), col. 743.
184. Rhys Williams, 'Churches unite to attack "damaging" Lottery', *Independent* (16/01/95).
185. Rhys Williams 'Labour urges £5M Lottery limit', *Independent* (16/01/95).
186. Capping jackpots has been demonstrated to adversely affect lottery sales in Sweden, Holland and Canada. Camelot Group plc, supplementary

memorandum submitted to National Heritage Committee, *The National Lottery Minutes of Evidence, H.C. 240 iii, Session 1995–96* (HMSO, London, 29/02/96), p. 57.

187. Luke FitzHerbert, *Winners and Losers: The Impact of the National Lottery* (Joseph Rowntree Foundation, London, July 1995), p. 28, and Richard Duce, 'Camelot "breeding addicts"', *The Times* (03/05/95).

188. National Gambling Impact Study Commission, *First Report*, p. 1-1.

189. Abt and McGurrin, 'Commercial gambling,' p. 414.

190. *Idem.*

191. Vicki Abt, James F. Smith and Eugene Martin Christiansen, *The Business of Risk: Commercial Gambling in Mainstream America* (University of Kansas Press, Lawrence, 1985), p. 148.

192. The Draw lottery is referred to as Lotto in the USA. *La Fleur's 2000 World Lottery Almanac* (TLF Publications Inc., Boyds, MD, 2000), pp. 317 and 319.

193. Oflot, *Research Programme 31/01/95–31/01/96*, sect. B1.

194. Oflot, *Social Research Programme 01/03/97–01/09/97* (Oflot, London, 1997), p. 11. In the first full year of the Midweek Draw, sales for the on-line Draw game increased by 22.5 per cent. Director General of the Lottery, *Annual Report 1997/98*, p. 1.

195. *Directions to the Director General*, Section 4, in Director General of the Lottery, *Annual Report 1993/94*, p. 29, app. F. This restriction was lifted from February 2000. National Lottery Commission, *Addendum 5 to Invitation to Apply* (National Lottery Commission, London, 04/02/00).

196. Oflot, *Research Programme 31/01/95–31/01/96*, sect. B2.

197. *Idem.*

198. Director General of the Lottery, *Annual Report 1997/98*, p. 1. The Operator, with the approval of Oflot, also promoted 20 superdraws during 1997/98, where the prize fund was increased (thereby reducing the Prize Target Shortfall) to attract greater levels of participation (*idem*).

199. Camelot, *Annual Report and Accounts 2000* (Camelot Group plc, Watford, 2000), p. 10.

200. Camelot, *Annual Report and Accounts 2001* (Camelot Group plc, Watford, 2001), p. 10.

201. Rhys Williams, 'Secrecy still name of game over Mr £17.9m', *Independent* (15/12/94).

202. Camelot, *Lottery Briefing Issue No. 6* (Camelot Group plc, Watford, spring 1997), p. 2.

203. Richard Brooks and Melanie Phillips, 'Poor losing most on the Lottery, new figures show', *Observer* (29/10/95).

204. I. Pilavin and M. Polakowski, 'Who plays the lottery? A comparison of patterns in Wisconsin and the Nation', *Institute for Research on Poverty Special Report*, no. 50 (January 1990), p. 14.

205. The average weekly Draw expenditure in July 1997 for those households of two adults and with income below £4500 p.a. was £3.69 for those playing twice weekly and £2.06 for those playing once per week, compared with £5.34 and £2.55 respectively for households with an income of between £15,500 and £24,999. Oflot, *Research Programme 01/03/97–01/09/97*, p. 8. In September 1998 average weekly expenditure on the Draw lottery for house-

holds with an income below £4500 stood at £3.68 for those playing twice weekly and £2.20 for those playing once per week, compared with £5.57 and £2.31 respectively for households with an annual income of between £15,500 and £24,999 (research carried out by NOP, between 9 and 15 September 1998 on 1683 adults). National Lottery Commission, *Social Research Programme Report No. 1* (National Lottery Commission, London, May 1999), p. 3 and p. 13, table 1.

206. Oflot, *Research Programme 31/01/95–31/01/96*, sect. B1, and Oflot, *Research Programme 01/06/96–01/03/97*, p. 6.

207. Oflot, *Research Programme 31/01/95–31/01/96*, sect. B1, and Oflot, *Research Programme 01/06/96–01/03/97*, Introduction.

208. Oflot, *Research Programme 01/06/96–01/03/97*, p. 10.

209. *Idem.*

210. *Idem.*

211. Oflot, *Research Programme 01/03/97–01/09/97*, p. 7.

212. Oflot, *Social Research Commissioned 01/02/96–01/06/96* (Oflot, London, 1996), p. 17.

213. National Lottery Commission, *Research Programme 09/98*, p. 16, table 4.

214. Oflot, *Research Programme 31/01/95–31/01/96*, sect. B2.

215. *Ibid.*, annex 1, p. 1, and annex 2, p. 17. Caution should be exercised due to the relatively small sample size of the sub-groups. Normal non-roll-over week research was carried out in July and September 1995 on 3585 people with an overall success rate of 48 per cent (*ibid.*, sect. B1 and annex 1).

216. *Ibid.*, annex 1, p. 4, and annex 2, p. 20. Again caution should be exercised regarding the small sub-group sample size.

217. *Ibid.*, annex 1, p. 5 and annex 2, p. 21. Again caution should be exercised regarding the small sub group sample size.

218. National Lottery Commission, *Research Programme 09/98*, p. 5.

219. *Ibid.*, p. 3.

220. Gaming Board for Great Britain, *Annual Report 1997/98* (The Stationery Office, London, 08/07/98), p. 2, para. 1.9.

221. Oflot, *Research Programme 01/06/96–01/03/97*, p. 20.

222. *Ibid.*, pp. 20–1.

223. *Idem.*

224. *Idem.*

225. D. B. Cornish, *Gambling: A Review of the Literature and Its Implications for Policy and Research* (Crown, London, 1978), pp. 152–3. See also J. Adler, 'Gambling, drugs and alcohol: a note on functional equivalents', *Issues in Criminology*, vol. 2, no. 1 (1966), pp. 111–18.

226. T. M. Martinez, *The Gambling Scene* (Charles C. Thomas, Springfield, IL, 1983), p. 156. This distinction between pathological and compulsive gambling is not recognized by Dr Fisher in the 1998 survey, who suggests that recent formal literature uses the term 'pathological' in favour of 'compulsive' to describe the more severe cases of problem gambling. National Lottery Commission, *Research Programme 09/98*, p. 14.

227. National Lottery Commission, *Research Programme 09/98*, p. 14, table 2.

228. Oflot, *Research Programme 01/06/96–01/03/97*, p. 10. Figures based on a UK adult population of 46.2 million with socio-economic group E comprising 18

per cent of this universe. Of 11,000 adults surveyed 0.9 per cent spent more than £10 in the draw preceding interview.

229. Director General of the Lottery, *Annual Report 1996/97*, p. 8.
230. *Idem.*
231. Gaming Board, *Annual Report 1996/97*, p. 60, para. 7.10.
232. *Idem.*
233. *Ibid.*, p. 9, para. 1.31.
234. Director General of the Lottery, *Annual Report 1996/97*, pp. 8–9.
235. FitzHerbert, Giussani and Hurd, *Lottery Yearbook 1996*, p. 294.
236. Director General of the Lottery, *Annual Report 1997/98*, p. 14, app. F.
237. FitzHerbert, Giussani and Hurd, *Lottery Yearbook 1996*, p. 294. The Director Generals did not permit non-cash prizes (Director General of the Lottery, *Annual Report 1997/98*, p. 5). In August 1999 the National Lottery Commission allowed Camelot to introduce a 'Winning Wallet' promotion whereby for a limited period prizes were offered including discounts on holidays for players buying both Draw and Instants tickets: 'This is your winning wallet' (Camelot Group plc, Watford, 1999). In June 2001 (in the face of disappointing sales) the top guaranteed prize was increased to £1 million (of which there were five prizes) and tickets were priced at £2. Camelot, The National Lottery launches the first ever Instants game with a top prize of £1 million (news release) (Camelot Group plc, Watford, 11/06/01).
238. *La Fleur's 2000 World Lottery Almanac*, pp. 321 and 324.
239. FitzHerbert, *Winners and Losers*, p. 28.
240. David Miers, 'The implementation and effects of Great Britain's National Lottery', *Journal of Gambling Studies*, vol. 12, no. 4 (winter 1996), p. 346.
241. *Idem.*
242. Dr Mark Griffiths (Psychology Division, Nottingham Trent University), cited by Dr Lynne Jones (MP Birmingham Selly Oak), House of Commons Official Report, *Parliamentary Debates* (HMSO, London, 03/07/95), col. 1087.
243. Griffiths, 'The National Lottery and Instant scratch cards', in FitzHerbert and Rhoades, *Lottery Yearbook 1997*, p. 25.
244. Griffiths, cited by Jones, col. 1087.
245. FitzHerbert, Giussani and Hurd, *Lottery Yearbook 1996*, p. 296.
246. Director General of the Lottery, *Annual Report 1995/96*, p. 19.
247. *Ibid.*, p. 20.
248. Griffiths, cited by Jones, col. 1087, and Dr E. Moran (consultant psychiatrist and Chairman of the National Council of Gambling), cited by FitzHerbert, Giussani and Hurd, *Lottery Yearbook 1996*, p. 293.
249. Director General of the Lottery, *Annual Report 1994/95*, p. 15, para. 2.11.
250. The Lotteries (Variation of monetary limits) Order No 1218 (1989).
251. Director General of the Lottery, *Annual Report 1995/96*, p. 17.
252. Oflot, *Research Programme 01/06/96–01/03/97*, p. 24.
253. National Lottery Commission, *Research Programme 09/98*, p. 4 and p. 9, fig. 1.
254. Oflot, *Research Programme 01/06/96–01/03/97*, p. 24. Average spending figures should be treated with caution as overall the survey failed to account for more than a third of actual sales. Both surveys carried out by NOP on 1797 adults in the January survey, Oflot, *Social Research 01/02/96–01/06/96*, p. 13; and on 1821 in the October survey, Oflot, *Research Programme 01/06/96–*

01/03/97, p. 4. In addition the January survey asked about scratch-cards in general and was not National Lottery–specific. Some commentators have suggested that the National Lottery's share of the total scratch-card market is around 80 per cent, Oflot, *Social Research 01/02/96–01/06/96*, p. 6.

255. National Lottery Commission, *Research Programme 09/98*, p. 20. Average spending figures should be treated with caution as overall the survey failed to account for more than 50 per cent of actual sales – implying average weekly expenditure could have been as high as £3.96 (*idem*).

256. Oflot, *Research Programme 01/03/97–01/09/97*, p. 6. Surveys conducted in April and July 1997 by NOP as part of an omnibus survey throughout the calendar year involving circa 9000 interviewees (*ibid.*, p. 3).

257. Oflot, *Social Research 01/02/96–01/06/96*, p. 7.

258. *Ibid.*, p. 8.

259. Oflot, *Research Programme 01/06/96–01/03/97*, p. 26.

260. *Ibid.*, p. 25. NB. The Report distinguishes between 'income' and 'socio-economic' groups which comprise the traditional standard (A–E) socio-economic grade classifications.

261. National Lottery Commission, *Research Programme 09/98*, pp. 3 and 4. Due to under-recording the figure of £5 could be as high as £7.50 (*ibid.*, p. 20).

262. Oflot, *Social Research 01/02/96–01/06/96*, p. 9.

263. Oflot, *Research Programme 01/06//96–01/03/97*, p. 26.

264. Oflot became involved with the charity GamCare in 1998 in coordinating a study on the incidence of gambling and problem gambling in the UK. Director General of the Lottery, *Annual Report 1997/98*, p. 2.

265. Horn, 'The courage to be counted', p. 304.

266. *La Fleur's 2000 World Lottery Almanac*, p. 309.

267. *Ibid.*, p. 313.

268. Paul Bellringer, 'Gambling and the National Lottery', FitzHerbert, Rahman and Harvey, *Lottery Yearbook 1999*, p. 12.

269. Paul Vallely 'Does the lottery add up?', *Independent* (04/06/99).

270. *Directions to the Director General*, Section 2 (1) (b), in Director General of the Lottery, *Annual Report 1993/94*, p. 28, app. F.

271. Director General of the Lottery, *Annual Report 1995/96*, p. 22.

272. *Idem*.

273. Kathleen Ward, 'It's not child's play', *Public Gaming International*, vol. 26, no. 11 (December 1998), pp. 11–13.

274. These church groups included the Church of England, the Catholic Church, the Methodists, the Church of Scotland, Baptists, the United Reformed Church, Quakers, Unitarians and Free Christian Churches. The declaration was also signed by the Salvation Army. Rhys Williams, 'Bottomley rejects Churches attack on scratchcards', *Independent* (25/10/95).

275. See Douglas, *British Charitable Gambling*, pp. 389–93.

276. Dr E. Moran, 'A generation of gamblers?', in FitzHerbert, Giussani and Hurd, *Lottery Yearbook 1996*, p. 293, and P. Bellringer (Director of GamCare), cited by Rosa Prince, 'Camelot told: stop sales to children', *Independent* (27/02/98).

277. National Heritage Committee, *The National Lottery Second Report, Vol. 1, 240–I Session 1995–96* (HMSO, London, 14/05/96), pp. xi–xii, paras 39–40.

278. Camelot, *Annual Review 1998* (Camelot Group plc, Watford, 1998), p. 18.

279. Bellringer, cited by Price.

280. Moran, 'A generation of gamblers?' in FitzHerbert, Guissani and Hurd, *Lottery Yearbook 1996*, p. 293.
281. National Heritage Committee, *The National Lottery Second Report*, p. xii, para. 39.
282. Dr Susan E. Fisher, *Gambling and Problem Gambling among Young People in England and Wales* (Centre for Research into the Social Impact of Gambling, University of Plymouth, January 1998, published by Oflot, February 1998), p. 35, table 12 and app. 2, p. 1.
283. Memorandum submitted by the National Council on Gambling to National Heritage Committee, *The National Lottery First Report*, H.C. *131, Session 1994–95* (HMSO, London, 26/01/95), p. 20, app. 2.
284. *Idem.*
285. *Idem.*
286. Dr Emanuel Moran, 'Majority of secondary school children buy tickets', *British Medical Journal*, vol. 311 (04/11/95), p. 1226.
287. Memorandum submitted by the National Council on Gambling, *The National Lottery First Report*, p. 20, app. 2.
288. Moran, 'A generation of gamblers?', in FitzHerbert, Guissani and Hurd, *Lottery Yearbook 1996*, p. 293.
289. David Alton MP, *House of Commons Official Report Parliamentary Debates* (Hansard, 25/10/95), col. 1056.
290. Independent Television Commission, 'Child's eye view', *Spectrum*, vol. 17 (1995), p. 24.
291. Fisher, *Gambling and Problem Gambling*, p. 1 and p. 57, table 26.
292. Jacinta Ashworth, Nicola Doyle and Nicholas Howat (BMRB Social Research), *Under 16s and the National Lottery Tracking Survey 2000* (National Lottery Commission, London, June 2001), p. 54, table 9a.
293. *Ibid.*, p. 55, table 9b.
294. Griffiths, 'The National Lottery and Instant scratch cards', in FitzHerbert and Rhoades, *Lottery Yearbook 1997*, p. 25.
295. Camelot, *Advertising Code of Practice* (January 1998), pp. 4–5.
296. Memorandum submitted by the National Council on Gambling, *The National Lottery First Report*, p. 20, app. 2.
297. *Idem.*
298. Moran, 'A generation of gamblers?' in FitzHerbert, Guissani and Hurd, *Lottery Yearbook 1996*, p. 293.
299. Gaming Board for Great Britain, *Annual Report 1994/95*, p. 4, para. 1.21.
300. *Idem.* This feature of the Instants game is borne out by Oflot-commissioned research. Problem gambling among children (12- to 15-year-olds) has been found to be statistically significant in connection with Instants but not the Draw game. Fisher, *Gambling and Problem Gambling*, p. 4.
301. The Lord Bishop of Oxford, *Official Report of the Grand Committee on the National Lottery Bill*, vol. 584, no. 90 (Hansard, 22/01/98), CWH 106.
302. National Heritage Committee, *The National Lottery Second Report*, p. xii, para. 39.
303. Director General of the Lottery, *Annual Report 1997/98*, p. 6.
304. Director General of the Lottery, *Annual Report 1995/96*, p. 19.
305. Camelot, *Annual Review 1998*, p. 22.

306. Camelot, *Annual Report and Accounts 1999*, p. 12, and Camelot, *Annual Report and Accounts 2000*, p. 11.
307. Director General of the Lottery, *Annual Report 1995/96*, p. 19.
308. Jane Woodhead, 'Young find it so easy to play Lottery', *Liverpool Daily Post* (24/02/96).
309. *Idem.*
310. FitzHerbert, Giussani and Hurd, *Lottery Yearbook 1996*, p. 296.
311. Oflot, *Social Research 01/02/96–01/06/96*, p. 20, para. 3(ii).
312. *Idem.*
313. Director General of the Lottery, *Annual Report 1995/96*, p. 19.
314. Director General of the Lottery, *Annual Report 1994/95*, p. 16, para. 2.12.
315. Director General of the Lottery, *Annual Report 1996/97*, p. 9.
316. Camelot, *Lottery Briefing*, issue no. 6 (Camelot Group plc, Watford, Spring 1997), p. 2.
317. Camelot, *Annual Report and Accounts 1997*, p. 17.
318. Camelot, *Lottery Briefing*, p. 2.
319. Oflot, *Research Programme 01/06/96–01/03/97*, p. 27.
320. Camelot, *Lottery Briefing*, p. 2.
321. Camelot, *Annual Report and Accounts 1997*, p. 16.
322. *Ibid.*, p. 17.
323. Fisher, *Gambling and Problem Gambling*, p. 2.
324. FitzHerbert, Rahman and Harvey, *Lottery Yearbook 1999*, p. 14.
325. *Idem.*
326. Director General of the Lottery, *Annual Report 1997/98*, p. 6.
327. Oflot, news release (Oflot, London, 26/02/98).
328. Memorandum submitted by Camelot Group plc to Culture, Media and Sport Committee, *Minutes of Evidence. First Report, Vol. II, H.C. 958–i, Session 1999–2000*, p. 6, para. 6.1.
329. Camelot, *Annual Report and Accounts 1999*, p. 6. This figure will increase to 10,000 visits each fiscal year during the second licence term. Camelot, *Camelot and Social Responsibility Interim Report 2000* (Camelot Group plc, Watford, 2001), p. 37, para. 8.1.4.
330. *Idem.*
331. Oflot, *Social Research 01/02/96–01/06/96*, pp. 20–1, para. 3(iv).
332. Dr Sue Fisher (research designer) (Report prepared by Jacinta Ashworth and Nicola Doyle), *Under 16s and the National Lottery* (National Lottery Commission, London, February 2000), pp. 6 and 7.
333. *Ibid.*, p. 8.
334. *Ibid.*, pp. 18, 19 and p. 44, table 7b.
335. Interviews carried out on 11,581, 12- to 15-year-olds from 15/06/00 to 21/07/00. Ashworth *et al.*, *op. cit.*, p. 1 and p. 32, chart 6a.
336. *Ibid.*, p. 32, chart 6a.
337. Ashworth *et al.*, *op. cit.*, p. 39, table 7a.
338. *Ibid.*, p. 41.
339. Camelot supports the introduction of such a scheme. Camelot, *Camelot and Social Responsibility Interim Report 2000*, p. 40, para. 8.3.2.
340. Neighbourhood Lottery Alliance Supplementary Memorandum submitted to Culture, Media and Sport Committee, *Minutes of Evidence. The Operation of the*

National Lottery. First Report, Vol. II, H.C. 958–ii, Session 1999–2000 (The Stationery Office, London, 16/11/00), p. 47. The idea is also supported by the Select Committee for Health, *idem.*

341. Camelot, *Annual Report 2001*, p. 5.
342. Camelot, *Camelot and Social Responsibility Interim Report 2000*, p. 40, para. 8.3.2.
343. Liz Hunt, 'Lottery "breeding generation of gamblers"', *Independent* (03/11/95).
344. Director General of the Lottery, *Annual Report 1995/96*, p. 18.
345. Sue Fisher, 'A preliminary study of underage spending on the National Lottery', in Oflot, *Social Research 31/01/95–31/01/96*, pp. 1–2.
346. *Ibid.*, p. 2. Of the 1762 12- to 15-year-olds surveyed between May and July for the health-related behaviour questionnaire, 97 failed to answer questions on the Lottery, resulting in a final sample of 1665. *Ibid.*, pp. 1–2.
347. *Ibid.*, p. 2.
348. *Ibid.*, pp. 2–3, p. 6, table 2, and p. 8, table 5.
349. *Ibid.*, pp. 3–4, p. 9, table 8, p. 10, table 9 and table 10.
350. Sue Fisher and John Balding, *A Second Preliminary Study of Underage Spending on the National Lottery* (Oflot, London, n.d., circa Dec 1995/Jan 1996), p. 1.
351. *Ibid.*, pp. 1–2.
352. *Ibid.*, p. 3, and p. 8, table 1.
353. *Ibid.*, p. 3, p. 8, table 1, and p. 10, table 5.
354. *Ibid.*, p. 4, p. 11, table 8, p. 12, table 9 and table 10.
355. *Ibid.*, p. 6.
356. *Ibid.*, p. 7.
357. Sue Fisher and John Balding, *Underage Participation in the National Lottery* (Oflot, London, 1996), p. 3.
358. *Ibid.*, p. iii and p. 5.
359. Because of problems experienced in developing the improved question format, a subset of 3724 children made this distinction in responding to the survey. *Ibid.*, p. iii.
360. *Idem.*
361. *Idem.*
362. *Ibid.*, pp. iv–v. All three surveys show a particularly strong association between under-age Lottery play (particularly the Instants game) and fruit machine gambling. The accusation that Instants tickets are like 'paper fruit machines' would appear to be borne out by this evidence.
363. Camelot, *Lottery Briefing*, p. 2.
364. Fisher and Balding, *Underage Participation*, p. iv and p. 21, table 10. While no relationship between socio-economic group and regular play was evidenced, regular players were more likely to be in receipt of their own income in excess of £5 per week from paid work or pocket money (as had been the case in the second report) with 18 per cent falling into this category compared with 6 per cent of other children; and regular players were more likely to come from an ethnic minority – 15 per cent compared with 9 per cent of other children (*ibid.*, p. 20, table 9).
365. *Ibid.*, p. 19, table 8, and p. 24, table 12. Caution should be exercised with regard to the validity of the regular players surveyed owing to the smallness of the sample.
366. *Idem.*

367. Fisher, *Gambling and Problem Gambling*, p. 1. Research designed and executed by Dr Fisher at the University of Plymouth's Centre for Research into the social impact of gambling and carried out on data collected by MORI from 9774 12- to 15-year-olds between 2 June and 4 July 1997. *Ibid.*, p. 1 and app. 2, p. 1.

368. *Ibid.*, p. 2, p. 28, table 6 (49 per cent of purchases were illegal, 51 per cent legal) and p. 29, table 7.

369. Age and access to personal income are themselves closely correlated.

370. Fisher, *Gambling and Problem Gambling*, p. 30.

371. *Idem.*

372. *Ibid.*, p. 29, table 7.

373. *Ibid.*, p. 25, table 5.

374. *Idem.*

375. *Ibid.*, p. 4. Problem gambling is identified in relation to an index of behaviours and psychological states known to be correlated with problem gamblers. *Idem.*

376. *Ibid.*, p. 42, table 17, and p. 43, table 18 (50 per cent of young people identified as problem gamblers had spent their money on other commercial scratch-cards in the week before interview).

377. Fisher, *Under 16s and the Lottery*, pp. 17 and 25.

378. *Ibid.*, p. 27, table 4d, and p. 48, table 8c.

379. The figure of 13.5 per cent given in the 1999 survey for 1997 is higher than the figure of 13 per cent which is actually included in the 1997 survey.

380. Fisher, *Under 16s and the Lottery*, p. 17.

381. *Ibid.*, pp. 19 and p. 31, table 5b (5 per cent of interviewees had spent more than £20 on non-National Lottery instant scratch-cards (2 per cent in 1997)). *Ibid.*, p. 35, table 5d.

382. *Ibid.*, p. 31, table 5b.

383. Ashworth *et al.*, *op. cit.*, p. 26, table 5d, and p. 25.

384. *Ibid.*, p. 25.

385. G. Moody, *Quit Compulsive Gambling* (Thorsons, Northampton, 1990), p. 109.

386. J. Livingston, *Compulsive Gamblers: Observations on Action and Abstinence* (Harper & Row, New York, 1974); R. L. Cluster, 'An overview of compulsive gambling', in P. A. Crone, S. F. Yoles, S. N. Kieffer and L. Krinsky (eds), *Addictive Disorders Update: Alcoholism, Drug Abuse, Gambling* (Human Scientific Press, 1982), cited by Sue Fisher; 'Gambling and pathological gambling in adolescents', *Journal of Gambling Studies*, vol. 9, no. 3 (Fall 1993), p. 286.

387. Fisher, *Gambling and Problem Gambling*, p. 8.

388. *Ibid.*, p. 52, table 23.

389. Fisher, *Under 16s and the Lottery*, p. 64, table 10d.

390. Ashworth *et al.*, *op. cit.*, p. 65, table 10d.

391. Rosa Prince, 'Camelot told: stop sales to children', *Independent* (27/02/98). Of those surveyed between February and July 1996, 2 per cent had missed school in order to play (17 per cent of regular players admitted to this). Fisher and Balding, *Underage Participation in the National Lottery*, p. 24, table 12. Caution should be exercised with regard to the validity of the regular players surveyed owing to the smallness of the sample. The larger survey carried out in the summer of 1997 revealed *inter alia* that of 4959 12- to 15-year-olds interviewed, 9 per cent had spent more than £10 gambling in one day, 15 per

cent had spent their school fare or dinner money on gambling, 12 per cent had stolen from their families to fund their gambling, 10 per cent had sold their possessions to fund their gambling and 14 per cent had lied about the extent of their gambling. Fisher, *Gambling and Problem Gambling*, pp. 5–6. Data relate to young people who had spent their own money on Instants scratch-cards or fruit machines in the last year. *Ibid.*, p. 5.

392. FitzHerbert and Rhoades, *Lottery Yearbook 1997*, p. 24.

393. Director General of the Lottery, *Annual Report 1997/98*, p. 6.

394. Robert A. Yaffe and Veronica J. Brodsky, 'Recommendations for research and public policy in gambling studies', *Journal of Gambling Studies*, vol. 13, no. 4 (winter 1997), p. 315.

395. Director General of the National Lottery, Financial penalties: principles and procedures (news release) (Office of the National Lottery, London, 10/07/98).

396. James Keulemans (Lottery Commission Public Affairs representative), telephone interview (20/04/99).

397. National Lottery Act 1998, Section 7. The Act also created a new body, The National Endowment for Science, Technology and the Arts (NESTA), to be funded from the New Opportunities Fund (*ibid.* Section 19). The 1998 Act in creating the new category reduced from 14/10/97 the share of the Distribution Fund going to the Arts, Sport, Heritage and Charities from 20 per cent to 16⅔ per cent and thus released 13⅓ per cent to be applied to the New Opportunity Fund (*ibid.*, Section 6). These percentages remained until October 1999 when the New Opportunities Fund percentage increased to 20 per cent and the Millennium Commission contribution reduced to 13⅓ per cent. FitzHerbert and Paterson, *Lottery Yearbook 1998*, p. 9.

398. Comptroller and Auditor General, *Evaluating the Applications*, p. 20, para. 3.4.

399. *Ibid.*, p. 12, para. 2.5.

400. *Ibid.*, p. 22, para. 3.9, p. 25, para. 3.14, and p. 30, para. 3.23.

401. Director General of the Lottery, *Annual Report 1994/95*, p. 14, para. 2.4.

402. Comptroller and Auditor General, *Evaluating the Applications*, p. 2, para. 4.

403. Comptroller and Auditor General, *Payments to the National Lottery Distribution Fund H.C. 678*, p. 14, para. 2.2.

404. 'Making a monster', *Independent on Sunday* (26/03/95).

405. *Idem.*

406. Camelot, *Annual Review 1998*, p. 15.

407. These bands are reproduced in each of Camelot's annual reports.

408. Camelot, *Annual Review 1998*, p. 15.

409. The Prize Target Shortfall is addressed further below. See table 3, page 71, in this volume.

410. Director General of the Lottery, *Annual Report 1995/96*, p. 44, app. A; *Annual Report 1996/97*, p. 23, app. A; *Annual Report 1997/98*, p. 8, app. A; NLC, *Annual Report 1998/99*, p. 13; NLC, *Annual Report 1999/2000* (The Stationery Office, London, 25/07/00), p. 20, app. A; and NLC, *Annual Report 2000/2001* (The Stationery Office, London, 12/07/01), p. 25, app. A.

411. Comptroller and Auditor General, *Evaluating the Applications*, pp. 35–6, para. 4.8 (i).

412. Director General of the Lottery, *Annual Report 1994/95*, p. 12, para. 1.14.

413. *Licence to Run the Lottery under Section 5*, p. 8, condition 2 (i).

414. Memorandum submitted by Camelot Group plc to National Heritage Committee, *Minutes of Evidence. H.C. 240, iii, Session 1995–96*, p. 46, para. 2 (a) (i).
415. *Licence to Run the Lottery under Section 5*, p. 8, condition 2 (i), Oflot, The National Lottery: preferred applicant announced (news release) (25/05/94), Table 2 and Director General of the Lottery, *Annual Report 1996/97*, p. 3.
416. Director General of the Lottery, *Annual Report 1996/97*, p. 6. The Director General and Oflot demonstrated some confusion over whether they did or did not have the power to impose financial penalties on Camelot for this failure. Cf. Peter Davis (Director General of the Lottery), *Minutes of Evidence. Twentieth Report*, p. 7, para. 58, and Memorandum submitted by Oflot to the National Heritage Committee, *Minutes of Evidence. H.C. 240, iii, Session 1995–96*, p. 60, para. 7.
417. Director General of the Lottery, *Annual Report 1996/97*, p. 3.
418. Oflot, The National Lottery: preferred applicant announced (news release) and *Licence to Run the Lottery under Section 5*, p. 8, condition 2 (i).
419. Comptroller and Auditor General, *Evaluating the Applications*, p. 36, para. 4.8.i., and Camelot, *Annual Report and Accounts 2000*, p. 11.
420. Comptroller and Auditor General, *Evaluating the Applications*, p. 36, para. 4.8.i.
421. Culture, Media and Sport Committee, *The Operation of the National Lottery. First Report, Vol. I, H.C. 56–I, Session 2000–2001* (The Stationery Office, London, 07/03/01), p. xi, para. 29.
422. National Heritage Committee, *Minutes of Evidence. H.C. 240, iii, Session 1995–96*, p. 47, para. (2); (ii) (c) Camelot, *Annual Report and Accounts 1997*, p. 24, Lynn Doolan (Camelot Lottery Line representative), telephone interview (28/09/98), Camelot, *Annual Report and Accounts 1999*, p. 15, Camelot, *Annual Report and Accounts 2000*, p. 10, and Camelot, *Annual Report and Accounts 2001*, p. 10.
423. Camelot, *Annual Report and Accounts 1996*, p. 2.
424. National Heritage Committee, *Minutes of Evidence. H.C. 240, iii, Session 1995–96*, p. 47, para. (2) (ii) (c); Doolan, telephone interview; Camelot, *Annual Report and Accounts 2000*, p. 4.
425. National Heritage Committee, *Minutes of Evidence. H.C. 240, iii, Session 1995–96*, p. 47, para. (2) (ii) (c).
426. Camelot, *Annual Report and Accounts 1997*, p. 13; Camelot, *Annual Review 1998*, p. 4; Doolan, telephone interview.
427. NLC, *Annual Report 1998/99*, p. 4.
428. Camelot, *Annual Report and Accounts 2000*, p. 10.
429. Camelot, *Annual Report and Accounts 2001*.
430. See Douglas, *British Charitable Gambling*, pp. 268–78.
431. National Lottery etc. Act 1993, Sections 48–52.
432. Calculations made from details provided at Table 3. These data lend support to critics of Instants who claim that the game's dynamics have more in common with the harder end of gambling and are quite distinct from those appertaining to the more benign Draw Lottery.
433. Camelot, *Annual Report and Accounts 1996*, p. 8.
434. Camelot, *Annual Report and Accounts 2001*, p. 25. See also Table 3 in this volume.

435. See also p. 175, fn. 475.
436. For the year ending 31 March 1999 society (charity) lotteries and local authority lotteries registered with the Gaming Board sold tickets valued at £161 million (the majority of which were scratch-cards). Societies (charities) and local authorities with proceeds from a lottery of less than £20,000 do not have to register with the Board. There is no central agency collecting data on these smaller lotteries. Gaming Board for Great Britain, *Annual Report 1997/ 98*, p. 60 para. 7.4 and Gaming Board for Great Britain, *Annual Report 1998/ 99*, p. 57, table 27.
437. Camelot, *Annual Review 1998*, p. 4.
438. FitzHerbert, Rahman and Harvey, *Lottery Yearbook 1999*, p. 9.
439. Broadcasting Complaints Commission, *The Bulletin*, no. 14 (24/09/98), p. 7.
440. *Directions to the Director General*, Section 2 (1) (b).
441. *Licence to Run the Lottery under Section 5*, condition 9 (2) (c).
442. Lord Skidelsky, *Official Report National Lottery Bill (H.L.)*, vol. 584, no. 82 (Hansard, London, 18/12/97), col. 739.
443. E. Colonius, 'The big payoff from lotteries', *Forbes* (25/03/91), p. 111.
444. Richard McGowan, *State Lotteries and Legalized Gambling* (Quorum Books, Westport, CT, 1994), pp. 63–4.
445. NLC, *Annual Report 1998/99*. pp. 20–1.
446. Camelot, *Annual Report and Accounts 1997*, p. 12. The sale of Instants fell from £877 million to £801 million between 1997 and 1998, Director General of the Lottery, *Annual Report 1997/98*, p. 8, app. A.
447. FitzHerbert and Paterson, *Lottery Yearbook 1998*, p. 10. Calculation can also be made by reference to Table 3.
448. NLC, *Annual Report 2000/01*, p. 11.
449. *Idem.*
450. Camelot, 'The National Lottery launches the first ever Instants game with a top prize of £1 million', news release.
451. National Lottery etc. Act 1993, Part I, Section 6.
452. Committee of Public Accounts, *Forty-First Report*, p. xiii, para. 32.
453. Miers, 'The implementation and effects of Britain's Lottery', p. 358.
454. *Idem* and Miers, 'Regulation and the public interest', p. 494.
455. Davis, *Minutes of Evidence. Forty-First Report*, p. 15, para. 148.
456. *Ibid.*, p. 15, para. 149.
457. Director General of the Lottery, *Annual Report 1997/98*, p. 5.
458. *Idem.*
459. *Idem.*
460. Vernons Lotteries Ltd, National Lottery football game ends (press release) (Vernons Lotteries Ltd, Liverpool, 16/04/99).
461. *Idem.*
462. NLC, *Annual Report 1998/99*, p. 5.
463. Camelot, *'Thunderball' Explanatory Leaflet* (Camelot Group plc, Watford, n.d., circa May/June 1999).
464. Camelot, *Annual Report and Accounts 2000*, p. 4.
465. *Directions to the Director General*, Section 2 (1) (a).
466. Director General of the Lottery, *Annual Report 1996/97*, p. 8.
467. This restriction was lifted in February 2000. See p. 118 in this volume.
468. *Directions to the Director General*, Sections 2 (2), 3 and 4.

469. Patricia A. McQueen, 'Alberta to vote on VLTs', *International Gaming and Wagering Business*, vol. 19, no. 9 (September 1998), pp. 111–12.
470. Miers, 'The implementation and effects of Britain's Lottery', p. 347.
471. Miers, 'Regulation and the public interest', p. 512.
472. *Idem.*
473. Director General of the Lottery, *Annual Report 1996/97*, p. 27, app. C.
474. James Keulemans (Oflot Public Affairs representative), telephone interview, (01/10/98).
475. Instants sales 1995/96 were £1523 million, 1996/97 £877 million, 1997/98 £801 million, 1998/99 £699 million, 1999/2000 £561 million, and 2000/01 £546 million. Figures taken from Oflot and the NLC's annual reports.
476. Comptroller and Auditor General, *Payments to the National Lottery Distribution Fund*, p. 15, para. 2.5. The Director General refused Camelot's request that the shortfall should be retained for future prizes. Memorandum submitted by Oflot to National Heritage Committee, *Minutes of Evidence. H.C. 240, iii, Session 1995–96*, p. 63, para. 26.
477. NLC, *Annual Report 2000/01*, p. 25, app. A.
478. Director General of the Lottery, *Annual Report 1996/97*, p. 7.
479. *Idem.*
480. Director General of the Lottery, *Annual Report 1995/96*, p. 23.
481. Comptroller and Auditor General, *Payments to the National Lottery Distribution Fund*, p. 20, fig. 6.
482. NLC, *Annual Report 2000/01*, p. 25, app. A.
483. Comptroller and Auditor General, *Payments to the National Lottery Distribution Fund*, p. 20, fig. 6.
484. NLC, *Annual Report 2000/01*, p. 25, app. A.
485. Comptroller and Auditor General, *Payments to the National Lottery Distribution Fund*, p. 17, para. 2.12.
486. *Idem.*
487. *Ibid.*, p. 20, fig. 6.
488. Simon Holden, 'BBC to pay £1/2 M a year for Lottery', *Liverpool Daily Post* (05/06/96).
489. *Idem.*
490. Neither Camelot nor the BBC are prepared to reveal the terms on which the contractual arrangements have been renewed, maintaining that this is 'commercially sensitive' information. Lynn Doolan (Camelot Lottery Line representative), telephone interview (05/10/98), and Erika Leonard (BBC production executive), correspondence from (18/03/99). By 2000 the annual fee stood at around £1 million of which £0.7 million was passed to the Distribution Fund. Tim Holley (Chief Executive of Camelot), *Minutes of Evidence Submitted to Culture, Media and Sport Committee. The Operation of the National Lottery First Report. Vol. II, H.C. 958 i, Session 2000–2001* (The Stationery Office, London, 09/11/00), p. 17, para. 41.
491. Director General of the Lottery, *Annual Report 1995/96*, p. 38.
492. Camelot, *Annual Report and Accounts 1997*, p. 13.
493. Director General of the Lottery, *Annual Report 1995/96*, p. 38.
494. Director General of the Lottery, *Annual Report 1996/97*, p. 6.
495. Director General of the Lottery, *Annual Report 1994/95*, p. 22.
496. Director General of the Lottery, *Annual Report 1995/96*, p. 38.

497. National Lottery Act 1998, Section (2) (3).
498. Comptroller and Auditor General, *Payments to the National Lottery Distribution Fund*, p. 19, fig. 6.
499. NLC, *Annual Report 2000/01*, p. 25, app. A.
500. Calculations derived from information included at Tables 1 and 3.
501. FitzHerbert and Paterson, *Lottery Yearbook 1998*, p. 10.
502. Sir George Russell (Chairman of Camelot), *Minutes of Evidence Submitted to the National Heritage Committee. H.C. 240, iii, Session 1995–96*, p. 49, para. 179.
503. Patrick Moon, 'The National Lottery and the economy in 1996', in FitzHerbert and Rhoades, *Lottery Yearbook 1997*, p. 31.
504. Diane Coyle, 'Delayed payouts by Lottery provide £2 billion boost for Treasury', *Independent* (16/09/96). See also Table 3.
505. Moon, 'The National Lottery', p. 32.
506. 'Bonus winners', *Daily Mail* (01/06/96).
507. Miers, 'Regulation and the public interest', p. 515.
508. E. Kent-Smith and S. Thomas, 'Luck had nothing to do with it. Launching the UK's largest consumer brand', *Journal of Market Research Society*, vol. 37, no. 2 (1995), p. 131. See also Committee of Public Accounts, *Forty-First Report*, p. ix, para. 9.
509. Kent-Smith and Thomas, 'Luck had nothing to do with it', p. 130.
510. Comptroller and Auditor General, *Evaluating the Applications*, p. 23, para. 3.14.
511. Director General of the Lottery, *Annual Report 1995/96*, p. 14.
512. Supplementary memorandum submitted by Camelot to National Heritage Committee, *Minutes of Evidence. H.C. 240, iii, Session 1995–96*, p. 58, para. 4 (a).
513. Camelot, *Annual Report and Accounts 1995*, p. 14, n. 13.
514. Supplementary memorandum submitted by Camelot to National Heritage Committee, *Minutes of Evidence. H.C. 240, iii, Session 1995–96*, p. 58, para. 4 (a).
515. Chris Blackhurst and Stephen Castle, 'Government swoops on lottery profit', *Independent on Sunday* (11/05/97).
516. Supplementary memorandum submitted by Camelot to National Heritage Committee, *Minutes of Evidence. H.C. 240, iii, Session 1995–96*, p. 59, para. 4 (d).
517. Marianne Macdonald, 'Camelot hits the jackpot with £10 M bonanza', *Independent* (07/06/95).
518. Camelot, *Annual Report and Accounts 1995*, pp. 33 and 38.
519. Macdonald, 'Camelot hits the jackpot'.
520. Camelot, *Annual Report and Accounts 1996*, p. 36.
521. Supplementary memorandum submitted by Camelot to National Heritage Committee, *Minutes of Evidence. H.C. 240, iii, Session 1995–96*, p. 59, para. 4 (d).
522. Camelot, *Annual Report and Accounts 1996*, p. 36, *Annual Report and Accounts 1997*, p. 35, and *Annual Review 1998*, p. 23.
523. Stephen Breyer, 'Analysing regulatory failure', p. 563.
524. Calculations (which exclude exceptional items) taken from Camelot's annual reports and accounts. Camelot itself expects post-tax profits to remain under 1 per cent over the period of the licence. Camelot, *Annual Report and Accounts 1996*, p. 2; Camelot, *Annual Review 1998*, p. 14; Camelot, *Annual Report and*

Accounts 1999, p. 29; Camelot, *Annual Report and Accounts 2000*, p. 24, and Camelot, *Annual Report and Accounts 2001*, p. 25.

525. *Labour Party Manifesto*, p. 31, and Smith, *The People's Lottery*, pp. 28–9.
526. T. La Fleur's *Lottery Annual Report 1994*, cited by Smith, *The People's Lottery*, p. 28.
527. See Table 3. Exceptional costs of £12 million were incurred by Camelot in FY 2001 and related to securing award of new Licence. Camelot, *Annual Report 2001*, p. 4.
528. Director General of the Lottery, *Annual Report 1995/96*, p. 35. The independent lottery expert Terri La Fleur ranked Camelot the most efficient lottery operator in the world for four consecutive years from 1997. Camelot, *Annual Report and Accounts 2000*, p. 4.
529. Camelot, *Annual Review 1998*, p. 22.
530. See Table 1 in this volume.
531. Camelot, *Annual Review 1998*, p. 14.
532. Director General of the Lottery, *Annual Report 1996/97*, p. 3. See also Table 3, p. 71, in this volume.
533. NLC, *Annual Report 1998/99*, p. 4.
534. See Table 1 in this volume.

Chapter 4

1. Marver H. Bernstein, *Regulating Business by Independent Commission* (Princeton University Press, Princeton, NJ, 1995), p. 88.
2. *Ibid.*, p. 91.
3. Conclusions to the Committee of Public Accounts, *Payments to the National Lottery Distribution Fund Twentieth Report* (The Stationery Office, London, 17/03/97), p. xviii, para. 52.
4. Peter Davis (Director General of the National Lottery), *Examination of Witnesses. Minutes of Evidence Taken Before the National Heritage Committee. H.C. 240, iii, Session 1995–96* (HMSO, London, 29/02/96), p. 67, para. 291.
5. Charles Wardle, *Minutes of Evidence Taken Before the PAC Twentieth Report* (The Stationery Office, London, 17/03/96), p. 10, para. 94.
6. Peter Davis, *Minutes of Evidence. Twentieth Report*, p. 10, para. 94.
7. Price Waterhouse Corporate Finance, *Regulated Industries: The UK Framework. Regulatory Brief 2* (Centre for the Study of Regulated Industries, London, 2nd edn, 1996), p. 59, para. 9.2.
8. National Lottery etc. Act 1993, Section 8 (3) (a).
9. Davis, *Minutes of Evidence Evaluating the Applications to Run the National Lottery and the Director General's Travel and Hospitality Arrangements Taken Before the Committee of Public Accounts on 11/12/95. Forty-First Report* (HMSO, London, 15/07/96), p. 24, para. 270.
10. David Miers, 'Regulation and the public interest: commercial gambling and the National Lottery', *Modern Law Review*, vol. 59, no. 4 (July 1996), p. 515.
11. *National Lottery Act 1998*, Section 2.
12. Director General of the National Lottery, *Annual Report 1995/96* (Oflot, London, 17/07/96), pp. 12–13.
13. Davis, *Minutes of Evidence. Twentieth Report*, p. 10, para. 95.

14. *Licence to Run the National Lottery under Section 5 of the National Lottery etc. Act 1993* (Oflot, London, July 1994), pp. 7–10, conditions 2 and 3.
15. Director General of the Lottery, *Annual Report (1995/96)*, p. 13.
16. By the time Peter Davis was appointed Regulatory Advisor to the Department of National Heritage in July 1993, the National Lottery Bill had passed through the Committee stage and was ready to go to the House of Commons for final reading before receiving Royal Assent in October 1993. James Keulemans (Oflot Public Affairs representative), telephone interview (05/03/99).
17. Bernstein, *Regulating Business*, p. 224.
18. *Idem.*
19. Director General of the National Lottery, *Annual Report 1996/97* (The Stationery Office, London, 26/06/97), p. 6.
20. Davis, *Minutes of Evidence. Twentieth Report*, p. 10, para. 94.
21. Robert A. Kagan, *Regulatory Justice* (Russell Sage Foundation, New York, 1978), p. 86.
22. Albert J. Reiss Jr, 'Selecting strategies of social control over organizational life', in Keith Hawkins and John M. Thomas (eds), *Enforcing Regulation* (Kluwer-Nijhoff Publishing, Boston, 1984), p. 26.
23. *Ibid.*, p. 24.
24. *Idem.*
25. 'Lottery risks huge fines', *Independent on Sunday* (29/05/94).
26. Reiss, 'Selecting strategies', p. 27.
27. *Idem.*
28. *Ibid.*, p. 28.
29. Martin Ricketts, 'Summary and conclusions', in Alan Peacock (ed.), *The Regulation Game* (Blackwell, Oxford, 1984), p. 158.
30. Davis, *Minutes of Evidence. Twentieth Report*, p. 4, para. 34.
31. National Heritage Committee, *The National Lottery Second Report, Vol. I, H.C. 240–I, Session 1995/96* (HMSO, London, 14/05/96), p. viii, para. 20.
32. Davis, *Minutes of Evidence. Twentieth Report*, p. 4, para. 34.
33. Director General of the Lottery, *Annual Report 1996/97*, introductory remarks.
34. 'UK Lottery', *Financial Times* (07/06/97).
35. Director General of the Lottery, *Annual Report 1996/97*, p. 7.
36. Keulemans, telephone interview (05/03/99).
37. Jean-Jacques Laffont and Jean Tirole, *A Theory of Incentives in Procurement and Regulation* (MIT Press, Cambridge, MA, and London, 1993), p. 644.
38. Cf. *National Lottery Act 1998*.
39. Alan Peacock and Ian Orton, 'The measurement of compliance costs', in Peacock (ed.), *The Regulation Game* (Blackwell, Oxford, 1984), p. 28.
40. Cento Veljanovski, 'The regulation game', in Cento Veljanovski, *Regulation and the Market* (Institute of Economic Affairs, London, 1991), p. 24.
41. *Ibid.*, p. 25.
42. *Ibid.*, pp. 24–5.
43. Peacock and Orton, 'The bargaining process as a means of implementing and enforcing regulations in the United Kingdom', in Peacock, *Regulation Game*, p. 97.
44. Committee of Public Accounts, *Twentieth Report*, p. ix, para. 8.
45. Director General of the Lottery, *Annual Report 1996/97*, p. 6.

46. *Idem*.
47. *Idem*.
48. Director General of the Lottery, *Annual Report 1995/96*, p. 19, and *Annual Report 1997/98*, (The Stationery Office, London, 09/07/98), p. 6.
49. Luke FitzHerbert and Lucy Rhoades (eds), *The National Lottery Yearbook 1997 Edition* (Directory of Social Change, London, 1997), p. 23.
50. 'It should be him', *The Times* (04/02/98).
51. National Heritage Committee, *The National Lottery Second Report*, p. xi, para. 37.
52. Robert Sheldon (former Chairman of the Commons Public Accounts Committee), cited by George Parker and Scheherazade Daneshkhu, 'Lottery regulator's rôle faces overhaul after GTech case', *Financial Times* (06/02/98). See also Joe Ashton (National Heritage Committee), *The National Lottery Minutes of Evidence. H.C. 240, iii, Session 1995–96* (HMSO, London, 29/02/96), p. 66, para. 281.
53. C. Smith (Secretary of State for Culture, Media and Sport), National Lottery Bill (Lords) (second reading) (07/04/98), col. 165.
54. *Idem*.
55. FitzHerbert and Rhoades, *Lottery Yearbook 1997*, p. 22. See Oflot's mission statement cited at pp. 14–15 in this volume.
56. John Vickers and George Yarrow, *Privatization: An Economic Analysis* (MIT Press, Cambridge, MA, and London, 1988), p. 36.
57. C. D. Foster, *Privatization, Public Ownership and the Regulation of Natural Monopoly* (Blackwell, Oxford and Cambridge, MA, 1992), p. 315.
58. *Ibid.*, p. 316.
59. Breyer, *Regulation and Its Reform* (Harvard University Press, Cambridge, MA, 1982), p. 79.
60. Foster, *Privatization*, p. 315.
61. *Ibid.*, p. 316.
62. *Ibid.*, p. 286.
63. Harriet Spicer (National Lottery Commissioner), *Minutes of Evidence Submitted to Culture, Media and Sport Committee. The Operation of the National Lottery. First Report. Vol. II, H.C. 958, iii, Session 1999–2000* (The Stationery Office, London, 23/11/00), p. 110, para. 292.
64. The Director General conceded that some of GTech's business practices, while acceptable in the United States, would not have been acceptable in this country. Davis, *Minutes of Evidence. Forty-First Report*, p. 25, para. 285.
65. Michael E. Levine and Jennifer L. Forrence, 'Regulatory capture, public interest and the public agenda: toward a synthesis', *Journal of Law, Economics and Organisation* (special issue) (1990), p. 167.
66. Bernstein, *Regulating Business*, p. 79.
67. *Idem*.
68. *Ibid.*, p. 154.
69. Foster, *Privatization*, p. 415.
70. James McCormick and Elizabeth Kendall, *A Flutter on the Future? Why the National Lottery Needs Citizens' Juries* (Institute for Public Policy Research, London, November 1995), p. 2.
71. John Stewart, Elizabeth Kendall and Anna Coote, *Citizens' Juries* (Institute for Public Policy Research, London, 1994), p. 11.

72. McCormick and Kendall, *A Flutter on the Future*, p. 2.
73. *Idem*.
74. Dr J. Cunningham, *Parliamentary Debates: House of Commons Official Report*, vol. 264, no. 149 (Hansard, HMSO, London, 25/10/95), col. 1032.
75. Smith, National Lottery Bill (Lords) (second reading), col. 165.
76. National Lottery Act 1998, Schedule I, Part II, Section 4.
77. John Stoker (Director General of the National Lottery), cited by John Frank-Keyes, 'Rebuilding the UK Lottery's image', *International Gaming and Wagering Business*, vol. 19, no. 7 (July 1998), p. 43.
78. Charles F. Phillips Jr, *The Economics of Regulation, Theory and Practice in the Transportation and Public Utilities Industries* (Richard D. Irwin, Homewood, IL, 1969), p. 718.
79. Horace M. Gray, 'The passing of the public utility concept', *Journal of Land and Public Utility Economics*, vol. 16, no. 1 (February 1940), p. 15.
80. *Ibid.*, p. 9.
81. Benefits from the Lottery accruing to society are not confined to the users or purchasers of the product, but extend to non-users (free riders) as well in the form of the Good Causes to which the Lottery's bounty is applied. Whether or not one buys a ticket, improved amenities and facilities in local communities that have received Lottery funding are a very visible and immediate benefit open to all. In this way the Lottery may be said to produce positive externalities or spillovers.
82. Cento Veljanovski, *The Future of Industry Regulation in the U.K.: A Report of Independent Inquiry* (European Policy Forum for British and European Studies, London, January 1993), p. 67.
83. R. G. Noll and B. M. Owen, *The Political Economy of Deregulation: Interest Groups in the Regulatory Process* (American Enterprise Institute for Public Policy Research, Washington, DC, and London, 1983), p. 32.
84. Bernstein, *Regulating Business*, p. 218. It is also noteworthy that in an effort to buttress the company's reputation, Camelot in the years ending March 1997 and March 1998 claimed to be the UK's most generous corporate donor in terms of the percentage of pre-tax profits (unconnected with monies passed to the Distribution Fund) donated to charities (9.46 per cent for 1997, 7.04 per cent for 1998, 4.47 per cent for 1999 and 4 per cent for 2000). In the calendar year 1999 the company donated 20.2 per cent of pre-tax profits (1999 includes value of donations in kind): *Corporate Citizen* (September 1997), cited by Camelot, *Annual Report and Accounts 1997* (Camelot Group plc, Watford, 1997), pp. 5, 10 and 35; Camelot, *Annual Review 1998* (Camelot Group plc, Watford, 1998), p. 12; Camelot, *Annual Report and Accounts 1999* (Camelot Group plc, Watford, 1999), p. 8; Camelot, 'Camelot tops list of UK's most generous companies' (press release) (Camelot, Watford, 02/10/98); Camelot, *Annual Report and Accounts 2000* (Camelot Group plc, Watford, 2000), p. 8; Camelot, *Annual Report and Accounts 2001* (Camelot Group plc, Watford, 2001), p. 7. The company also launched a television advertising campaign in the spring of 1999, highlighting some of the Good Causes that are in receipt of National Lottery funding. During the financial year 1998/99 Camelot appointed a Director for Social Responsibility and committed the company to a comprehensive social audit of the Lottery (the Report was published early in 2000 and is referred to elsewhere in the text). Paul Vallely, 'Does the

Lottery add up?', *Independent* (04/06/99). Finally in August 1999, Camelot agreed with the government to withdraw Lottery terminals from the premises of retailers found guilty of selling smuggled alcohol or tobacco. Colin Brown, 'Lottery ban on bootleg traders' shops', *Independent* (17/08/99).

85. Abuses associated with lotteries *per se* had led to their general ban (with some limited exceptions) between 1826 and 1934. See Andrew Douglas, *British Charitable Gambling 1956–1994* (The Athlone Press, London, 1995), pp. 265–6.

86. National Heritage Committee, *Minutes of Evidence. The National Lottery, H.C. 240–I, Session 1995–96* (HMSO, London, 20/02/96), p. xi, para. 35.

87. Miers, 'Regulation and the public interest', p. 516.

88. Peacock and Orton, 'The bargaining process', in Peacock, *Regulation Game*, p. 97.

89. Committee of Public Accounts, *Forty-first Report*, p. vii, para. xvii.

90. Virginia Bottomley (Secretary of State for National Heritage), 'Letter to Peter Davis (Director General of the National Lottery) (19/12/95)', cited in Committee of Public Accounts, *Appendices to Minutes of Evidence. Forty-first Report*, p. 61, app. 4, and Committee of Public Accounts, *Forty-first Report*, p. viii, para. xxi, and p. xviii, para. 64.

91. An Advisory Group Report, *The National Lottery Initiatives and Recommendations* (Labour Party, London, 1996), p. 6.

92. Conclusion to the Committee of Public Accounts, *Twentieth Report*, p. xviii, para. 52.

93. *Idem.*

94. The Director General also had the power (which he chose not to exercise) of alternatively allowing the Prize Target Shortfall to be used for prizes in the following year. National Heritage Committee, *The National Lottery Second Report*, p. viii, para. 20.

95. Report of the Comptroller and Auditor General, *Payments to the National Lottery Distribution Fund, H.C. 678, Session 1995–96* (National Audit Office, HMSO, London, 23/07/96), p. 50, para. 4.16.

96. National Lottery etc. Act 1933, Section 8 (3) (a).

97. Comptroller and Auditor General, *Payments to the National Lottery Distribution Fund*, p. 50, para. 4.16 (b).

98. *Ibid.*, p. 50, para. 4.16 (a).

99. Committee of Public Accounts, *Twentieth Report*, pp. vii and xvi.

100. National Heritage Committee, *The National Lottery Second Report*, p. viii, para. 20.

101. Director General of the National Lottery, *Annual Report 1993/94* (HMSO, London, 01/11/94), p. 5.

102. Davis, *Minutes of Evidence. Twentieth Report*, p. 13, para. 20.

103. Conclusions to Committee of Public Accounts, *Twentieth Report*, p. xvi, para. 41.

104. *Idem.*

105. *Idem.*

106. Keulemans, telephone interview (05/03/99).

107. Committee of Public Accounts, *Twentieth Report*, pp. vi–vii, paras xi–xii.

108. *Ibid.*, p. vii, para. xii.

109. Keulemans, telephone interview (05/03/99).

110. Committee of Public Acounts, *Twentieth Report*, p. vii, para. xiii.
111. *Ibid.*, p. xiv, para. 33.
112. Davis, *Minutes of Evidence. Twentieth Report*, p. 15, para. 150.
113. Iain Vallance (Chairman of British Telecommunications PLC), Speech to Annual General Meeting (30/07/92).
114. Catherine Price, 'Economic regulation of privatised monopolies', in Peter M. Jackson and Catherine M. Price (eds), *Privatisation and Regulation: A Review of the Issues* (Longman, Essex, 1994), p. 81.
115. *Idem.*
116. See p. 25 in this volume, including p. 156 n. 18.
117. Conclusions to Committee of Public Accounts, *Twentieth Report*, p. x, para. 10.
118. Committee of Public Accounts, *Twentieth Report*, p. ix, para. 7.
119. *Ibid.*, p. vi, para. viii.
120. M. Rankin, 'The cabinet and the agencies: towards accountability in British Columbia', *University of British Columbia Law Review*, vol. 19 (1985), p. 36.
121. Bernstein, *Regulating Business*, p. 87.
122. *Ibid.*, p. 92.
123. *Ibid.*, p. 87.
124. Veljanovski, *Industry Regulation in the U.K.*, p. 77.
125. *Ibid.*, p. 80.
126. Standing Order No 122 – (1) cited by Committee of Public Accounts, *Forty-first Report*, p. ii. Oflot's expenditure (£2.4 million for financial year 1997/98) was covered by money transferred from the Distribution Fund. Director General of the Lottery, *Annual Report 1993/94*, p. 15, para. 10.2, and *Annual Report 1997/98*, p. 19, app. I.
127. Anthony I. Ogus, *Regulation: Legal Form and Economic Theory* (Clarendon Press, Oxford, 1994), p. 104.
128. Peter Boulding, *Whither Regulation? Current Developments in Regulated Industries*. 1997 occasional Paper 7 (Centre for the Study of Regulated Industries, London, 1997), p. 5, para. 1.3.1.
129. Ogus, *Regulation*, p. 104.
130. Veljanovski, *Industry Regulation in the U.K.*, p. 69.
131. Alan Williams (Lab), Mike Hall (Lab), *Minutes of Evidence. Twentieth Report*, *passim*, and Robert Maclennan (Lib Dem), Angela Eagle (Lab) and Alan Williams (Lab), *Minutes of Evidence. Forty-first Report*, *passim*.
132. Peter Davis (Director General of the National Lottery), memorandum submitted to the PAC (26/01/96), Committee of Public Accounts, *Forty-first Report*, p. 40, app. 3.
133. *Idem.*
134. Clerk to the Committee of Public Accounts, copy of part of letter to Director General (10/01/96), *Forty-first Report*, p. 38, app. 3.
135. *Idem.*
136. Davis, *Minutes of Evidence. Forty-first Report*, p. 9, para. 87, and Robert Sheldon (Chairman), *Minutes of Evidence. Forty-first Report*, p. 9, para. 89.
137. Peter Davis (Director General of the National Lottery), copy of part of letter to the clerk to the PAC (26/01/96), Committee of Public Accounts, *Forty-first Report*, p. 39, app. 2.
138. Davis, memorandum submitted to the PAC (26/01/96), Committee of Public Accounts, *Forty-first Report*, p. 40, app. 3.

139. Committee of Public Accounts, *Forty-first Report*, p. xv, para. 40, and Conclusions to Committee of Public Accounts, *Forty-first Report*, p. xvii, para. 57.

140. Davis, *Minutes of Evidence. Forty-first Report*, p. 1, para. 1.

141. Conclusions to Committee of Public Accounts, *Forty-first Report*, p. xvii, para. 56.

142. Davis, *Minutes of Evidence. Forty-first Report*, p. 1, para. 1.

143. Committee of Public Accounts, *Forty-first Report*, p. vii, para. xvi. See also Report of the Comptroller and Auditor General, *Evaluating the Applications to Run the National Lottery, H.C. 569 Session 1994–95* (National Audit Office, HMSO, London, 07/07/95), p. 8, para. 1.16.

144. Michael Stern, *Minutes of Evidence. Twentieth Report*, p. 14, paras. 142–3, and Comptroller and Auditor General, *Payments to the National Lottery Distribution Fund*, p. 10, para. 1.8.

145. Davis, *Minutes of Evidence. Twentieth Report*, p. 14, para. 143.

146. Michael Carpenter (Treasury solicitor), memorandum from the Treasury Solicitor (05/12/96), *Minutes of Evidence. Twentieth Report*, p. 22, app. I, annex A.

147. *Idem.*

148. Williams, *Minutes of Evidence. Twentieth Report*, p. 8, para. 82.

149. Committee of Public Accounts, *Twentieth Report*, p. xiii, para. 27.

150. Conclusions to the Committee of Public Accounts, *Twentieth Report*, p. xviii, para. 54. These areas (referred to earlier) related to delays in getting compliance programmes established, security issues at the retail level and the matter of interest accruing to Camelot rather than the Distribution Fund on certain accounts (*idem*).

151. Nigel Gale (Director of the National Audit Office), telephone interview (30/03/99).

152. Report of the Comptroller and Auditor General, *National Lottery Distribution Fund Accounts. H.C. 269, Session 1997–98* (The Stationery Office, London, 04/03/99), p. 7.

153. Department of National Heritage, *Nineteenth Report. CM 2990, Session 1994–95* (HMSO, London, October 1995), p. 11. See also General Conclusions to Committee of Public Accounts, *Twentieth Report*, p. xviii, para. 49.

154. Department of National Heritage, Treasury Minute to Nineteenth Report, p. 11, para. 38, and Comptroller and Auditor General, *Payments to the National Lottery Distribution Fund*, p. 11, fig. 2.

155. *Idem.* The Treasury minute also affirmed the position taken by the Treasury solicitor that under the National Audit Act of 1983 the Comptroller and Auditor General did not have access to Camelot's books as it was a private sector company and not a public body as defined in Sections 6 and 7 of the Act. See also Committee of Public Accounts, *Twentieth Report*, p. xviii, para. 49.

156. Comptroller and Auditor General, *Payments to the National Lottery Distribution Fund*, p. 10, para. 1.9.

157. *Idem.*

158. *Idem.*

159. National Lottery Act 1998, Sections 1 and 5. N.B. The National Audit Office does not enjoy similar access to the records of the companies responsible for running the public utilities. Gale, Telephone interview (30/03/99).

160. William R. Eadington, 'Ethical and policy considerations in the spread of commercial gambling', in Jan McMillen (ed.), *Gambling Cultures: Studies in History and Interpretation* (Routledge, London, 1996), p. 244.

161. Julie Ault (Deputy Director of the Ohio Lottery Problem Gambling Awareness Dept), cited by Kathleen Ward, 'Lotteries address responsible play', *Public Gaming International*, vol. 26, no. 8 (September 1998), p. 31.

162. Charles Singer, 'The ethics of gambling', in Colin S. Campbell and John Lowman (eds), *Gambling in Canada: Golden Goose or Trojan Horse? A Report from the First National Symposium on Lotteries and Gambling* (School of Criminology, Simon Fraser University, British Columbia, 1989), p. 287.

163. Alex Rubner, *The Economics of Gambling* (Macmillan, London, 1966), p. 77.

164. Gaming Board for Great Britain, *Annual Report 1996/97* (The Stationery Office, London, 10/07/97), p. 7, para. 1.25.

165. Culture, Media and Sport Committee, *The Operation of the National Lottery. First Report, vol. I, H.C. 56–I, Session 2000–2001*, p. xxxii, para. 122.

166. *Idem*. Cf. Sir Alan Budd (Chairman), *Gambling Review Report* (The Stationery Office, London, CM5206, July 2001). N.B. Responsibility for policy on gambling was transferred from the Home Office to the Department for Culture, Media and Sport during the summer of 2001. Gaming Board for Great Britain, *Annual Report 2000/01* (The Stationery Office, London, 11/07/01), p. 7, para. 1.3.

167. Culture, Media and Sport Committee, *The Operation of the National Lottery. First Report, vol. I, H.C. 56–I, Session 2000–2001*, p. xxxii, para. 24.

168. Jerome Skolnick, *House of Cards* (Little, Brown, Boston, 1978), pp. 174–5.

169. FitzHerbert, Rahman and Harvey (eds), *The National Lottery Yearbook 1999 Edition* (Directory of Social Change, London, 1999), p. 7. See also Lea Paterson, 'How lucky Treasury is all-round winner', *The Times* (31/08/99).

170. Director General of the Lottery, *Annual Report 1993/94*, p. 6.

171. Department for Culture, Media and Sport, 'Government announces names of the new Lottery Commissioners' (news release) (25/01/99).

172. Tom Weyman-Jones, 'Deregulation', in Jackson and Price (eds), *Privatisation and Regulation*, p. 114.

173. Ben W. Lewis, 'Emphasis and misemphasis in regulatory policy', in William G. Shepard and Thomas G. Gies (eds), *Utility Regulation, New Directions in Theory and Practice* (Random House, New York, 1996), p. 245.

174. James Keulemans (National Lottery Commission Public Affairs representative), telephone interview (08/04/99).

175. *National Lottery Act 1998*, Section 2.

176. *Ibid.*, Section 5.

177. Lord Skidelsky, *Official Report of the Grand Committee on the National Lottery Bill (H.L.), Vol. 584, No. 87* (Hansard, London, 19/01/98), CWH7.

178. P. W. Macavoy, W. T. Stanbury, George Yarrow and R. J. Zeckhauser, *Privatization and State-Owned Enterprises* (Kluwer Academic Publishers, Boston, 1989), p. 25.

179. Comptroller and Auditor General, *Payments to the National Lottery Distribution Fund*, p. 8, para. 1.6.

180. Graham, *Is There a Crisis in Regulatory Accountability? Discussion Paper 13* (Centre for the Study of Regulated Industries, London, 1995), pp. 38–9.

181. A. Davis and J. Willman, *What Next? Agencies, Departments and the Civil Service* (Institute of Public Policy Research, London, 1991), p. 33.
182. Cento Veljanovski, 'The Power of the Regulator', in Adam Smith Institute, *But Who Will Regulate the Regulators?* (Adam Smith Institute, London, 1993), p. 25.
183. Foster, *Privatization*, p. 417.
184. *Idem.*

Chapter 5

1. The staff of Oflot were transferred to the new National Lottery Commission on 1 April 1999. Their status also changed from civil servants (at Oflot) to public-sector employees (at the National Lottery Commission). As a government department the costs of Oflot were funded from the Parliamentary Vote Supply, with administrative costs net of Section 5 and Section 6 Licence fees received being recoverable from the Distribution Fund. Oflot's expenditure was typically of the order of £2.5 million p.a. Funding for the Lottery Commission has been by way of Grant in Aid from the Department of Culture, Media and Sport, and is also recoverable from the Distribution Fund. Director General of the National Lottery, *Annual Report 1994/95* (HMSO, London, 16/10/95), p. 6, paras 6.3 and 6.5. *Annual Report 1997/98* (The Stationery Office, London, 09/07/98), p. 19, App. i, and James Keulemans, telephone interview (08/04/99).
2. Irwin M. Stelzer, 'Lessons for UK regulation from recent US experience', in M. E. Beesley (ed.), *Regulating Utilities: A Time for Change? Readings 44* (Institute of Economic Affairs, London, 1996), pp. 191 and 196.
3. Department of CMS (news release) (25/01/99).
4. Andreas Whittam Smith, 'Sack the Lottery Commissioners before it's too late', *Independent* (09/10/00)
5. James Keulemans (National Lottery Commission Public Affairs representative), telephone interview (20/04/99).
6. *Idem.*
7. *National Lottery Act 1998*, Schedule I, Part II, Section 4.
8. John Stoker (Director General of the National Lottery), cited by John Frank-Keyes, 'Rebuilding the UK Lottery's image', *International Gaming and Wagering Business*, vol. 19, no. 7 (July 1998), p. 43.
9. C. D. Foster, *Privatization, Public Ownership and the Regulation of Natural Monopoly* (Blackwell, Oxford and Cambridge, MA, 1992), p. 416.
10. Mark Harris (Chief Executive of the National Lottery Commission), telephone interview (07/10/99).
11. *Idem.*
12. Catherine Price, 'Economic regulation of privatized monopolies', in Peter M. Jackson and Catherine M. Price (eds), *Privatization and Regulation: A Review of the Issues* (Longman, Harlow, 1994), p. 86.
13. Stelzer, 'Lessons for UK regulation', pp. 191 and 196.
14. Price, 'Economic regulation', p. 82.
15. Stelzer, 'Lessons for UK regulation', p. 191.

16. *Idem.*
17. Joy Copley, 'Lottery to be run by team of five', *Daily Telegraph* (02/04/98).
18. Harris, telephone interview (07/10/99).
19. See Stelzer, 'Lessons for UK regulation', *passim.*
20. See, for example, James McCormick and Elizabeth Kendall, *A Flutter on the Future? Why the National Lottery Needs Citizens' Juries* (Institute of Public Policy Research, London, November 1995), *passim.*
21. Eamonn Butler, 'But who will regulate the regulators?', in Adam Smith Institute, *But Who Will Regulate the Regulators?* (Adam Smith Institute, London, 1993), p. 3.
22. Stelzer, 'Lessons for UK regulation', p. 190.
23. Director General of the National Lottery, 'Financial penalties: principles and procedures' (news release) (Office of the National Lottery, London, 10/07/98).
24. *Idem.*
25. *Idem.*
26. National Lottery Act 1998, Section 2 (2) (b), and National Lottery etc. Act 1993, Section 21 (2).
27. National Lottery Act 1998, Section 2 (1) (9) (a).
28. *Ibid.,* Section 3.
29. Director General of the Lottery, 'Financial penalties' (news release) (10/07/98).
30. Lord Redesdale, *Official Report of the Grand Committee on the National Lottery Bill (H.L),* Vol. 584, No. 87, CWH8.
31. Lord McIntosh of Haringey, *Official Report of the Grand Committee on the National Lottery Bill (H.L.),* Vol. 584, No. 87, CWH8.
32. National Lottery Commission, *Annual Report 1998/99* (The Stationery Office, London, 20/07/99), p. 6.
33. Lord McIntosh, *Official Report of the Grand Committee on the NL Bill (H.L.),* Vol. 584, No. 87, CWH8 and CWH11.
34. James Keulemans (Lottery Commission Public Affairs representative), telephone interview (28/04/99).
35. Cento Veljanovski, 'The economics of regulatory enforcement', in Keith Hawkins and John M. Thomas (eds), *Enforcing Regulation* (Kluwer-Nijhoff Publishing, Boston, 1984), p. 176.
36. See p. 180 n 84.
37. Alan Peacock and Ian Orton, 'The bargaining process as a means of implementing and enforcing regulations in the United Kingdom', in Alan Peacock (ed.), *The Regulation Game* (Blackwell, Oxford, 1984), p. 97.
38. *Idem.*
39. Dr J. Cunningham, *Parliamentary Debates: House of Commons Official Report.* Vol. 264, No. 149 (Hansard, HMSO, London, 25/10/95), col. 1022.
40. *Idem.*
41. An Advisory Group Report, *The National Lottery Initiatives and Recommendations* (Labour Party, London, 1996), p. 5. The introduction to the Report, written by the Shadow Secretary of State for National Heritage, Dr J. Cunningham, maintained that while the Report was not a statement of Labour Party policy, it formed an invaluable foundation for a future Labour government's approach to the Lottery (*ibid.,* p. 4).

42. *Ibid.*, p. 6.
43. Chris Smith (Secretary of State for Culture, Media and Sport), *The People's Lottery (White Paper)* Cm 3709 (The Stationery Office, London, July 1997).
44. *Ibid.*, p. 29.
45. National Lottery Commission, 'Regulator announces basis for granting next Lottery Licence' (news release) (National Lottery Commission, London, Ref 4/05–99, 29/07/99).
46. *Idem.*
47. Harris, telephone interview (07/10/99).
48. National Lottery Commission, *The Next Licence to Run the National Lottery: Statement of Main Principles* (National Lottery Commission, London, July 1999), p. 2, appended to NLC, 'Regulator announces basis for granting next Licence' (news release) (29/07/99).
49. *Idem.*
50. NLC, 'Regulator announces basis for granting next Licence'.
51. NLC, *The Next Licence to Run the Lottery*, p. 3, and *Invitation to Apply for a Licence under Section 5 of the National Lottery etc. Act 1993* (National Lottery Commission, London, November 1999), pp. 54–9, conditions 10.2 and 10.3.
52. Henry B. Hansmann, 'The rôle of non profit enterprise', *Yale Law Journal*, vol. 89, no. 5 (April 1980), p. 838.
53. *Idem.*
54. National Lottery Commission, 'Good Causes and Lottery players will win from new Lottery terms' (news release) (National Lottery Commission, London, Ref 12/99, 30/11/99).
55. NLC, *Invitation to Apply*, p. 54, condition 10.2.
56. *Idem.*
57. *Idem.*
58. Mark Slattery (Head of Public Affairs to National Lottery Commission), telephone interview (10/12/99).
59. NLC, *Invitation to Apply*, p. 58, condition 10.3.
60. National Lottery Commission, *Draft Invitation to Apply for a Licence under Section 5 of the National Lottery etc. Act 1993* (National Lottery Commission, London, September 1999), p. 8, condition 1.5.
61. The draft Invitation to Apply (and subsequently the Invitation to Apply) and the draft Section 5 Licence are consistent with and build on the 'Statement of main principles'. Mark Harris (Chief Executive of the National Lottery Commission), correspondence from (29/09/99). Soundings were taken from bidders and suppliers in connection with the design of the draft Invitation to Apply which formed the basis for the final Invitation to Apply. Mark Harris (Chief Executive of the National Lottery Commission), correspondence from (10/12/99). In addition the Invitation to Apply reserved the right of the NLC to make changes to the Invitation to Apply at any time. *Invitation to Apply*, p. 17, condition 3.3.
62. NLC, *The Next Licence to Run the Lottery*, p. 1.
63. *Ibid.*, p. 4.
64. Anthony I. Ogus, *Regulation: Legal Form and Economic Theory* (Clarendon Press, Oxford, 1994), p. 322.
65. *Idem.*

66. NLC, *The Next Licence to Run the Lottery*, p. 3, and *Invitation to Apply*, pp. 35–6, condition 7.2.
67. Clare Garner, 'Camelot directors gamble on pay cuts in fight for lottery licence', *Independent* (02/02/00).
68. Dan Gledhill, 'Camelot to cut profits by half', *Independent on Sunday* (27/02/00).
69. *Invitation to Apply*, pp. 94–5, condition 14.4.
70. National Lottery Commission, *Addendum 3 to Invitation to Apply* (National Lottery Commission, London, January 2000), p. 2.
71. See p. 73 in this volume.
72. National Lottery Commission, *Addendum 5 to Invitation to Apply* (National Lottery Commission, London, 04/02/00).
73. *Idem*.
74. *Invitation to Apply*, pp. 14–15, condition 2.9.
75. David P. Baron, 'Design of regulatory mechanisms and institutions', in Richard Schmalensee and Robert D. Willig (eds), *Handbook of Industrial Organization, Vol. II* (Elsevier Science Publishers, Amsterdam, North Holland, 1989), p. 1406.
76. *Idem*.
77. Camelot, *Camelot and Social Responsibility Social Report 1999* (Camelot Group plc, Watford, 2000), p. 9, para. 8.4.1, and p. 10, para. 8.4.2.
78. *Ibid.*, p. 8, para. 8.4.1.
79. Consignia Enterprises Ltd's participation as a shareholder in the Camelot consortium *qua* a wholly owned subsidiary of Consignia plc was contingent on Camelot's Licence being renewed. *Ibid.* p. 3, para. 3.1, n. iv. CEL became an equal 20 per cent shareholder in the Camelot consortium on 13/03/01. Camelot, *Annual Report and Accounts (2001)*, p. 15.
80. Steve Boggan, 'Post Office joins new Camelot bid', *Independent* (07/08/99).
81. 'Camelot nosedive', *Independent* (24/11/99).
82. Andrew Sparrow, 'Branson pledges fortune to lottery', *Daily Telegraph* (25/08/00).
83. National Lottery Commission, 'Bids for the next National Lottery Licence 2001–2008: Commission announces identities of bidders' (news release) (National Lottery Commission, London, ref 05/2000, 29/02/00).
84. Mark Slattery (Head of Public Affairs to National Lottery Commission), telephone interview (01/03/00).
85. The People's Lottery Ltd, 'Branson announces "profit for good causes" bid for National Lottery Licence' (news release) (Finsbury Ltd, London, 13/12/99) and Finsbury representative (PR Agency for the People's Lottery), telephone interview (01/03/00).
86. The People's Lottery Ltd, news release (13/12/99). It is noteworthy that one of the partners of The People's Lottery – Automated Wagering International (AWI) – was involved in the Arizona Lottery fiasco of the early 1990s (see page 35 in this volume). Jon Ashworth and Raymond Snoddy, 'Branson gambles on putting fun back into Lottery', *The Times* (14/12/99).
87. NLC, 'Bids for the next Licence' (news release) (29/02/00).
88. Jon Ashworth, 'Late challenge to Lottery's two-horse race', *The Times* (01/03/00).

89. *Idem.*
90. Detailed information on the bids remained confidential during the bidding process.
91. Ogus, *Regulation*, p. 329. To help offset the advantage to the incumbent the NLC took steps to ensure potential bidders for the next Licence were furnished with details of Camelot's network of independent retailers. National Lottery Commission, 'National Lottery Commission to supply retailer details to bidders for the next Licence' (news release) (National Lottery Commission, London, Ref 14/99, 06/12/99).
92. National Lottery Commission, *The Next Licence to Operate the National Lottery, Essential Background and Timetable* (National Lottery Commission, London, 30/11/99).
93. Ogus, *Regulation*, p. 329.
94. Daniel F. Spulber, *Regulation and Markets* (MIT Press, Cambridge, MA, and London, 1989), p. 267.
95. V. P. Goldberg, 'Regulation and administered contracts', *Bell Journal of Economics*, vol. 7, no. 2 (autumn 1976), p. 443.
96. *Idem.*
97. NLC, *The Next Licence to Run the Lottery*, p. 6.
98. *Invitation to Apply*, p. 64, condition 10.11.
99. Peter Davis (Director General of the National Lottery), *Minutes of Evidence. H.C. 240–III, Session 1995–96* (HMSO, London, 29/02/96), p. 71, para. 327.
100. NLC, *The Next Licence to Run the Lottery*, p. 6.
101. See Oliver E. Williamson, 'Franchise bidding for natural monopolies in general and with respect to CATV', *Bell Journal of Economics*, vol. 7, no. 1 (spring 1976), pp. 83–91.
102. Announcement of the preferred bidder was initially to be made by end of June 2000, with the new Licence starting October 2001. NLC, 'Regulator announces basis for granting next Licence' (news release) (29/07/99).
103. George J. Stigler, *The Citizen and the State* (University of Chicago Press, Chicago, 1975), p. 105.
104. Cf. *Draft Invitation to Apply*, pp. 49–50, condition 9.5, and pp. 127–8, conditions 21.5–21.6.
105. NLC, 'Good Causes and Lottery players will win from the new Lottery terms' (news release) (30/11/99).
106. 'No-win for the Lottery contenders', *The Times* (01/12/99). It may be possible to sell the existing terminals to other lotteries overseas, and so defray the loss. *Idem.*
107. NLC, 'Good Causes and Lottery players will win'.
108. Dominic Kennedy, 'Camelot plans to fall back on rival lottery', *The Times* (18/03/00).
109. Lotteries (Prizes and Expenses: Variation and Prescription of Percentage Limits) Order 1997 (SI 43/1997).
110. Camelot was part of the consortium that won the Licence to run the South African Lottery in 1999. Patricia A. McQueen, 'South Africa picks up Uthingo', *International Gaming and Wagering Business*, vol. 20, no. 8 (August 1999), p. 1.
111. Martin K. Perry, 'Vertical integration: determinants and effects', in Schmalensee and Willig (eds), *Handbook. Vol. II*, p. 185.

112. Alfred E. Kahn, *The Economics of Regulation: Principles and Institutions. Vol. 2* (John Wiley, New York, 1970), p. 256.
113. Spulber, *Regulation and Markets*, p. 489.
114. Peter Davis, *Minutes of Evidence Evaluating the Applications to Run the Lottery and the Director General's Travel Arrangements Taken before the Committee of Public Accounts on 11/02/95. Forty-first Report* (HMSO, London, 15/07/96), p. 5, para. 34.
115. Perry, 'Vertical integration', p. 206, and C. W. Baden Fuller, 'Article 86 EEC: economic analysis of the existence of a dominant position', in A. I. Ogus and C. G. Veljanovski (eds), *Readings in the Economics of Law and Regulation* (Clarendon Press, Oxford, 1984), p. 220.
116. Spulber, *Regulation and Markets*, p. 489.
117. Davis, *Minutes of Evidence. Forty-first Report*, p. 18, para. 191. See also *Licence to Run the Lottery*, pp. 147–150, Schedule 8, Condition 23.
118. 'National Lottery – game theory', *The Economist* (30/10/93), p. 33.
119. Sir Richard Branson, *Minutes of Evidence Submitted to Culture, Media and Sport Committee. The Operation of the National Lottery. First Report, Vol. II, H.C. 958–i, Session 1999–2000* (The Stationery Office, London, 09/11/00), p. 33, para. 139.
120. Williamson, 'Franchise bidding', p. 85.
121. Severin Carrell, 'Improved returns will boost bid by Camelot', *Independent* (30/09/00).
122. Matthew Taylor, 'New Labour's lucky ticket', *Guardian* (24/08/00).
123. Michael Harrison, 'Humbug must not lay low the kingdom of Camelot', *Independent* (31/05/97).
124. *Idem.*
125. NOP cited by The People's Lottery (news release).
126. Lord McNally, *National Lottery Bill (H.L.). Official Report, Vol. 584, No. 82* (Hansard, London, 18/12/97), col. 779.
127. Jackson and Price, *Privatisation and Regulation*, pp. 11–12.
128. Harvey Averch and Leland L. Johnson, 'Behavior of the firm under regulatory constraint', *American Economic Review*, vol. LII, no. 3 (June 1962), p. 1052.
129. *Idem.*
130. *Idem.*
131. Report of the Comptroller and Auditor General, *Evaluating the Applications to Run the National Lottery. H.C. 569, Session 1994–95* (National Audit Office, HMSO, London, 07/07/95), p. 5, fig. 1, and p. 27, para. 3.18.
132. Lord Skidelsky, *Official Report of the Grand Committee on the N.L. Bill (H.L.). Vol. 584, No. 87*, CWH2.
133. Richard A. Posner, 'Natural monopoly and its regulation', in Paul W. Macavoy (ed.), *The Crisis of the Regulatory Commissions* (W. W. Norton, New York, 1970), p. 35.
134. *Idem.*
135. *Ibid.*, pp. 35–6.
136. William J. Baumol, 'Reasonable rules for rate regulation: plausible policies for an imperfect world', in Macavoy (ed.), *Regulatory Commissions*, p. 195.
137. Tim Holley, *Minutes of Evidence Submitted to Culture, Media and Sport Committee. The Operation of the National Lottery. First Report. Vol. II, H.C. 958–i, Session 2000–2001* (The Stationery Office, London, 09/11/00), p. 22, para. 94.
138. Posner, 'Natural monopoly', p. 36.

139. J. A. Schumpeter (trans. R. Opie), *The Theory of Economic Development* (Cambridge, MA, 1936).

140. Baumol, 'Reasonable rules', p. 195.

141. Jean-Jacques Laffont and Jean Tirole, *A Theory of Incentives in Procurement and Regulation* (MIT Press, Cambridge, MA, and London, 1993), p. 664.

142. Cento Veljanovski, *The Future of Industry Regulation in the U.K.: A Report of Independent Inquiry* (European Policy Forum for British and European Market Studies (London, January 1993), p. 67.

143. For example, in the area of Lottery ticket sales through routes other than the retail environment (e.g. telephones, interactive television and the Internet) which the Invitation to Apply sought proposals on (and details of which were included in both bids). *Invitation to Apply*, pp. 88–9, condition 13.7.

144. It should not be forgotten that the Distribution Fund already enjoys a greater percentage of income than that which is retained by the Operator as ticket sales rise through different tranches.

145. Sue Slipman (Director for Social Responsibility for Camelot), cited by Vallely 'Does the Lottery add up?' (04/06/99).

146. Holley, *Minutes of Evidence. First Report*, p. 15, para. 16.

147. Posner, 'Natural monopoly', p. 37.

148. Charles F. Phillips Jr, *The Economics of Regulation, Theory and Practice in the Transportation and Public Utility Industries* (Richard D. Irwin, Homewood, IL, 1969), p. 722.

149. William F. Butler, 'The business outlook plus some thoughts on business regulation', *Telephony* (19/09/65), p. 25.

Chapter 6

1. Severin Carrell, 'Both bidders for Lottery are told: "It won't be you"', *Independent* (24/06/00).

2. *Idem.*

3. Dan Gledhill, 'Camelot hit by fall in lottery sales', *Independent on Sunday* (02/07/00).

4. 'Branson in waiting', *Guardian* (24/08/00).

5. National Lottery Commission, *Neither Bid Meets Statutory Criteria* (Open Document) (National Lottery Commission, London, ref. 13/00, 23/08/00), p. 1.

6. *Idem.*

7. Gledhill, 'Camelot hit by fall in lottery sales' (02/07/00).

8. NLC, Open Document, p. 4, para. 9.

9. *Idem.*

10. Philip Johnston, 'GTech kept computer fault secret for over two years', *Daily Telegraph* (24/08/00).

11. Severin Carrell and Andrew Mullins, 'The GTech cover-up that left Camelot exposed', *Independent* (24/08/00), and Jon Ashworth and Raymond Snoddy, 'Secrecy over blunder signalled end of road', *The Times* (24/08/00).

12. NLC, Open Document, p. 4, para. 10.

13. *Idem.*

14. Carrell and Mullins, 'The GTech cover-up' (24/08/00), and David Usborne,

'GTech clears out top executives amid fury over lottery cover-up', *Independent* (07/07/00).

15. *Idem.* The NLC's investigations resulted in Camelot paying over £115,000 to the prize fund, and also compensating retailers. NLC, *Annual Report (2000/01)*, p. 14.

16. See pp. 35–6 in this volume.

17. Matt Wells, 'How the magic went out of a legend', *Guardian* (24/08/00).

18. NLC, Open Document, p. 4, para. 13.

19. *Ibid.*, p. 5, para. 13.

20. *Ibid.*, p. 5, para. 14.

21. Ashworth and Snoddy, 'Secrecy over blunder'.

22. Scheherazade Daneshkhu and Sheila Jones, 'Glitches in the system prove end to lottery reign', *Financial Times* (24/08/00).

23. NLC, Open Document, p. 6, para. 17, and p. 7, para. 25.

24. *Ibid.*, p. 9, para. 32.

25. Gledhill, 'Camelot hit by fall in lottery sales'.

26. NLC, Open Document, p. 9, para. 33.

27. Director General of the National Lottery, *Annual Report 1995/96* (HMSO, London, 17/07/96), p. 44, app. A, and National Lottery Commission, *Annual Report 1999/2000* (The Stationery Office, London, 25/07/00), p. 20, app. A.

28. NLC, Open Document, p. 8, para. 27.

29. The NLC Open Document devoted more space to the GTech deception and its ramifications than any other single issue.

30. There is some doubt as to whether the Commission is legally competent to impose fines on the Licensee (Camelot) for the failings of a third party (GTech). Mark Slattery (Head of Public Affairs to National Lottery Commission), telephone interview (29/12/00).

31. NLC, Open Document, p. 10, para. 35.

32. *Idem.*

33. *Ibid.*, p. 10, para. 36.

34. *Idem.*

35. Cordelia Brabbs, 'How Branson's bid hit the jackpot', *Marketing* (31/08/00), p. 13.

36. 'It could be him', *The Economist*, vol. 356, no. 8185 (26/08/00), p. 28.

37. Julia Snoddy, 'Pledge to create daily allowance', *Guardian* (24/08/00).

38. The People's Lottery Ltd (press release) (Finsbury Ltd, London, 23/08/00).

39. Tampering with Lotto game formats can be a fraught business. In 1999 the Florida State Lottery changed their Lotto game format along similar lines to those proposed by The People's Lottery and suffered a 25 per cent fall in sales. Dan Gledhill, 'Camelot claims punters hate Branson's rollovers', *Independent on Sunday* (10/09/00).

40. Dan Gledhill and Colin Brown, ' "People's Lottery" idea flopped in US', *Independent on Sunday* (10/12/00), and Tim Holley, *Minutes of Evidence Submitted to Culture, Media and Sport Committee. The Operation of the National Lottery. First Report. Vol. II, H.C. 958–i, Session 2000–2001*, p. 19, para. 63.

41. Gledhill and Brown, ' "People's Lottery" idea flopped'.

42. Andrew Mullins, 'Bigger jackpots designed as lure for the people', *Independent* (24/08/00).

43. *Idem.*

44. NLC, Open Document, p. 11, para. 38.
45. Henry Palmer and David Benady, 'Bring on the Branson', *Marketing Week* (31/08/00), p. 21.
46. *Idem.*
47. *Idem.*
48. The People's Lottery (press release) (23/08/00).
49. NLC, Open Document, p. 8, para. 27. The People's Lottery pledge to Good Causes was marginally higher than Camelot's. Although not released by the Commission, speculation in the press claimed that The People's Lottery had offered up to 6.9 per cent more than Camelot. Severin Carrell, 'Lottery regulators say sorry to Camelot over fiasco', *Independent* (07/10/00).
50. NLC, Open Document, p. 11, para. 39.
51. Julia Snoddy, 'Pledge to create daily allowance', and Raymond Snoddy 'Branson gambles £3M on lottery', *The Times* (25/08/00).
52. Mullins, 'Bigger jackpots' (24/08/00).
53. Julia Snoddy, 'Pledge to create daily allowance'. Suppliers were not shareholders; The People's Lottery was wholly owned by a holding company which was itself limited by guarantee. The directors of The People's Lottery (who were also members of the holding company) were Simon Burridge, Chief Executive, and six non-executive directors: Sir Richard Branson (Chairman); John Jackson of Virgin; Henry King, Chairman of Rentokil Initial; Caroline Marland, former Managing Director of Guardian Newspapers; Don Cruickshank, Chairman of the London Stock Exchange and Scottish Media Group; and Michael Blakenham, a director of Sotheby's. *Idem.*
54. Severin Carrell, 'Camelot launches legal bid to block Branson takeover', *Independent* (26/08/00).
55. 'Branson's chance', *The Times* (24/08/00).
56. 'It's a Lottery', *Daily Telegraph* (24/08/00).
57. Dame Helena Shovelton (Chairwoman of National Lottery Commission), *Newsnight* interview (BBC Television, 21/09/00).
58. 'It's a Lottery', *Daily Telegraph*.
59. 'Branson in waiting', *Guardian*.
60. Severin Carrell and Paul Waugh, 'The Lottery: it's a rollover', *Independent* (24/08/00).
61. Scheherazade Daneshkhu and Christopher Adams, 'Branson agrees to £50 M lottery "net"', *Financial Times* (25/08/00).
62. John Cassy, 'Camelot wins legal review', *Guardian* (30/08/00).
63. 'Lottery losers', *Financial Times* (30/08/00).
64. Severin Carrell, 'Camelot buys GTech UK and seeks to bid again for Lottery', *Independent* (07/09/00).
65. Under this arrangement GTech continues to act as software supplier, but has no management input.
66. David Teather, 'Camelot lottery ruling blow to Branson', *Guardian* (22/09/00).
67. Andrew Norfolk, 'Camelot wins its place in lottery bid shoot-out', *The Times* (22/09/00).
68. David Teather, 'Camelot takes its chance,' *Guardian* (22/09/00).
69. *Idem.*
70. *Idem.*

71. Robert A. Kagan, *Regulatory Justice* (Russell Sage Foundation, New York, 1978), pp. 14–15.
72. Michael Fordham (public law barrister, Blackstone Chambers, London), cited by Frances Gibb, 'Victory is the first against a powerful regulator', *The Times* (22/09/00).
73. Norfolk, 'Camelot wins its place' (22/09/00).
74. Teather, 'Camelot lottery ruling' (22/09/00). The deadline talks with The People's Lottery ended on 23 September. John Mason, Scheherazade Daneshkhu and Christopher Adams, 'Camelot back in Lottery race', *Financial Times* (22/09/00).
75. 'The National Lottery should cease to be a monopoly', *Independent* (22/09/00).
76. David Teather, 'Branson the victor attacks Camelot', *Guardian* (25/08/00).
77. *Idem.*
78. 'The National Lottery should cease to be a monopoly'.
79. Patience Wheatcroft, 'Get round a table with Camelot', *The Times* (22/09/00).
80. *Idem.*
81. 'Meddling Ministers', *Independent* (07/10/00).
82. Carrell, 'Lottery regulators say sorry', *Independent* (07/10/00).
83. Raymond Snoddy, 'The lottery is about money, not charity – and Branson knows it', *Marketing* (31/08/00), p. 14.
84. See p. 35 in this volume and p. 188 n. 86.
85. Cahal Milmo, 'Branson software is acceptable say lottery officials', *Independent* (28/08/00).
86. *Idem.*
87. Jon Ashworth, 'Back in the running but with very little to smile about', *The Times* (22/09/00).
88. *Idem.*
89. Dianne Thompson (Chief Executive of Camelot), *Minutes of Evidence submitted to Culture, Media and Sport Committee. The Operation of the National Lottery. First Report. Vol. II, H.C. 958–i, Session 1999–2000* (The Stationery Office, London, 09/11/00), p. 13, para. 8.
90. David Teather, 'Group needs another £50M', *Guardian* (24/08/00).
91. Edward Heathcoat Amory, 'Key questions that demand answers now', *Daily Mail* (22/09/00), and 'Branson must guarantee lottery dream', *Guardian* (25/08/00).
92. Paul Murphy, 'Branson and the bravura biographer', *Guardian* (22/09/00).
93. *Idem.*
94. *Idem.*
95. Severin Carrell, 'Judge's ruling puts Camelot back in running for lottery', *Independent* (22/09/00).
96. 'Rollover for Camelot?', *Financial Times* (05/10/00).
97. Severin Carrell, 'Improved returns will boost bid by Camelot', *Independent* (30/09/00).
98. 'Unlucky lottery', *Guardian* (22/09/00), 'Loaded dice', *Financial Times* (22/09/00) and 'The National Lottery should cease to be a monopoly' (22/09/00).
99. Carrell, 'Lottery regulators say sorry' (07/10/00).

100. Frances Gibb and Andrew Pierce, 'Blighted Lottery watchdog sacks its lawyers', *The Times* (05/10/00).

101. *Idem.*

102. *Idem.*

103. Harriet Spicer, *Minutes of Evidence Submitted to Culture, Media and Sport Committee. The Operation of the National Lottery. First Report. Vol. II, H.C. 958–iii, Session 1999–2000* (The Stationery Office, London, 09/11/00), p. 115, para. 325.

104. Carrell, 'Lottery regulators say sorry' (07/10/00).

105. Marie Woolf, 'Smith gives Lottery to former mandarin', *Independent* (13/10/00).

106. Severin Carrell, 'Lottery watchdog chief backs his board', *Independent* (26/10/00).

107. Ashworth, 'Back in the running' (22/09/00).

108. *Idem.*

109. Ann McElvoy, 'Will Branson be the fall guy for new Labour?', *Independent* (12/10/00)

110. Sheherazade Daneshkhu, 'Camelot's second big lottery win', *Financial Times* (20/12/00).

111. National Lottery Commission, *Statement of Reasons for the Decision of the National Lottery Commission on the Grant of a Licence to Run the National Lottery* (National Lottery Commission, London, 19/12/00), p. 2, para. 7.

112. *Ibid.*, pp. 3–4, para. 16.

113. *Ibid.*, p. 4, para. 17.

114. Ivan Viehoff and Ian Jones, *Franchise Auctions in Uncertain Market Conditions – a Toolbox of Techniques* (National Economic Research Associates, London, March 1995), p. 5.

115. *Idem.*

116. NLC, *Statement of Reasons*, p. 4, paras 19–20, and p. 6, para. 30.

117. *Ibid.*, p. 5, para. 22.

118. *Ibid.*, p. 6, para. 30.

119. *Ibid.*, p. 5, para. 25, and 'Honourable defeat', *The Times* (20/12/00).

120. NLC, *Statement of Reasons*, p. 3, para. 12.

121. 'Lottery spins into reverse', *Financial Times* (20/12/00).

122. Lord Burns (Chairman of National Lottery Commission), *Minutes of Evidence Submitted to Culture, Media and Sport Committee. The Operation of the National Lottery. First Report. Vol. II, H.C. 56–iii, Session 2000–2001* (The Stationery Office, London, 18/01/01), p. 205, para. 552.

123. National Lottery Commission, 'Commission announces its decision on the next National Lottery Licence' (news release) (National Lottery Commission, London, Ref. 24/00, 19/12/00).

124. NLC, *Statement of Reasons*, p. 3, paras 11 and 14.

125. National Lottery Commission, statement by Hilary Blume (National Lottery Commission, London, 19/12/00).

126. *Idem.*

127. 'Camelot's second coming', *Guardian* (20/12/00).

128. NLC, *Statement of Reasons*, p. 3, para. 13.

129. See p. 136 in this volume.

130. Slattery, telephone interview (29/12/00).
131. NLC, *Statement of Reasons*, p. 3, para. 14.
132. Sean O'Neill, 'Camelot chief wins £400,000 licence bonus', *Daily Telegraph* (21/12/00). It was finally determined that the new Licence would run from 27 January 2002 to 31 January 2009. National Lottery Commission, 'Funding from National Lottery set to stay high' (news release) (National Lottery Commission, London, 27/06/01). It is instructive that a condition of the second Licence requires Camelot to co-operate for up to two years prior to the end of the Licence period, with regard to the possible handover of the Lottery to a new operator. NLC, *Annual Report 2000/01*, p. 24.
133. David Teather, 'Branson delays decision on legal action over National Lottery loss', *Guardian* (21/12/00).
134. *Idem.*
135. Sandra Laville, 'Branson bows out of battle for lottery', *Daily Telegraph* (11/01/01).
136. Scheherazade Daneshkhu, 'Branson not to challenge "cowardly" decision', *Financial Times* (11/01/01).
137. *Idem.*

Chapter 7

1. Severin Carrell, 'Lottery faces shake-up after licence fiasco', *Independent* (19/12/00).
2. *Idem.*
3. Professor Ian Walker (Department of Economics, University of Warwick), *Minutes of Evidence Submitted to Culture, Media and Sport Committee. The Operation of the National Lottery. First Report. Vol. II, H.C. 958–ii, Session 1999–2000* (The Stationery Office, London, 16/11/00), p. 99, para. 280.
4. David Teather, 'Branson delays decision on legal action over National Lottery loss', *Guardian* (21/12/00), and Chris Smith (Minister for Culture, Media and Sport), *Minutes of Evidence to Culture, Media and Sport Committee. The Operation of the National Lottery. First Report. Vol. II, H.C. 56–iii, Session 2000–2001* (The Stationery Office, London, 18/01/01), p. 230, para. 692.
5. *Culture, Media and Sport Committee. The Operation of the National Lottery. First Report. Vol. I, H.C. 56–i, Session 2000–2001* (The Stationery Office, London, 07/03/01), p. xxix, para. 109.
6. Teather, 'Branson delays decision' (21/12/00).
7. Robert Baldwin and Martin Cave, *Franchising as a Tool of Government* (Centre for the Study of Regulated Industries, London, 1996), p. 28, sect. 2.1.6.
8. C. D. Foster, *Privatization, Public Ownership and the Regulation of Natural Monopoly* (Blackwell, Oxford and Cambridge, MA, 1992), p. 159.
9. Smith, *Minutes of Evidence. First Report*, p. 222, para. 640.
10. Steve Boggan, 'Branson: I will never again make lottery bid', *Independent* (11/01/01).
11. Scheherazade Daneshkhu, Francesco Guerrera and Cathy Newman, 'Camelot snatches prize from Branson', *Financial Times* (20/12/00). The People's Lottery had sought legal advice as to whether or not it could sue the National Lottery Commission to recover a portion of its bid cost. In 28 days

alone, following the August decision by the Commission to negotiate exclusively with The People's Lottery, the Company spent £5 million. Andrew Pierce, 'Branson bows out of "farce" over the lottery', *The Times* (11/01/01).

12. *Culture, Media and Sport Committee. The Operation of the National Lottery. First Report*, p. xxx, para. 115.
13. Antony W. Dnes, 'Franchising, natural monopoly and privatisation', in Cento Veljanovski (ed.), *Regulation and the Market* (Institute of Economic Affairs, London, 1991), p. 229.
14. Baldwin and Cave, *Franchising as a Tool*, p. 14, sect. 1.4.3.
15. Daniel F. Spulber, *Regulation and Markets* (MIT Press, Cambridge, MA, and London, 1989), p. 267.
16. Dnes, 'Franchising', p. 229.
17. *Idem.*
18. Baldwin and Cave, *Franchising as a Tool*, p. 14, sect. 1.4.3.
19. *Idem.*
20. *Idem.*
21. 'Honourable defeat', *The Times* (20/12/00).
22. Following the problems with GTech, under the terms of the new Licence the Commission can require any contract entered into by Camelot to contain provisions relating to internal controls and to include reporting arrangements to the National Lottery Commission as well as Camelot. National Lottery Commission, *Annual Report 2000/01*, p. 23.
23. National Lottery Commission, 'Funding from National Lottery to stay high' (news release) (National Lottery Commission, London, 27/06/01).
24. National Lottery Commission, *Statement of Reasons, Decision of the National Lottery Commission on the Grant of a Licence to Run the National Lottery*, (National Lottery Commission, London, 19/12/00), p. 4, para. 18.
25. A Lottery Extra game launched by Camelot in mid-November 2000, which involves the player spending an extra £1 and selecting six numbers in a separate section of their Draw Lottery tickets, was projected to generate as much as an extra £60 million in sales each month. Actual sales up to the end of January 2001 were only £11 million a month. Severin Carrell, 'Lottery game fails to reverse slump in ticket sales', *Independent* (06/02/01).
26. Gaming Board, *Annual Report 2000/01*, p. 10, para. 1.14.
27. Budd, *Gambling Review*, p. 2, para. 1.6, and p. 187, para. 35.13. Turnover on the Irish National Lottery fell by between 15 per cent and 22 per cent when side-betting on the outcome of the Lottery was made legal. Camelot, *Statement by Camelot Group plc in Respect of the Gambling Review* (Camelot Group plc, Watford, 17/07/01). Camelot's performance will also be influenced fundamentally by the degree to which the Regulator permits it to offer new types of gambling products.
28. Dnes, 'Franchising', p. 218.
29. Burns, *Minutes of Evidence. First Report*, p. 208, para. 570.
30. Ian Walker and Juliet Young, 'The dummies' guide to lottery design', memorandum submitted to Culture, Media and Sport Committee. *The Operation of the National Lottery. First Report. Vol. II, H.C. 958–ii, Session 1999–2000* (The Stationery Office, London, 16/11/00), p. 90, para. 58.
31. *Idem.*

32. *Idem.*
33. The government will be reviewing the arrangements for the award of the Licence(s) in 2009. Smith, *Minutes of Evidence. First Report*, p. 222, para. 639.
34. Severin Carrell, 'Smith considers seizing control of National Lottery', *Independent* (07/02/01).
35. Burns, *Minutes of Evidence. First Report*, pp. 205–6, para. 555, and p. 208, para. 569, and *Culture, Media and Sport Committee. The Operation of the National Lottery First Report*, p. xxxi, para. 119.
36. Alfred E. Kahn, *The Economics of Regulation: Principles and Institutions*, vol. 2 (John Wiley, New York, 1970), p. 326.
37. John Kay and John Vickers, 'Regulatory reform: an appraisal', in Giandomenico Majone (ed.), *Deregulation or Re-regulation? Regulatory Reform in Europe and the United States* (Pinter, London, 1990), p. 232.
38. Patricia Day and Rudolf Klein, *Accountabilities, Five Public Services* (Tavistock Publications, London, 1987), p. 28.
39. *Idem.*
40. Foster, *Privatization*, p. 414.
41. Clair Wilcox and William G. Shepherd, *Public Policies Toward Business* (Richard D. Irwin, Homewood, IL, 1975, 5th edn), p. 321.
42. *Idem.*
43. *Culture, Media and Sport Committee. The Operation of the National Lottery. First Report*, p. xxi, para. 69.
44. Mark Call, 'Privatisation, regulation and the consumer', in Adam Smith Institute, *But Who Will Regulate the Regulators?* (Adam Smith Institute, London, 1993), p. 27.
45. Cosmo Graham, *Is There a Crisis in Regulatory Accountability? Discussion Paper 13* (Centre for the Study of Regulated Industries, London, 1995), pp. 50–1.
46. John Kay, 'The future of UK utility regulation', in M. E. Beesley (ed.), *Regulating Utilities: A Time for Change? Readings 44* (Institute of Economic Affairs, London, 1996), p. 145.
47. Bardach and Kagan, *op. cit.*, p. 348.
48. Day and Klein, *Accountabilities*, p. 27.
49. *Culture, Media and Sport Committee. The Operation of the National Lottery. First Report*, p. xli, para. (xxiv).

INFORMATION REQUIRED FROM APPLICANTS

The Invitation to Apply gave applicants very detailed guidance on the information required . . .

1. **General Information**

   General Information, e.g. regarding company directors, key employees and major shareholders.

   Organization Structure. Management Approach, i.e. commitment to good corporate governance.

   Lottery Personnel, e.g. steps taken to ensure their integrity, prevent fraud etc.

   Relevant Experience of the Applicant.

2. **Licence Commitments**

   Proportion of revenue to be paid to the NLDF. Proportion of revenue to be paid in prizes. Target Launch date and proposed number of retail outlets.

   Retail Build-up throughout licence period. Minimum Marketing Expenditure from 1 April 1999.

   Proposed Commercial Ancillary Activities. Systems Development Plan.

3. **Business Plan**

   Summary Business Plan and Accounting Statements for each year of the licence. Staffing and Remuneration proposals. Pre-operational and Development Expenditure proposed. Business Plan for proposed Commercial Ancillary Activities.

4. **Game Plan**

   Proposals for Game Design and Portfolio. Proportion of prize money in '2' above to be paid out in different games.

   Plans for Section 6 Licence(s).

5. **Retail Distribution Plan**

   The number, mix and distribution of proposed outlets at the peak of proposed Retail Coverage.

Retail Build-up, i.e. the number, mix and distribution of retail outlets throughout the licence period.

Financial Arrangements with Retailers, i.e. proposed commission.

Commitments already received from Retailers to sell lottery tickets. Details of Non-Independent Retail Outlets, i.e. those wholly/partly owned by applicant. Any proposals for Attended Vending Machines. Any proposals for Payments and Receipts by Customers other than at Retail Outlets, e.g. subscriptions, Proposals for selection, support and control of retailers.

Proposals for sales force to manage the retail network.

6. **Marketing Plan**

Proposed Total Marketing Expenditure analysed by type of expenditure and game involved over the licence period.

Advertising and Promotion plan. Proposed strategy for Public Relations over the licence period.

7. **Customer Services and Customer Relations**

Proposed Information Strategy and Complaints procedures.

Systems for Prize distribution and communication with winners. Code of Practice on Customer Relations. Performance Standards, e.g. for speed of prize payment.

8. **Security of Prize Money and Banking**

Proposals for Security for Prize Monies. Banking arrangements.

9. **Game Playing Processes and Controls**

Proposed Player and Ticket Services, including design specification of equipment to be used. Retailer Support Services, e.g. repairing faults. Systems for recording tickets. System for validating prize claims.

Method of validating and delivering prize pay-outs. Equipment and systems used to draw results.

10. **The Lottery Systems**

Systems and Service Design and Installation. Security and Resilience of proposed systems. Process Assurance, e.g. audit logs etc. Arrangements for Internal Audit. Cash Management, i.e. ticket reconciliation, transaction matching etc.

Source: National Audit Office precis based on the Invitation to Apply for a Section 5 Licence in Comptroller and Auditor General, *Evaluating the Applications to run the National Lottery* (National Audit Office, HMSO, London, 3 July 1995) p. 10, fig. 3.

OHIO LOTTERY – PLEASE PLAY RESPONSIBLY

Please Play Responsibly

The Ohio Lottery Commission wants you to enjoy playing Ohio Lottery games and to play them responsibly.

No matter how successful you may be at playing games that require skill, or games of chance, unless you manage your money well, you can still end up spending more than you budget.

You must manage your gaming expenditures to ensure both safety and enjoyment.

· **NEVER** gamble with borrowed money.

· **Bet** with your head and not your heart.

· **Work** out your weekly or monthly recreation spending budget, and don't go over it.

· **Only** spend what you can afford to lose when playing.

· **Never** increase your bets when losing.

· **If** you must increase your bets, only do so when winning.

Gambling should be a pleasurable experience. Borrowing money to play, spending above your budget or using money allocated for other purposes is not only unwise but can lead to more significant problems for yourself and your family.

We want you to enjoy playing the Ohio Lottery games and to enjoy the experience. Achieve this goal by setting limits for yourself in your gaming activities.

Remember: Bet with your head...Not above it.
Gambling is not the Problem...
Problem Gambling Is.

William G. Howell, Executive Director
Julie Ault, Deputy Director
Problem Gambling Awareness Department

UNDER **PERSONS UNDER THE AGE OF EIGHTEEN (18) ARE PROHIBITED FROM PLAYING THE OHIO LOTTERY.**

An Equal Opportunity Employer & Service Provider.
William G. Howell · *Director*   PLEASE PLAY RESPONSIBLY
If you or someone you know has a gambling problem, please call · **1-800-589-9966**

If you or someone you know has a gambling problem, help is available by calling:
1-800-589-9966
PLEASE PLAY RESPONSIBLY
THE OHIO LOTTERY

PLEASE PLAY RESPONSIBLY

Source: Miscellaneous leaflets and labels (Ohio State Lottery, USA, 1999)

CAMELOT AND CONSORTIUM MEMBERS' FINANCIAL BENEFIT FROM OPERATING LOTTERY TO 31 MARCH 2001

			£m
A	Camelot cumulative profit	pre-tax	427.20
		post-tax	287.80
B	Cadbury Schweppes		
	Capital, stock and revenue		2.70
	Dividends		45.66
	Consortium tax relief		30.50
C	De La Rue		
	Capital, stock and revenue (including contract termination compensation)		32.50
	Dividends		45.66
	Consortium tax relief		13.30
D	GTech		
	Capital, stock and revenue (includes £27.9m. since disposal of shareholding)		124.20
	Dividends		14.26
E	ICL		
	Capital, stock and revenue		105.70
	Dividends		29.99
	Consortium tax relief		18.10

F   Thales Electronics (formerly Racal)
      Capital, stock and revenue   119.90
      Dividends   45.66
      Consortium tax relief   8.20

G   Consignia
      Capital, stock and revenue   5.70

Source: Camelot's reports and accounts for each year to 31 March 2001. *Note*: Cumulative dividends up to the end of 31 March 2001 were £181.23m. This figure is likely to more than double, for a special reserve has been allowed to accumulate to protect prize winners in the event of the Operator's insolvency (See *Licence to Run the Lottery*, p. 81, Condition 33). The National Lottery Commission has allowed this reserve to be released, and as a result Camelot's shareholders should receive an extraordinary distribution (in two instalments between May 2001 and May 2002) of around £100m. In addition the Operator can be expected to pay dividends as a by-product of its trading success. Mark Slattery (Head of Public Affairs to National Lottery Commission), telephone interview (28 March 2001). It is not unreasonable to assume that cumulative dividends up to May 2002 will approach £250m.

BIBLIOGRAPHY

Publications

Abt, Vicki, James F. Smith and Eugene Martin Christiansen, *The Business of Risk: Commercial Gambling in Mainstream America* (University of Kansas, Lawrence, 1985).

Asch, P., *Consumer Safety Regulation* (Oxford University Press, 1988).

Baden Fuller, C. W., 'Article 86 EEC: economic analysis of the existence of a dominant position', in A. I. Ogus and C. G. Veljanovski (eds), *Readings in the Economics of Law and Regulation* (Clarendon Press, Oxford, 1984).

Baldwin, Robert and Martin Cave, *Franchising as a Tool of Government* (Centre for the Study of Regulated Industries, London, 1996).

Bardach, Eugene and Robert A. Kagan, 'Conclusion: responsibility and accountability', in Eugene Bardach and Robert A. Kagan (eds), *Social Regulation: Strategies for Reform* (Institute for Contemporary Studies, CA, 1982).

——*Going by the Book: The Problem of Regulatory Unreasonableness* (Temple University Press, Philadelphia, 1982).

Baron, David P., 'Design of regulatory mechanisms and institutions', in Richard Schmalensee and Robert D. Willig (eds), *Handbook of Industrial Organization. Vol. II* (Elsevier Science Publishers, Amsterdam, 1989).

Baumol, William J., 'Reasonable rules for rate regulation: plausible policies for an imperfect world', in Paul W. Macavoy (ed.), *The Crisis of the Regulatory Commissions* (W. W. Norton, New York, 1970).

Bernstein, Marver H., *Regulating Business by Independent Commission* (Princeton University Press, Princeton, NJ, 1995).

Boulding, Peter, *Whither Regulation? Current Developments in Regulated Industries. Occasional Paper 7* (Centre for the Study of Regulated Industries, London, 1997).

Breyer, Stephen, *Regulation and Its Reform* (Harvard University Press, Cambridge, MA, 1982).

——'Regulation and deregulation in the United States: airlines, telecommunications and antitrust', in Giandomenico Majone (ed.), *Deregulation or Reregulation? Regulatory Reform in Europe and the United States* (Pinter, London, 1990).

Butler, Eamonn 'But who will regulate the regulators?', in Adam Smith Institute, *But Who Will Regulate the Regulators?* (Adam Smith Institute, London, 1993).

Call, Mark, 'Privatisation, regulation and the consumer', in Adam Smith Institute, *But Who Will Regulate the Regulators?* (Adam Smith Institute, London, 1993).

Clotfelter, Charles T. and Philip J. Cook, *Selling Hope: State Lotteries in America* (Harvard University Press, Cambridge, MA, 1989).

Cluster, R. L., 'An overview of compulsive gambling', in P. A. Crone, S. F. Yoles, S. N. Kieffer and L. Krinsky (eds), *Addictive Disorders Update: Alcoholism, Drug Abuse, Gambling* (Human Scientific Press, New York, 1982).

Cornish, D. B., *Gambling: A Review of the Literature and Its Implications for Policy and Research* (Crown, London, 1978).

Currie, David, 'Regulating utilities – the Labour view', in M. E. Beesley (ed.), *Regulating Utilities: Broadening the Debate. Readings 46* (Institute of Economic Affairs, London, 1997).

Davis, A. and J. Willman, *What Next? Agencies, Departments and the Civil Service* (Institute of Public Policy Research, London, 1991).

Day, Patricia and Rudolf Klein, *Accountabilities, Five Public Services* (Tavistock Publications, London, 1987).

Dnes, Antony W., 'Franchising, natural monopoly and privatisation', in Cento Veljanovski (ed.), *Regulation and the Market* (Institute of Economic Affairs, London, 1991).

Douglas, Andrew, *British Charitable Gambling 1956–1994* (The Athlone Press, London, 1995).

Eadington, William R., 'Ethical and policy considerations in the spread of commercial gambling', in Jan McMillen (ed.), *Gambling Cultures: Studies in History and Interpretation* (Routledge, London, 1996).

Evans, Graham and Judy White, *The Economic and Social Impact of the National Lottery* (University of North London Press, Centre for Leisure and Tourism Studies, London, 1996).

FitzHerbert, Luke, *Winners and Losers: The Impact of the National Lottery* (Joseph Rowntree Foundation, London, July 1995).

FitzHerbert, Luke, Celia Guissani and Howard Hurd (eds), *The National Lottery Yearbook 1996 Edition* (Directory of Social Change, London, 1996).

FitzHerbert, Luke and Mark Paterson (eds), *The National Lottery Yearbook 1998 Edition* (Directory of Social Change, London, 1998).

FitzHerbert, Luke, Faisel Rahman and Stan Harvey (eds), *The National Lottery Yearbook 1999 Edition* (Directory of Social Change, London, 1999).

FitzHerbert, Luke and Lucy Rhoades (eds), *The National Lottery Yearbook 1997 Edition* (Directory of Social Change, London, 1997).

Foster, C. D., *Privatization, Public Ownership and the Regulation of Natural Monopoly* (Blackwell, Oxford and Cambridge, MA, 1992).

Giddings, Philip, 'The Treasury Committee and the Next Steps agencies', in Philip Giddings (ed.), *Parliamentary Accountability* (Macmillan, London, 1995).

Graham, Cosmo, *Is There a Crisis in Regulatory Accountability? Discussion Paper 13* (Centre for the Study of Regulated Industries, London, 1995).

Griffiths, Mark, *Adolescent Gambling* (Routledge, London, 1995).

——'The National Lottery and Instant scratch cards: some comments on research', in Luke FitzHerbert and Lucy Rhoades (eds), *The National Lottery Yearbook 1997 Edition* (Directory of Social Change, London, 1997).

Jackson, Peter M. and Catherine M. Price, 'Privatisation and regulation: a review of the issues', in Peter M. Jackson and Catherine M. Price (eds), *Privatisation and Regulation: A Review of the Issues* (Longman, Harlow, 1994).

Kagan, Robert A., *Regulatory Justice* (Russell Sage Foundation, New York, 1978).

Kahn, Alfred E., *The Economics of Regulation: Principles and Institutions. Vol. 2* (John Wiley, New York, 1970).

Karcher, Alan J., *Lotteries* (Transaction Publishers, New Brunswick, NJ, 1989).

Kay, John, 'The future of UK utility regulation', in M. E. Beesley (ed.), *Regulating Utilities: A Time for Change? Readings 44* (Institute of Economic Affairs, London, 1996).

Kay, John and John Vickers, 'Regulatory reform: an appraisal', in Giandomenico Majone (ed.), *Deregulation or Re-regulation? Regulatory Reform in Europe and the United States* (Pinter, London, 1990).

Laffont, Jean-Jacques and Jean Tirole, *A Theory of Incentives in Procurement and Regulation* (MIT Press, Cambridge, MA, and London, 1993).

La Fleur's 1996 World Lottery Almanac (TLF Publications Inc., Boyds, MD, 1996).

The 1998 La Fleur's World Lottery Almanac (TLF Publications Inc., Boyds, MD, 6th edn, 1998).

La Fleur's 1999 World Lottery Almanac (TLF Publications Inc., Boyds, MD, 7th edn, 1999).

La Fleur's 2000 World Lottery Almanac (TLF Publications Inc., Boyds, MD, 2000).

Lewis, Ben W., 'Emphasis and misemphasis in regulatory policy', in William G. Shephard and Thomas G. Gies (eds), *Utility Regulation: New Directions in Theory and Practice* (Random House, New York, 1996).

Livingston, J., *Compulsive Gamblers: Observations on Action and Abstinence* (Harper & Row, New York, 1974).

Macavoy, P. W., W. T. Stanbury, George Yarrow and R. J. Zeckhauser, *Privatization and State-owned Enterprises* (Kluwer Academic Publishers, Boston, 1989).

Martinez, T. M., *The Gambling Scene* (Charles C. Thomas, Springfield, IL, 1983).

McCormick, James and Elizabeth Kendall, *A Flutter on the Future? Why the National Lottery Needs Citizens' Juries* (Institute for Public Policy Research, London, November 1995).

McGowan, Richard, *State Lotteries and Legalized Gambling* (Quorum Books, Westport, CT, 1994).

Miers, David, 'The national regulation of gambling and the completion of the internal market in the European Community', in William R. Eadington and Judy A. Cornelius (eds), *Gambling and Public Policy* (University of Nevada, Reno, 1991).

——'Objectives and systems in the regulation of commercial gambling', in Jan

McMillen (ed.), *Gambling Cultures: Studies in History and Interpretation* (Routledge, London, 1996).

Miles, Robert H. and Arvind Bhambri, *The Regulatory Executives* (Sage, Thousand Oaks, CA, 1983).

Mitnick, Barry M., *The Political Economy of Regulation* (Columbia University Press, New York, 1980).

Moody, G., *Quit Compulsive Gambling* (Thorsons, Northampton, 1990).

Moon, Patrick, 'The National Lottery and the economy in 1996', in Luke FitzHerbert and Lucy Rhoades (eds), *The National Lottery Yearbook 1997 Edition* (Directory of Social Change, London, 1997).

Moran, E., 'A generation of gamblers?', in Luke FitzHerbert, Celia Guissani and Howard Hurd (eds), *The National Lottery Yearbook 1996 Edition* (Directory of Social Change, London, 1996).

Noll, Roger G., 'Government regulatory behaviour: a multi-disciplinary survey and synthesis', in Roger G. Noll (ed.), *Regulatory Policy and the Social Sciences* (University of California Press, Los Angeles and Berkeley, 1985).

Noll, R. G. and B. M. Owen, *The Political Economy of Deregulation: Interest Groups in the Regulatory Process* (American Enterprise Institute for Public Policy Research, Washington and London, 1983).

Ogus, Anthony I., *Regulation: Legal Form and Economic Theory* (Clarendon Press, Oxford, 1994).

Owen, Bruce M. and Ronald Braeutigam, *The Regulation Game* (Billinger Publishing, Cambridge, MA, 1978).

Peacock, Alan and Ian Orton, 'The bargaining process as a means of implementing and enforcing regulations in the United Kingdom', in Alan Peacock (ed.), *The Regulation Game* (Blackwell, Oxford, 1984).

——'The measurement of compliance costs', in Alan Peacock (ed.), *The Regulation Game* (Blackwell, Oxford, 1984).

Pendleton Herring, E., *Public Administration and the Public Interest* (McGraw-Hill, New York and London, 1936).

Perry, Martin K., 'Vertical integration: determinants and effects', in Richard Schmalensee and Robert D. Willig (eds), *Handbook of Industrial Organization. Vol. II* (Elsevier Science Publishers, Amsterdam, 1989).

Phillips Charles F., Jr, *The Economics of Regulation, Theory and Practice in the Transportation and Public Utility Industries* (Richard D. Irwin, Homewood, IL, 1969).

Posner, Richard A., 'Natural monopoly and its regulation', in Paul W. Macavoy (ed.), *The Crisis of the Regulatory Commissions* (W. W. Norton, New York, 1970).

Price, Catherine, 'Economic regulation of privatised monopolies', in Peter M. Jackson and Catherine M. Price (eds), *Privatisation and Regulation: A Review of the Issues* (Longman, Harlow, 1994).

Reiss, Albert J., Jr, 'Selecting strategies of social control over organizational life', in Keith Hawkins and John M. Thomas (eds), *Enforcing Regulation* (Kluwer-Nijhoff Publishing, Boston, 1984).

Ricketts, Martin, 'Summary and conclusions', in Alan Peacock (ed.), *The Regulation Game* (Blackwell, Oxford, 1984).

Rubner, Alex, *The Economics of Gambling* (Macmillan, London, 1966).

Schumpeter, J. A. (trans. R. Opie), *The Theory of Economic Development* (Harvard University Press, Cambridge, MA, 1936).

Simon, H. A., *Administrative Behavior* (Free Press, New York, 1975).

Singer, Charles, 'The ethics of gambling', in Colin S. Campbell and John Lowman (eds), *Gambling in Canada: Golden Goose or Trojan Horse? A Report from the First National Symposium on Lotteries and Gambling* (School of Criminology, Simon Fraser University, Vancouver, 1989).

Skolnick, Jerome, *House of Cards* (Little, Brown, Boston, 1978).

Smith, C. M. and S. P. Monkcom, *The Law of Betting, Gaming and Lotteries* (Butterworth, London, 1987).

Souter, David, 'A stakeholder approach to regulation', in Dan Corry, David Souter and Michael Waterson, *Regulating Our Utilities* (Institute for Public Policy Research, London, 1991).

Spulber, Daniel F., *Regulation and Markets* (MIT Press, Cambridge, MA, and London, 1989).

Stelzer, Irwin M., 'Lessons for UK regulation from recent US experience', in M. E. Beesley (ed.), *Regulating Utilities: A Time for Change? Readings 44* (Institute of Economic Affairs, London, 1996).

Stewart, John, Elizabeth Kendall and Anna Coote, *Citizens' Juries* (Institute for Public Policy Research, London, 1994).

Stigler, George J., *The Citizen and the State* (University of Chicago Press, Chicago, 1975).

The Shorter Oxford English Dictionary (on Historical Principles), *Vol. II* (Clarendon Press, Oxford, 3rd edn, 1978).

Veljanovski, Cento, 'The economics of regulatory enforcement', in Keith Hawkins and John M. Thomas (eds), *Enforcing Regulation* (Kluwer-Nijhoff Publishing, Boston, 1984).

——'The regulation game', in Cento Veljanovski, *Regulation and the Market* (Institute of Economic Affairs, London, 1991).

——*The Future of Industry Regulation in the UK: A Report of Independent Inquiry* (European Policy Forum for British and European Market Studies, London, January 1993).

——'The power of the regulator', in Adam Smith Institute, *But Who Will Regulate the Regulators?* (Adam Smith Institute, London, 1993).

Vickers, John and George Yarrow, *Privatization: An Economic Anlaysis* (MIT Press, Cambridge, MA, and London, 1988).

Viehoff, Ivan and Ian Jones, *Franchise Auctions in Uncertain Market Conditions – a Toolbox of Techniques* (National Economic Research Associates, London, March 1995).

Weyman-Jones, Tom, 'Deregulation', in Peter M. Jackson and Catherine M. Price (eds), *Privatisation and Regulation: A Review of the Issues* (Longman, Harlow, 1994).

Wilcox, Clair, *Public Policies Toward Business* (Richard D. Irwin, Homewood, IL, 1966).
Wilcox, Clair and William G. Shepherd, *Public Policies Toward Business* (Richard D. Irwin, Homewood, IL, 1995, 5th edn).

Reports

Alton, David, *House of Commons Official Report. Parliamentary Debates* (Hansard, HMSO, London, 25/10/95).
An Advisory Group Report, *The National Lottery Initiatives and Recommendations* (Labour Party, London, 1996).
Ashton, Joe (National Heritage Committee), *The National Lottery. Minutes of Evidence, HC 240–iii, Session 1995–96* (HMSO, London, 29/02/96).
Ashworth, Jacinta, Nicola Doyle and Nicholas Howat (BMRB Social Research) *Under 16s and the National Lottery Tracking Survey 2000* (National Lottery Commission, London, June 2001).
Branson, Sir Richard, *Minutes of Evidence Submitted to Culture, Media and Sport Committee. The Operation of the National Lottery First Report. Vol. II, H.C. 958–i, Session 1999–2000* (The Stationery Office, London, 09/11/00).
Brooke, Rupert (Secretary of State for National Heritage), *Minutes of Evidence National Lottery etc. Bill. 389–i, Session 1992–93* (HMSO, London, 13/01/93).
Budd, Sir Alan, *Gambling Review Report* (The Stationery Office, London, CM5206, July 2001).
Burns, Lord (Chairman of the National Lottery Commission), *Minutes of Evidence Submitted to Culture, Media and Sport Committee. The Operation of the National Lottery. First Report. Vol. II, H.C. 56–iii, Session 2000–2001* (The Stationery Office, London, 18/01/01).
Camelot, *Annual Report and Accounts 1997* (Camelot Group plc, Watford, 1997).
——*Annual Review 1998* (Camelot Group plc, Watford, 1998).
——*Annual Report and Accounts 1999* (Camelot Group plc, Watford, 1999).
——*Annual Report and Accounts 2000* (Camelot Group plc, Watford, 2000).
——*Camelot and Social Responsibility Social Report 1999* (Camelot Group plc, Watford, 2000).
——*Annual Report and Accounts 2001* (Camelot Group plc, Watford, 2001).
——*Camelot and Social Responsibility Interim Report 2000* (Camelot Group plc, Watford, 2001).
——Memorandum submitted to Culture, Media and Sport Committee, *Minutes of Evidence. The Operation of the National Lottery. First Report. Vol. II, H.C. 958–i, Session 1999–2000* (The Stationery Office, London, (09/11/00).
——Supplementary memorandum submitted to National Heritage Committee, *The National Lottery. Minutes of Evidence. H.C. 240–iii, Session 1995–96* (HMSO, London, 29/02/96).
Carpenter, Michael (Treasury solicitor), *Memorandum from the Treasury Solicitor*

(05/12/96), *Minutes of Evidence Taken Before the PAC. Twentieth Report* (The Stationery Office, London, 17/03/97).

Clerk to the Committee of Public Accounts, copy of part of letter to Director General (10/01/96). *Forty-first Report* (HMSO, London 15/07/96).

Committee of Public Accounts, *Evaluating the Applications to Run the National Lottery and the Director General's Travel and Hospitality Arrangements. Forty-first Report* (HMSO, London 15/07/96).

——*Payments to the National Lottery Distribution Fund. Twentieth Report* (The Stationery Office, London, 17/03/97).

Comptroller and Auditor General, Report of the, *Evaluating the Applications to Run the National Lottery. H.C. 569, Session 1994–95* (National Audit Office, HMSO, London, 07/07/95).

——*National Lottery Distribution Fund Accounts. H.C. 269, Session 1997–98* (The Stationery Office, London, 04/03/99).

——*Payments to the National Lottery Distribution Fund. H.C. 678, Session 1995–96* (National Audit Office, HMSO, London, 23/07/96).

Culture, Media and Sport Committee. The Operation of the National Lottery. First Report. Vol. I, H.C. 56–i, Session 2000–2001 (The Stationery Office, London, 07/03/01).

Cunningham, J., *Parliamentary Debates: House of Commons Official Report. Vol. 264, No. 149* (Hansard, HMSO, London, 25/10/95).

Davis, Peter (Director General of the National Lottery), Copy of part of letter to the clerk to the PAC (26/01/96), Committee of Public Accounts, *Forty-first Report* (HMSO, London 15/07/96).

——*Examination of Witnesses. Minutes of Evidence Taken Before the National Heritage Committee. H.C. 240–iii, Session 1995–96* (HMSO, London, 29/02/96).

——*Memorandum submitted to the PAC* (26/01/96), Committee of Public Accounts, *Forty-first Report* (HMSO, London, 15/07/96).

——*Minutes of Evidence Evaluating the Applications to Run the National Lottery and the Director General's Travel and Hospitality Arrangements Taken Before the Committee of Public Accounts on 11/12/95. Forty-first Report* (HMSO, London 15/07/96).

——*Minutes of Evidence Taken Before the Committee of Public Accounts. Twentieth Report* (The Stationery Office, London, 17/03/97).

——*Minutes of Evidence Taken Before the Committee of Public Accounts* (13/11/96), *Payments to the National Lottery Distribution Fund. Twentieth Report. H.C. 99, Session 1996–97* (The Stationery Office, London, 17/03/97).

——*Minutes of Evidence to PAC Payments to the NLDF. Twentieth Report* (The Stationery Office, London, 17/03/97).

Dean, Peter (Chairman), *Report of the Gaming Board for Great Britain 1998/99* (The Stationery Office, London, 14/07/99).

Director General of the National Lottery, *Annual Report 1993/94* (HMSO, London, 01/11/94).

——*Annual Report 1994/95* (HMSO, London, 16/10/95).

——*Annual Report 1995/96* (HMSO, London, 17/07/96).

——*Annual Report 1996/97* (The Stationery Office, London, 26/06/97).

——*Annual Report 1997/98* (The Stationery Office, London, 09/07/98).

Eagle, Angela (Lab), *Minutes of Evidence Taken Before the PAC. Forty-first Report* (HMSO, London, 15/07/96).

Fisher, Susan E., 'A preliminary study of underage spending on the National Lottery', in Oflot, *Social Research 31/01/95–31/01/96* (Oflot, London, 1996).

——*Gambling and Problem Gambling among Young People in England and Wales* (Centre for Research into the Social Impact of Gambling, University of Plymouth, January 1998, published by Oflot, February 1998).

——(Research designer) (Report prepared by Jacinta Ashworth and Nicola Doyle), *Under 16s and the National Lottery* (National Lottery Commission, London, February 2000).

Fisher, Sue and John Balding, *A Second Preliminary Study of Underage Spending on the National Lottery* (Oflot, London, n.d., circa Dec. 1995/Jan. 1996).

——*Underage Participation in the National Lottery* (Oflot, London, 1996).

Gaming Board for Great Britain, *Annual Report 1993/94* (HMSO, London, 11/07/94).

——*Annual Report 1994/95* (HMSO, London, 11/07/95).

——*Annual Report 1995/96* (HMSO, London, 11/07/96).

——*Annual Report 1996/97* (The Stationery Office, London, 10/07/97).

——*Annual Report 1997/98* (The Stationery Office, London, 08/07/98).

——*Annual Report 1998/99* (The Stationery Office, London, 14/07/99).

——*Annual Report 2000/01* (The Stationery Office, London, 11/07/01).

Griffiths, Dr Mark (Psychology Division, Nottingham Trent University), cited by Dr Lynne Jones (MP Birmingham Selly Oak), *House of Commons Official Report. Parliamentary Debates* (HMSO, London, 03/07/95).

Hall, Mike (Lab), *Minutes of Evidence Taken Before the PAC. Twentieth Report* (The Stationery Office, London, 17/03/97).

Holley, Tim (Chief Executive of Camelot), *Minutes of Evidence Submitted to Culture, Media and Sport Committee. The Operation of the National Lottery. First Report. Vol. II, H.C. 958–i, Session 2000–2001* (The Stationery Office, London, 09/11/00).

Leicester, Lord Bishop of, *National Lottery Bill. House of Lords. Vol. 584, No. 82* (Hansard, 18/12/97).

Maclennan, Robert (Lib Dem), *Minutes of Evidence Taken Before the PAC. Forty-first Report* (HMSO, London 15/07/96).

McIntosh, Lord of Haringey, *Official Report of the Grand Committee on the National Lottery Bill (H.L.). Vol. 584, No. 87* (Hansard, London, 19/01/98).

McNally, Lord, *National Lottery Bill (H.L.). Official Report. Vol. 584, No. 82* (Hansard, London, 18/12/97).

National Council on Gambling, Memorandum submitted by the National Council on Gambling to National Heritage Committee, *The National Lottery First Report. H.C. 131, Session 1994–95* (HMSO, London, 26/01/95).

National Heritage Committee, *Minutes of Evidence. The National Lottery. H.C. 240–i, Session 1995–96* (HMSO, London, 20/02/96).

——*The National Lottery Second Report. Vol. 1, 240–i, Session 1995–96* (HMSO, London, 14/05/96).

National Heritage, Department of, *Nineteenth Report. Cm 2990. Session 1994–95* (HMSO, London, October 1995).

National Lottery Commission, *Annual Report 1998/99* (The Stationery Office, London, 20/07/99).

——*Annual Report 1999/2000* (The Stationery Office, London, 25/07/00).

——*Annual Report 2000/1* (The Stationery Office, London, 12/07/01).

——*Social Research Programme Report No. 1* (National Lottery Commission, London, May 1999).

Neighborhood Lottery Alliance, Supplementary memorandum submitted to Culture, Media and Sport Committee, *Minutes of Evidence. The Operation of the National Lottery. First Report. Vol. II, H.C. 958–ii, Session 1999–2000* (The Stationery Office, London, 16/11/00).

Oflot, Memorandum submitted by Oflot to the National Heritage Committee, *Minutes of Evidence. H.C. 240–iii, Session 1995–96* (HMSO, London, 29/02/96).

——*Social Research Commissioned 01/02/96–01/06/96* (Oflot, London, 1996).

——*Social Research Commissioned 31/01/95–31/01/96* (Oflot, London, 1996).

——*Social Research Commissioned 01/03/97–01/09/97* (Oflot, London, 1997).

Oxford, The Lord Bishop of, *Official Report of the Grand Committee on the National Lottery Bill. Vol. 584, No. 90* (Hansard, 22/01/98).

Pilavin, I. and M. Polakowski, 'Who plays the lottery? A comparison of patterns in Wisconsin and the Nation', in *Institute for Research on Poverty Special Report No. 50* (January 1990).

Price Waterhouse Corporate Finance, *Regulated Industries: the UK Framework. Regulatory Brief 2* (Centre for the Study of Regulated Industries, London, 2nd edn, 1996).

Rafferty, Anne, QC, *Enquiry into National Lottery Application Allegations* (Temple, London, 31/05/96)

Redesdale, Lord, *Official Report of the Grand Committee on the National Lottery Bill (H.L). Vol. 584, No. 87* (Hansard, London, 19/01/98).

Russell, Sir George (Chairman of Camelot), *Minutes of Evidence Submitted to the National Heritage Committee. H.C. 240–iii, Session 1995–96* (HMSO, London, 29/02/96).

Sheldon, Robert (Chairman) *Minutes of Evidence Taken Before the PAC. Forty-first Report* (HMSO, London 15/07/96).

Skidelsky, Lord, *Official Report National Lottery Bill (H.L.). Vol. 584, No. 82* (Hansard, London, 18/12/97).

——*Official Report of the Grand Committee on the National Lottery Bill (H.L.). Vol. 584, No. 87* (Hansard, London, 19/01/98).

Smith, C. (Minister for Culture, Media and Sport), *Minutes of Evidence to Culture, Media and Sport Committee. The Operation of the National Lottery. First Report. Vol. II, H.C. 56–iii, Session 2000–2001* (The Stationery Office, London, 18/01/01).

——National Lottery Bill (Lords) (second reading) (07/04/98).

Spicer, Harriet (National Lottery Commissioner), *Minutes of Evidence Submitted to Culture, Media and Sport Committee. The Operation of the National Lottery, First Report. Vol. II, H.C. 958–i, Session 1999–2000* (The Stationery Office, London, 23/11/00).

Stern, Michael, *Minutes of Evidence Taken Before the PAC. Twentieth Report* (The Stationery Office, London, 17/03/97).

Thompson, Dianne (Chief Executive Designate of Camelot), *Minutes of Evidence to Culture, Media and Sport Committee. The Operation of the National Lottery, First Report. Vol. II, H.C. 958–i, Session 1999–2000* (The Stationery Office, London, 09/11/00).

Walker, Professor Ian (Department of Economics, University of Warwick), *Minutes of Evidence to Culture, Media and Sport Committee. The Operation of the National Lottery, First Report. Vol. II, H.C. 958–ii, Session 1999–2000* (The Stationery Office, London, 16/11/00).

Walker, Ian and Juliet Young, 'The dummies' guide to lottery design', Memorandum submitted to *Culture, Media and Sport Committee. The Operation of the National Lottery, First Report. Vol. II, H.C. 958–ii, Session 1999–2000* (The Stationery Office, London, 16/11/00).

Wardle, Charles, *Minutes of Evidence Taken Before the PAC. Twentieth Report* (The Stationery Office, London, 17/03/97).

Williams, Alan (Lab), *Minutes of Evidence Taken Before the PAC. Twentieth Report* (The Stationery Office, London, 17/03/97).

Government Publications

Commission of the European Communities, *Gambling in the Single Market – a Study of the Current Legal and Market Situation. Vol. I* (Office for Official Publications of the European Communities, Luxembourg, 1991).

Culture, Media and Sport, Department of, 'Government announces names of the new Lottery Commissioners' (news release) (25/01/99).

Directions to the Director General of the National Lottery under Section 11 of the National Lottery etc. Act 1993 (Department of National Heritage, 16/12/93).

Home Office, *A National Lottery Raising Money for Good Causes CM 1861* (HMSO, London, March 1992).

National Gambling Impact Study Commission, *Final Report* (National Gambling Impact Study Commission, Washington, DC, June 1999).

Progress in the Next Steps initiative, *The Government's Reply to the Eighth Report from the Treasury and Civil Service Committee, CM 1263 Session 1989–90* (HMSO, London, October 1990).

Smith, Chris (Secretary of State for Culture Media and Sport), *The People's Lottery* (Cm 3709, July 1997).

Newspapers/Magazines

Corporate Citizen

(September 1997).

Daily Mail

'Bonus winners' (01/06/96).
Brogan, Benadict, 'Lottery bosses told to beware crooked traders' (30/08/96).
Burt, Jason, 'Camelot told: we may halt Lottery' (07/03/98).
Deans, John and Jason Burt, 'Bottomley tells churchmen to count their good fortune' (05/01/96).
Dixon, Cyril, 'Lottery Supremo offered Branson bribe over lunch' (14/01/98).
Heathcoat Amory, Edward, 'Key questions that demand answers now' (22/09/00).

Daily Telegraph

Copley, Joy, 'Lottery to be run by team of five' (02/04/98).
Foster, Peter, 'How Camelot lost the biggest prize' (24/08/00).
'It's a Lottery' (24/08/00).
Johnston, Philip, 'GTech kept computer fault secret for over two years' (24/08/00).
——'Why Lottery watchdog failed to bite' (04/02/98).
Laville, Sandra, 'Branson bows out of battle for lottery' (11/01/01).
O'Neil, Sean, 'Camelot Chief wins £400,000 licence bonus' (21/12/00).
Sparrow, Andrew, 'Branson pledges fortune to lottery' (25/08/00).
Tweedie, Neil, 'There's always a bottom line, what can I do for you personally? Everyone needs something' (03/02/98).
'2.6 million lottery offers seized' (09/06/90).

Dallas Morning News

Kuempel, George and Tom Steinert-Threlkeld, 'Lottery firm's tactics gall rivals; GTech notes clean record, seeks new challenges' (17/04/94).

The Economist

'It could be him', Vol. 356, No. 8185 (26/08/00).
'The National Lottery – an easy going lot' Vol. 340, No. 7981 (31 Aug–Sept 1996).
'National Lottery – game theory' (30/10/93).

Evening Standard

Pryer, Nick, 'Big Lottery fiddle probe' (25/04/95).

Financial Times

Daneshkhu, Scheherazade, 'Branson not to challenge 'cowardly' decision' (11/01/01).
——'Camelot's second big lottery win' (20/12/00).
Daneshkhu, Scheherazade and Christopher Adams, 'Branson agrees to £50 M lottery "net"' (25/08/00).
Daneshkhu, Scheherazade, Francesco Guerrera and Cathy Newman, 'Camelot snatches prize from Branson' (20/12/00).
Daneshkhu, Scheherazade and Sheila Jones, 'Glitches in the system prove end to lottery reign' (24/08/00).
'Loaded dice' (22/09/00).
'Lottery losers' (30/08/00).
'Lottery spins into reverse' (20/12/00).
Mason, John, Scheherazade Daneshkhu and Christopher Adams, 'Camelot back in Lottery race' (22/09/00).
Mason, John and Richard Tomkins, 'Serious blow for world's biggest Lottery operator' (03/02/98).
Parker, George and Scheherazade Daneshkhu, 'Lottery regulator's rôle faces overhaul after Gtech case' (06/02/98).
'Rollover for Camelot?' (05/10/00).
Snoddy, Raymond, 'Lottery chief summoned to talks' (29/05/97).
'UK Lottery' (07/06/97).

Forbes

Colonius, E., 'The big payoff from lotteries' (25/03/91).

Guardian

Ahmad, Kamal, 'Bribes verdict ignites Lottery crisis' (03/02/98).
——'Lottery operator Camelot dumps UK shareholder' (02/04/98).
Bannister, Nicholas, 'Watchdogs held at bay' (05/02/98).
'Branson in waiting' (24/08/00).
'Branson must guarantee lottery dream' (25/08/00).
'Camelot's second coming' (20/12/00).
Cassy, John, 'Camelot wins legal review' (30/08/00).
Lowe, Roger, Keith Harper and Celia Watson, 'Labour hits the profiteers for six' (07/06/97).
Murphy, Paul, 'Branson and the bravura biographer' (22/09/00).
Snoddy, Julia, 'Pledge to create daily millionaire' (24/08/00).
Taylor, Matthew, 'New Labour's lucky ticket' (24/08/00).

Teacher, Andrew, 'Camelot lottery ruling blow to Branson' (22/09/00).
——'Camelot takes its chance' (22/09/00).
Teather, David, 'Branson delays decision on legal action over National Lottery loss' (21/12/00).
——'Branson the victor attacks Camelot' (25/08/00).
——'Group needs another £50M' (24/08/00).
'Unlucky lottery' (22/09/00).
Wells, Matt, 'How the magic went out of a legend' (24/08/00).

Independent

Blackhurst, Chris, 'Man who has pride in being boring' (13/12/95).
Boggan, Steve, 'Branson: I will never again make lottery bid' (11/01/01).
——'Post Office joins new Camelot bid' (07/08/99).
——'Victory of the Lottery fat-cats' (07/06/97).
Brown, Colin, 'Lottery ban on bootleg traders' shops' (17/08/99).
'Camelot nosedive' (24/11/99).
Camelot 'Thunderball' advertisement (07/06/99).
Carrell, Severin, 'Both bidders for Lottery are told: "It won't be you"' (24/06/00).
——'Camelot buys GTech UK and seeks to bid again for Lottery' (07/09/00).
——'Camelot launches legal bid to block Branson takeover' (26/08/00).
——'Improved returns will boost bid by Camelot' (30/09/00).
——'Judge's ruling puts Camelot back in running for lottery' (22/09/00).
——'Lottery faces shake-up after licence fiasco' (19/12/00).
——'Lottery game fails to reverse slump in ticket sales' (06/02/01).
——'Lottery regulators say sorry to Camelot over fiasco' (07/10/00).
——'Lottery watchdog chief backs his board' (26/10/00).
——'Smith considers seizing control of National Lottery' (07/02/01)
Carrell, Severin and Andrew Mullins, 'The GTech cover-up that left Camelot exposed' (24/08/00).
Carrell, Severin and Paul Waugh, 'The Lottery: it's a rollover' (24/08/00).
Coyle, Diane, 'Delayed payouts by Lottery provide £2 billion boost for Treasury' (16/09/96).
Garner, Clare, 'Camelot directors gamble on pay cuts in fight for lottery licence' (02/02/00).
Harrison, Michael, 'Humbug must not lay low the kingdom of Camelot' (31/05/97).
Hunt, Liz, 'Lottery "breeding generation of gamblers"' (03/11/95).
Macdonald, Marianne, 'Camelot hits the jackpot with £10 M bonanza' (07/06/95).
——'Camelot plays £40M hand to launch Lottery' (04/11/94).
McElvoy, Anne, 'Will Branson be the fall guy for New Labour?' (12/10/00).
'Meddling Ministers' (07/10/00).
Milmo, Cahal, 'Branson software is acceptable say lottery officials' (28/08/00).

Mullins, Andrew, 'Bigger jackpots designed as lure for the people' (24/08/00).
Prince, Rosa, 'Camelot told: stop sales to children' (27/02/98).
'The jury's verdict damned the lottery regulator too' (03/02/98).
'The National Lottery should cease to be a monopoly' (22/09/00).
'The winners: £1.5M a week for Camelot' (03/06/98).
Toynbee, Polly, 'The man from the ministry of culture' (03/06/97).
'Unsackable should not mean unaccountable' (21/12/95).
Usborne, David, 'GTech clears out top executives amid fury over lottery cover-up' (07/07/00).
Vallely, Paul, 'Does the lottery add up?' (04/06/99).
——'It's a Lottery but Camelot has earned its dosh' (30/05/97).
Whittard Smith, Andreas, 'Sack the Lottery Commissioners before it's too late' (09/10/00).
Williams, Rhys, 'Bottomley rejects Churches attack on scratchcards' (25/10/95).
——'Churches unite to attack "damaging" Lottery' (16/01/95).
——'Labour urges £5M Lottery limit' (16/01/95).
——'Secrecy still name of game over Mr £17.9M' (15/12/94).
Woolf, Marie, 'Smith gives Lottery job to former mandarin' (13/10/00).

Independent on Sunday

Blackhurst, Chris and Stephen Castle, 'Government swoops on lottery profit' (11/05/97).
'English soundbites' (08/06/97).
Farrelly, Paul, 'Camelot accused' (21/01/96).
Gledhill, Dan, 'Camelot claims punters hate Branson rollovers' (10/09/00).
Gledhill, Dan and Colin Brown, '"People's Lottery" idea flopped in US' (10/12/00).

International Gaming and Wagering

Gledhill, Dan, 'Camelot hit by fall in lottery sales' (02/07/00).
——'Camelot to cut profits by half' (27/02/00).
Goodchild, Sophie, 'Lottery glitch leaves winners out of pocket' (21/05/00).
'Lottery risks huge fines' (29/05/94).
'Making a monster' (26/03/95).
Frank-Keyes, John, 'Rebuilding the UK Lottery's image', vol. 19, no. 7 (July 1998).
McQueen, Patricia A., 'Alberta to vote on VLTs', vol. 19, no. 9 (September 1998).
——'South Africa picks Uthingo', vol. 20, no. 8 (August 1999)
McQueen, Patricia A. and John Frank-Keyes, 'GTech buyout boosts Camelot', vol. 19, no. 5 (May 1998).

Liverpool Daily Post

Holden, Simon, 'BBC to pay £1/2 M a year for Lottery' (05/06/96).
Woodhead, Jane, 'Young find it so easy to play Lottery' (24/02/96).

Marketing

Brabbs, Cordelia, 'How Branson's bid hit the jackpot' (31/08/00).
Snoddy, Raymond, 'The Lottery is about money, not charity – and Branson
    knows it' (31/08/00).

Marketing Week

Palmer, Henry and David Benady, 'Bring on the Branson' (31/08/00).

Observer

Brooks, Richard and Melanie Phillips, 'Poor losing most on the Lottery, new
    figures show' (29/10/95).

Public Gaming International

'Compulsive gambling? Lotteries are not a problem', vol. 19, no. 5 (May 1991).
'Lottery jurisdiction response to problem gambling', vol. 26, no. 9 (October
    1998).
Ward, Kathleen, 'It's not child's play', vol. 26, no. 11 (December 1998).
——'Lotteries address responsible play', vol. 26, no. 8 (September 1998).

Sunday Telegraph

Alderson, Andrew, 'Will this man's numbers finally come up?' (20/02/00).

The Times

Ashworth, Jon, 'Back in the running but with very little to smile about'
    (22/09/00).
——'Compromise likely on Camelot pay' (06/06/97).
——'Late challenge to Lottery's two-horse race' (01/03/00).
Ashworth, Jon and Oliver August, 'Cutting American Lifeline would spell the
    end of Camelot's reign' (04/02/98).
Ashworth, Jon and Raymond Snoddy, 'Branson gambles on putting fun back
    into Lottery' (14/12/99).
——'Secrecy over blunder signalled end of road' (24/08/00).
Bale, Joanna, 'Peter Davis sacked as Lottery chief' (04/02/98).
Bale, Joanna, and Andrew Pierce, 'Davis did not deserve humiliation, says
    wife' (05/02/98).

'Branson's chance' (24/08/00).

'Camelot "breeding addicts"' (03/05/95).

Gibb, Frances, 'Victory is the first against a powerful regulator' (22/09/00).

Gibb, Frances and Andrew Pierce, 'Blighted Lottery watchdog sacks its lawyers' (05/10/00).

'Honourable defeat' (20/12/00).

'It should be him' (04/02/98).

Kennedy, Dominic, 'Camelot plans to fall back on rival lottery' (18/03/00).

Midgely, Carol, 'Changes drive punters away' (04/02/98).

——'How life turned too exciting for dull accountant' (02/04/98).

——'Lottery chiefs ordered to give up bonus' (03/06/97).

Midgley, Carol and Jon Ashworth, 'GTech to sell Lottery stake in £51M deal' (02/04/98).

Miller, Robert, 'Lottery tickets seized in £100M scam inquiry' (27/09/95).

Norfolk, Andrew, 'Camelot wins its place in lottery bid shoot-out' (22/09/00).

'No – win for the Lottery contenders' (01/12/99).

Paterson, Lea, 'How lucky Treasury is all-round winner' (31/08/99).

Pierce, Andrew, 'Branson bows out of "farce" over the lottery' (11/01/01).

'Smith in Camelot' (07/06/97).

Snoddy, Raymond, 'Branson gambles £3M on lottery' (25/08/00).

Webster, Philip and Joanne Bale, 'Peter Davis sacked as Lottery chief' (04/02/98).

Wheatcroft, Patience, 'Get round a table with Camelot' (22/09/00).

Which?

'The National Lottery – who wins who loses?' (Consumers' Association, January 1997).

Reviews/Journals/Periodicals

Abt, Vicki and Martin C. McGurrin, 'Commercial gambling and values in American society: the social construction of risk', *Journal of Gambling Studies*, vol. 8, no. 4 (winter 1992).

Adler, J. 'Gambling, drugs and alcohol: a note on functional equivalents' *Issues in Criminology*, vol. 2, no. 1 (1966).

Averch, Harvey and Leland L. Johnson, 'Behavior of the firm under regulatory constraint', *American Economic Review*, vol. LII, no. 3 (June 1962).

Bernstein, Marver H., 'The regulatory process: a framework for analysis', *Law and Contemporary Problems*, vol. 6 (1961).

Boer, Larry de, 'Jackpot size and Lotto sales: evidence from Ohio 1986–1987', *Journal of Gambling Studies*, vol. 6, no. 4 (Winter, 1990).

Breyer, Stephen, 'Analyzing regulatory failure: mismatches, less restrictive alternatives and reform', *Harvard Law Review*, vol. 92, no. 3 (January 1979).

Broadcasting Complaints Commission, *The Bulletin*, no. 14 (24/09/98).

Butler, William F., 'The business outlook plus some thoughts on business regulation' *Telephony* (19/09/65).

Caudill, S. B., S. K. Johnson and F. G. Mixon, 'Economies of scale in state lotteries – an update and statistical test', *Applied Economics Letters*, vol. 2, no. 4 (Department of Economics, Auburn University, 1995).

Coups, Elliot, Geoffrey Haddock and Paul Webley, 'Correlates and predictors of lottery play in the United Kingdom', *Journal of Gambling Studies*, vol. 14, no. 3 (Fall, 1998).

Fisher, Sue, 'Gambling and pathological gambling in adolescents', *Journal of Gambling Studies*, vol. 9, n. 3 (Fall 1993).

Goldberg, V. P., 'Regulation and administered contracts', *Bell Journal of Economics*, vol. 7, no. 2 (autumn 1976).

Gray, Horace M., 'The passing of the public utility concept', *Journal of Land and Public Utility Economics*, vol. 16, no. 1 (February 1940).

Hansmann, Henry B., 'The rôle of non profit enterprise', *Yale Law Journal*, vol. 89, no. 5 (April 1980).

Horn, Bernard P., 'The courage to be counted', *Journal of Gambling Studies*, vol. 13, no. 4 (winter 1997).

Independent Television Commission, 'Child's eye view', *Spectrum*, vol. 17 (1995).

Jackson, T. H., 'The fresh start policy in bankruptcy law', *Harvard Law Review*, vol. 98 (1983).

Kelly, Joseph M., 'British Gaming Act of 1968', *New York Law School Journal of International and Competition Law*, vol. 8 (1986).

Kent-Smith, E. and S. Thomas, 'Luck had nothing to do with it. Launching the UK's largest consumer brand', *Journal of Market Research Society*, vol. 37, no. 2 (1995).

Levine, Michael E. and Jennifer L. Forrence, 'Regulatory capture, public interest and the public agenda: toward a synthesis', *Journal of Law, Economics and Organisation* (special issue 1990).

McCaffery, Edward J., 'Why people play lotteries and why it matters', *Wisconsin Law Review* (1994).

McGowan, Richard, 'The ethics of gambling research: an agenda for mature analysis', *Journal of Gambling Studies*, vol. 13, no. 4 (winter 1997).

Miers, David, 'Regulation and the public interest: commercial gambling and the National Lottery', *Modern Law Review*, vol. 59, no. 4 (July 1996).

——'The implementation and effects of Great Britain's National Lottery', *Journal of Gambling Studies*, vol. 12, no. 4 (winter 1996).

Moran, Emanuel, 'Majority of secondary school children buy tickets', *British Medical Journal*, vol. 311 (04/11/95).

Osborne, Judith A., 'Licensing without law: legalized gambling in British Columbia', *Canadian Public Administration – Administration Publique du Canada*, vol. 35, no. 1 (1992).

Persaud, Raj (Consultant psychiatrist), 'Letter', *British Medical Journal*, vol. 311 (04/11/95).

Rankin, M., 'The cabinet and the agencies: towards accountability in British Columbia', *University of British Columbia Law Review*, vol. 19 (1985).

Rogers, Paul, 'The cognitive psychology of lottery gambling: a theoretical review', *Journal of Gambling Studies*, vol. 14, no. 2 (summer 1998).

Stearns, James M. and Shaheena Borna, 'The ethics of lottery advertising: issues and evidence', *Journal of Business Ethics*, vol. 14, no. 1 (1995).

Williamson, Oliver E., 'Franchise bidding for natural monopolies in general and with respect to CATV', *Bell Journal of Economics*, vol. 7, no. 1 (spring 1976).

Wilson, Graham K. 'Social regulation and explanations of regulatory failure', *Political Studies*, vol. 32 (1984).

Yaffe, Robert A. and Veronica J. Brodsky, 'Recommendations for research and public policy in gambling studies', *Journal of Gambling Studies*, vol. 13, no. 4 (winter 1997).

Interviews/Correspondence

Bottomley, Virginia (Secretary of State for National Heritage), 'Letter to Peter Davis' (Director General of the National Lottery) (19/12/95).

Doolan, Lynn (Camelot Lottery Line Representative), Telephone interview (28/09/98 and 05/10/98).

Farley, Gail (Camelot Lottery Line Team Manager, Player Services Division), Correspondence from (ref GF/SRI/99/02/813436, 03/08/99).

Finsbury Ltd representative (PR Agency for The People's Lottery), Telephone interview (01/03/00).

Gale, Nigel (Director of the National Audit Office), Telephone interview (30/03/99).

Harris, Mark (Chief Executive of the National Lottery Commission), Correspondence from (29/09/99 and 10/12/99) and Telephone interview (07/10/99).

Keulemans, James (Oflot Public Affairs representative), Telephone interviews (01/10/98, and 05/03/99).

Keulemans, James (National Lottery Commission Public Affairs representative), Telephone interviews (08/04/99, 20/04/99 and 28/04/99).

Leonard, Erika (BBC production executive), Correspondence from (18/03/99).

Shovelton, Dame Helena (Chairman of National Lottery Commission), *Newsnight* interview (BBC Television, 21/09/00).

Simard, Melissa (Public Relations account co-ordinator to Connecticut Lottery), Telephone interview (27/04/98).

Slattery, Mark (Head of Public Affairs to National Lottery Commission), Telephone interviews (08/07/99, 10/12/99, 01/03/00, 29/12/00, and 28/03/01).

Legislation

Betting and Gaming Act 1960
Gaming Act 1968
Lotteries (Prizes and Expenses: Variation and Prescription of Percentage Limits)
    Order 1997 (SI43/1997)
National Lottery etc. Act 1993
National Lottery Act 1998
The Lotteries (Variation of Monetary Limits) Order, no. 1218 (1989)
The National Lottery Regulations 1994 (no. 189)

Miscellaneous

Camelot, *Advertising Code of Practice* (Camelot Group plc, Watford, January, 1998).

——'Camelot tops list of UK's most generous companies' (press release) (Camelot Group plc, Watford, 02/10/98).

——*Lottery Briefing Issue, no. 6* (Camelot Group plc, Watford, Spring 1997).

——*The Advertising Code of Practice* (Camelot Group plc, Watford, 2nd edn, November 1995).

——'The National Lottery launches the first ever Instants game with a top prize of £1 million' (news release) (Camelot Group plc, Watford, 11/06/01).

——*Statement by Camelot Group plc in respect of the Gambling Review* (Camelot Group plc, Watford, 17/07/01).

——'This is your winning wallet' (Camelot Group plc, Watford, 1999).

——*Thunderball' explanatory leaflet* (Camelot Group plc, Watford, n.d., circa May/June 1999).

Director General of the National Lottery, 'Financial penalties: principles and procedures' (news release) (Office of the National Lottery, London, 10/07/98).

Kinsey, R. K., 'The rôle of lotteries in public finance' (PhD thesis, Columbia University, Canada, 1959).

Labour Party Manifesto (April 1997).

Licence to Run the National Lottery under Section 5 of the National Lottery etc. Act 1993 (Oflot, London, July 1994).

Miscellaneous leaflets and labels (Ohio State Lottery, USA, 1999).

National Lottery Commission, *Addendum 3 to Invitation to Apply* (National Lottery Commission, London, January 2000).

——*Addendum 5 to Invitation to Apply* (National Lottery Commission, London, 04/02/00).

——'Commission announces its decision on the next National Lottery Licence' (news release) (National Lottery Commission, London, Ref. 24/00, 19/12/00).

——*Draft Invitation to Apply for a Licence under Section 5 of the National Lottery etc. Act 1993* (National Lottery Commission, London, September 1999).

——'Funding from National Lottery set to stay high' (news release) (National Lottery Commission, London, 27/06/01).

——'Good Causes and Lottery players will win from the new Lottery terms' (news release) (National Lottery Commission, London, Ref. 12/99, 30/11/99).

——*Invitation to Apply for a Licence under Section 5 of the National Lottery etc. Act 1993* (National Lottery Commission, London, November 1999).

——'National Lottery Commission to supply retailer details to bidders for the next lottery Licence' (news release) (National Lottery Commission, London, Ref. 14/99, 06/12/99).

——*Neither Bid Meets Statutory Criteria* (Open Document) (National Lottery Commission, London, Ref. 13/00, 23/08/00).

——'Regulator announces basis for granting next Lottery Licence' (news release) (National Lottery Commission, London, Ref. 4/05–99, 29/07/99).

——Statement by Hilary Blume (National Lottery Commission, London, 19/12/00).

——*Statement of Reasons for the Decision of the National Lottery Commission on the Grant of a Licence to Run the National Lottery* (National Lottery Commission, London, 19/12/00).

——*The Next Licence to Operate the National Lottery, Essential Background and Timetable* (National Lottery Commission, London, 30/11/99).

——*The Next Licence to Run the National Lottery: Statement of Main Principles* (National Lottery Commission, London, July 1999).

The National Lottery Company Ltd, 'Branson announces "profit for good causes" bid for National Lottery' (news release) (Finsbury Ltd, London, 13/12/99).

——'The People's Lottery Ltd' (press release) (Finsbury Ltd, London, 23/08/00).

Office of the National Lottery, (news release) (Oflot, London, 26/02/98).

——The Director General of the National Lottery. Background note (Oflot, London, n.d.).

——'The National Lottery: preferred applicant announced' (news release) (Oflot, London, 25/05/94).

——Stoker, John (Acting Director General to the National Lottery), Note re GTech appended to news release (Oflot, London, 09/04/98).

Vallance, Iain (Chairman of British Telecommunications plc), *Speech to Annual General Meeting* (30/07/92).

Vernons Lotteries Ltd, 'National Lottery football game ends' (press release) (Vernons Lotteries Ltd, Liverpool, 16/04/99).

INDEX